T0073603

Microprediction

Microprediction

Building an Open AI Network

Peter Cotton

The MIT Press
Cambridge, Massachusetts
London, England

The MIT Press would like to thank the anonymous peer reviewers who provided comments on drafts of this book. The generous work of academic experts is essential for establishing the authority and quality of our publications. We acknowledge with gratitude the contributions of these otherwise uncredited readers.

This book was set in Sabon by Westchester Publishing Services. Printed and bound in the United States of America.

Library of Congress Cataloging-in-Publication Data

Names: Cotton, Peter, author.
Title: Microprediction : building an open ai network / Peter Cotton.
Description: Cambridge, Massachusetts: The MIT Press, [2022] | Includes
    bibliographical references and index.
Identifiers: LCCN 2022001006 (print) | LCCN 2022001007 (ebook) |
    ISBN 9780262047326 (hardcover) | ISBN 9780262371339 (ebook) |
    ISBN 9780262371346 (pdf)
Subjects: LCSH: Strategic planning. | Artificial intelligence–Economic
    aspects. | Organizational change.
Classification: LCC HD30.28 .C6956 2022 (print) | LCC HD30.28 (ebook) |
    DDC 658.4/012–dc23/eng/20220615
LC record available at https://lccn.loc.gov/2022001006
LC ebook record available at https://lccn.loc.gov/2022001007

10 9 8 7 6 5 4 3 2 1

To know of and put to use a machine not fully employed, or somebody's skill which could be better utilized, or to be aware of a surplus stock which can be drawn upon during an interruption of supplies, is socially quite as useful as the knowledge of better alternative techniques.

—Hayek (1945), *The Use of Knowledge in Society*

To my mother, who taught me to question pyramids.

Contents

The Pitch

Quants are meek. This is good because we will inherit the Earth. It's not so good when it comes to influencing the perception of quantitative work, or its future—the topic of this book.

These days, everybody wants to be a data scientist. I get it, but I'm not heavily vested in vague terminology like data science or artificial intelligence. In these pages, I set out to effect a qualitative change in your perception of whatever-you-want-to-call-it and where it is going. I feel no obligation to defend any of the edifice that has arisen in recent years.

Ironically, I am asymptotically the world's most productive data scientist—as you will eventually discover—and unlike most, I'm prepared to tell you that most "new" activity can be broken down into standard, commodity, repeated quantitative tasks and delivered at much lower cost. (If I may be colloquial, data science is a rip-off.)

These repeated tasks I speak of go by many names in industry, which is part of the problem. In this book, I mostly use only one word: microprediction. That is the act of making thousands or millions of predictions of the same type over and over again.

This book explores the nature of microprediction from the perspective of economics, statistics, decision-making under uncertainty, and privacy-preserving computation.

Informed by progress in those fields, I ask basic questions. What is the best way to produce and distribute high-quality microprediction at arbitrarily low cost and thus help businesses of all sizes? Is microprediction an individual or a collective activity? What things, currently described as artificial intelligence (AI), can't be decomposed into microprediction?

It is very hard to reconcile the answers with artisan data science. Instead, the conclusion reached is that the world is missing a public utility, and companies are missing an important abstraction in their strategies, which might enable them to use it.

That utility is a vast collection of live streams of data, inhabited by autonomous self-navigating models that crawl from one to the next and make predictions. I invite you to help me create it because the world is not short of algorithms. I conclude it is short of micromanagers of algorithms, as I refer to them, who are autonomous algorithm chauffeurs.

If an algorithm can drive a car from New York to San Francisco, it ought to be able to find its way from a code repository to a business problem without human intervention. The main difficulty is the failure to reduce business problems to a combination of canonical microprediction tasks.

This book is aimed at *all* potential contributors to a prediction web, as it might be described. You can supply code, or launch algorithms, or create new feeds, or supply mathematical insight, or help in any number of technical ways.

You can also help by socializing the idea or adding to the demand for *explicit* versus implicit microprediction—by nudging your data scientists to send their model residuals to their nearest microprediction "oracle." Five lines of Python won't kill anyone.

However you choose to come at this topic, I hope that some of you will come to see the prediction network as a long felt unmet need. A microprediction microeconomy is not an easy thing to bring about. It might take time. It may never reach critical scale without happenstance. Perhaps your picking up this book, or searching "microprediction" to find working prototypes, is precisely what is required.

1

Overview

Imagine awaking one day to a world in which every aspect of every business, large or small, is quantitatively optimized to the nth degree. Imagine that this optimization derives its strength, ultimately, from advanced mathematical technique applied to decision-making under uncertainty and that this is informed by trillions of data points drawing in every conceivable quantity that might reasonably be deemed relevant to the task at hand.

In this scenario, every activity is optimized, not just the production line of companies that can afford to hire data scientists and lay down expensive analytics infrastructure. Every small business benefits, including the guy selling beer and peanuts at the baseball game. Every individual benefits and cost is negligible. A democratic artificial intelligence (AI) miracle has occurred.

This book asks only one hypothetical question: how did this come about? Among all possible explanations for this seemingly unlikely outcome, we set out to determine the one with the highest probability.

1.1 Half of Statistics

We will have some minor terminological challenges that are entirely other people's fault. So I must be crystal clear about one thing—only half an AI miracle is contemplated.

I consider the use of applied statistics to the optimization of relatively fast-moving operational problems only. We shall assume the instrumentation of those processes throws off sufficient data for so-called data-hungry methods to work well, or at least enough data to mechanically assess competing approaches. We shall assume that quantitative challenges *of the same kind* are thrown up over and over again—thousands or millions of times.

Methods termed *machine learning* are therefore bound to play a key role. There isn't a mathematically useful delineation of that field from statistics or parts of applied mathematics, for that matter, but one finds oneself trading accuracy for brevity and slipping into the use of *machine learning* to describe a collection of methods that work surprisingly well when data is plentiful.

That's not entirely fair to any tribe, and the related schism in the field of statistics is discussed with marginally more nuance in chapter 6. But my point is not to assert superiority of machine learning over inferential statistics or anything else. Rather, in the fine mathematical tradition, I merely wish to simplify my task to one that can be solved.

Rather than tripping on terminological sensitivities, I prefer the vulgarity of referring to my domain of problems as "half of statistics," although I'll let the reader decide what fraction of "applied something" really constitutes my scope. You may decide it is very close to zero or very close to one.

Arguing for the latter, so many things will be instrumented in the future that it's tempting to say that data-rich problems are the bigger half—although of course I mean that in a short-term, commercial sense (since human survival or extinction should probably appear on the scales as well).

Arguing for the former, the inherent statistical difficulty of a task approaches zero in the limit of infinite data, assuming that past is prologue. All you need is a nearest neighbor search.

In a somewhat related vein, press coverage of artificial intelligence breakthroughs has reinforced the idea, pun intended, that bespoke statistical modeling can be discarded since algorithms can learn in model-free ways.

In *Reward Is Enough*, a recent essay by Silver, Singh, Precup, and Sutton, pioneers of reinforcement learning, it is suggested that the objective of maximizing reward is "enough to drive behaviour that exhibits most if not all attributes of intelligence that are studied in natural and artificial intelligence, including knowledge, learning, perception, social intelligence, language and generalisation."[1]

My goal is more modest. I use the term *microprediction* in an attempt to avoid any impression otherwise. I emphasize the problem domain (as distinct from which methods might work), and it is hoped the term *microprediction* can deanchor some readers from unhelpful connotations of one-off events. That said, we are most certainly talking about prediction.

Semantics aside, in chapter 2, we'll allow our mind's eye to pan across a world of business problems and how they can be transformed with a sprinkling of *frequently repeated* prediction pixie dust. Suffice to say that the larger that opportunity is, the more important our contemplations will be. And the domain is growing rapidly.

Carrying forward the ambiguity in the word "half," I'll boldly assert that half of statistics—so defined—is half of AI. Part of the case rests on chapter 8, where we consider frequently repeated conditional prediction of so-called value functions.

What is important, I feel, is to focus solely on frequently repeated prediction and data-rich problems and not covet the other half of statistics.

I don't want the world
I just want your half
—Ana Ng, *They Might be Giants*

It is my assertion that companies have failed, in large part, to properly delineate the two and reorganize accordingly.

1.2   Cost

Now that we know we are concerned with only half an AI democratic miracle, I'll move from the delineation of the problem domain to the assessment of quality.

A simple way to set the standard is to propose that *almost everything* will be predicted almost as well as *anything* is today. If that is our ambition, then cost is the only reason the miracle I describe can seemingly be reduced to absurdity. Cost *is* the problem.

Let's examine a small part of today's analytic world where no expense is spared. We view a hugely profitable market making firm. It is well positioned to hire the best and brightest minds it can throw money at. It burns through a ten-figure technology budget, year after year, and leans on a virtually unlimited ability to store and process data.

This trading firm possesses a high level of organizational mathematical maturity, almost certainly represented in the technical acumen of senior management and flowing all the way down. It trains formidable intellectual firepower at a very precise and narrow task: determining the probabilistic representation of the near future of a finite set of security prices.

The firm does this because accuracy means profit. In chapters 2 and 7, I'll give formal examples of that direct connection, but for now, I ask you not to fixate on the details of any given task where accuracy helps but rather how implausible it is that most ordinary businesses, including small ones, could achieve as high a level of predictive proficiency as this well-funded organization.

I ask you to consider the enormity of the expense and the incredible undertakings of this trading company over many years. No doubt this has consumed the best intellectual years of a large interdisciplinary team. All this energy, ultimately, is dedicated to the creation and maintenance of a continuously changing probabilistic description of a set of live numbers.

Those numbers are of economic significance, it must be said—but nonetheless they are a tiny, mostly unrepresentative sample of the set of all quantities that instrument our personal and commercial lives. (It is possible, but unlikely, that a single number under study by this firm will materially help a surgeon, a pilot, or an operator at a nuclear plant make a crucial, real-time decision.)

Every story needs an antagonist. Ours is the cost of bespoke analytics. This antagonist is abstract, admittedly, although it can be personified with relative ease. I will take aim at highly paid data scientists in their role as human managers of models, or other humans, and I'm poking fun at my own quixotic aspiration to learn a fraction of all applied mathematical technique.

My theme is that human-managed production of intelligence—at least the portion directed at repeated tasks—cannot remain competitive. If we view all the undertakings by individuals and businesses on this planet as important and if, for the sake of this thought experiment, we place every instrumented quantity they might care about on a par with security market prices, then there is seemingly no way to fund similarly high-quality prediction and business optimization across the board.

But we can let our minds wonder and consider how this seemingly insurmountable challenge might eventually be tackled. I think we can find a different economic equilibrium. Working in our favor are the properties of data and models—the infinitesimal lightness and ease of replication. Data is free, eventually, in a more surprising way as well. We can utilize the predictive power of data without it being revealed to us.

The future of AI is a first principles exercise, not an extrapolation of industry trends.

1.3   The Problem

Talent scarcity dictates that only a tiny fraction of humanity's activities will benefit from applied mathematics the same way our supposed trading firm does. What will firms much smaller than our fictional market maker use? What *do* they use?

Here's one mildly disturbing data point. Recently, I examined what is by far the most commonly downloaded open-source forecasting package in the Python ecosystem. I found, as others before me had, that it was poorly conceived and frequently performed worse than a simple moving average.[2]

If this is in any way indicative of firms' ability to discern the quality of analytic tools, then they really will be at the mercy of others. Bear in mind that at many companies, things are worse, because you can't find someone proficient in Python to begin with.

It is true that we all will benefit from artificial intelligence, sooner or later. I happen to believe in a second coming of the Excel paperclip, and this time it will be hyperintelligent. There will be other gifts bestowed upon us by large firms as intelligence creeps into every product, but this kind of artificial intelligence arrives on someone else's terms, not yours.

What we won't have is our own personal data science team or the ability to play the AI poker game with a strong hand. We'll end up folding and giving away most of our data for nothing. A high fixed cost of quantitative business optimization translates into a small number of occasions when a firm—never mind an individual—takes charge of its own quantitative destiny. Most of the time, the marginal return on investment simply doesn't justify this.

At first glance, there is no way around this. The creation, deployment, and maintenance of quantitative devices that improve business operations include endeavors with all the hallmarks of expense. It is risky and iterative, and involves highly skilled employees wrestling with data (rarely cheap) and rapidly changing technology.

Even larger firms, it must be said, struggle to organize data and models. We are all aware of the limitations of companies viewed as larger brains—even at rare institutions where efficient communication of mathematical ideas is part of the culture (mostly, it isn't). The sound of mathematics being organized by large corporations is hardly the purr of a well-designed machine—more like the bleep, screech, and ding of a dial-up modem from the 1990s.

If large firms falter, it's hardly surprising if individuals, organizations, and small- to medium-sized enterprises also fail, given more limited resources. They are excluded in important ways from data science for the foreseeable future.

1.4 The Solution

This dire situation is surely the moment to introduce our protagonist. The hero of our story must render, at negligible cost yet uncanny accuracy, repeated short-term predictions of all quantities of interest to all companies and individuals.

In this book, I ask you to contemplate a mesh of automated, economically aware, reward-seeking prediction algorithms. They are not subject to the same limitations as people. But they substitute for people by arranging the capability for, and executing on, repeated prediction. Thereby, they stand a chance of collectively orchestrating model and data search—by weaving an increasingly rich and powerful microprediction web.

Separate business logic will leverage this web for all manner of tailored commercial or individual use. But that logic can usually be limited. On the other hand, the microprediction production encapsulates the truly hard part of the task and the ongoing, painful, iterative work required for constantly improving performance.

In this manner, commodity repeated prediction capability will enhance company bottom lines *as if* the work was undertaken by a huge well-sponsored team of top-flight applied mathematicians and developers. Our little algorithmic heroes must render this pragmatic, even though, in the vast majority of instances, such an investment seems economically ridiculous today.

Some algorithms might be self-contained prediction algorithms. But most will be middle managers and middlemen, categories that bring out prejudices like no other. (How fortunate that mid-twentieth-century economists can free us from our predispositions, as I discuss in chapter 4.)

Our hero needs a name and hereafter will be known as the "micromanager." That's not the most heroic-sounding role, I grant you. But the micromanager competes as voraciously as a trader in the old Chicago pits—when it chooses to do the heavy lifting. The micromanager can also be like a manager for a football team, with tasks that include recruiting, rewarding, punishing, and sometimes giving up on algorithms or data.

A micromanager sets out to solve on a microscopic scale and an ongoing basis an economic problem that is rather subtle—one certain to defy a singular solution. That problem is how to produce as much predictive power as possible at the lowest possible cost.

My role is to provide more concrete mental models for that problem and what a micromanager might look like. I do so in chapter 5, without wishing to limit anyone's imagination. It is the ultimate role of the micromanager to unburden the consumer of repeated prediction of all the things we are accustomed to paying for—in effort, money, and developer time.

However, in assessing the micromanager's utility, I'm afraid it is up to you to meditate on what millions of these miniature mechanical minstrels might materialize. And yes, this is the part where I play the dreamy visionary and you follow my extended arm toward the horizon. That prediction web hovering before you is a vast lattice of quantities, each one predicted as accurately, minutes hence, as it could reasonably be if the best minds turned their attention to it.

So forget all other connotations of "micromanager." No, the micromanager is not the annoying nontechnical boss whose bike-shedding churns the front-end developers. Not in this story.

1.5   Bespoke AI on Tap

What if, in the future, the mere specification of a repeated prediction task was synonymous with its solution? That is the case once the microprediction web, prediction web, or microprediction network (if you prefer) comes to be.

In a prediction web, every node is a competitively predicted stream of data. Every stream gets *better* treatment than that reserved for the AAPL ticker. Depending on how the game is played, not only will the mean be predicted well (the only part markets get right, for the most part) but so too the volatility, higher moments, distributional properties, and the fine structure of its codependence with other related quantities.

The AI miracle requires that anyone is able to source their own repeated predictions—say by sending their own live data. Only then is microprediction, and what comes with it, fully democratized. So the prediction web will include a myriad of numbers whose computation would not, in any other paradigm, come close to being economically sustainable.

For this reason, I urge the reader not to anchor to the well-established concept of a prediction market. Although prediction markets are lauded universally by economists and undoubtedly are underutilized (due to regulation, mostly), they also lower the expectations of what a prediction web might achieve.

A prediction web need not be a limited catalog of things that interest many people at once—although there is little harm in including when the train will arrive or which NFL players will gain yards in the next play. (Nor is there any need to pander to humans, their lame insistence on user interfaces, and other evolutionary traits that probably doom us—at least as far as our ability to compete with machines on data-hungry tasks is concerned.)

What is essential is that micromanagers endowed with economic desire are sufficiently hungry for new food—something that reflects on their own running and navigation costs. In a sufficiently competitive prediction web, your data is attacked with the same ferocity as market prices are today, even though the rewards are much smaller.

1.6 Oracles

I shall work backward from the aspiration of high-quality on-demand repeated prediction.

In chapter 3, we begin with a gentle examination of what an interface to a prediction network might look like. I use the term *pseudo-oracle* to describe a micromanager providing a gateway into the prediction web. It is a step-down transformer of sorts—thus providing a connection between a seething swarm of hungry algorithms and your business problem or application.

These gateways aspire to be "forever" functions. In theory, you never need to change your code, but the results just get better over time and, to within a cost multiple, as good as they can be. We can try to reason as to what they must do, in order to meet this "microprediction oracle" requirement. Of course, they ultimately draw their power from the diversity of algorithms and data around us.

In drawing conclusions, I shall assume that finding the right data for a given prediction problem is an immensely difficult task. I will assume the same of model search too, because it has been a century—probably many—since the time of the mathematical polymath.

I grant you that it would help, on the second front, if someone came up with a model that did everything and that possibility, or at least a useful component of it, is put forward by Pedros Domingos, author of *The Master Algorithm*.

Domingos suggests the possibility of an algorithm that could elegantly capture the power of most of the existing ones.[3] He invites contributions, but until a master algorithm is found, oracles might be the best bet.

A more modest version of Domingos's vision constitutes the field of automated model search, which has advanced quickly in recent years. However, the crucial question is whether pyramids of humans are the best organizers of the production of autonomous prediction. That isn't the only way.

1.7 Orchestrating Prediction

Thus begins the clash of civilizations.

To create the best repeated short-term prediction at a low cost, should humans organize in a large, well-funded automated machine learning company? Or can the production of automated model selection be drawn together by other mechanisms? Rather obviously, loose collections of volunteers working on open-source software also advance the needle.

But in this work, I focus on the price mechanism as a much more fine-grained orchestration principle, and I draw attention to the severe limitations of central planning. My response to Domingos's invitation to create the master algorithm is to hope that we are already living in one— the economy. It's merely that this master algorithm is far too cumbersome to achieve our microprediction objective, unless we change it.

I'm very fond of the rich tapestry of algorithms that are available to us today, many of which can help with creating a microprediction web. However, the economy itself coerces us not through Bayesian message passing, iterative proportional sampling, or anything from the statistical toolbox. It does not send us extrasensory messages so we can implement federated gradient descent or particle swarm optimization.

No, we are controlled by the price mechanism. That is, and likely always will be, how the macroscopic world organizes the production of prediction. Firms compete. They buy and sell data and analytics. This is the highest level at which analytics is organized. Other organizing principles, like Gantt charts, come in below.

The question I pose is whether we need those secondary levels of orchestration if the price mechanism is let loose. The price mechanism is an old but miraculous device. But its relative efficacy is an economic question breathed entirely new life when we focus on repeated prediction specifically. That is the discussion in chapter 4.

1.8 Small Rewards and Friction

The reader may disagree, but I believe the veracity of my thesis rests on whether extremely small rewards are enough. (The relationship between repeated commoditized tasks and everything known as AI is something I owe the reader—but it is mathematical and engineering busywork, at some level. So too privacy preservation is a journey beginning in chapter 9 whose eventual destination is, I hope, somewhat obvious.)

Let's reflect momentarily on the success or otherwise of large rewards. In general, "perfecting" rapidly repeated prediction is a hopeless task. Most quantities can be causally linked to dozens of others, who in turn might be influenced by hundreds of others and so forth.

Certainly, when we look at existing asset markets, betting exchanges, or prediction markets, we don't see what everyone would call complete success.

But you have to set the bar somewhere and not make the perfect the enemy of the good. I take the position that a stock price is a short-term prediction (of itself) that is astoundingly good. If you are inclined to complain about the quality of that prediction, then you and I are not talking about the same kind of AI miracle—and I wish you well achieving your more ambitious variety.

There is an inefficient markets literature of sorts that accidentally bolsters my case, rather than weakening it, because it simply highlights that the main thing preventing graduate students from making markets more efficient isn't inherent statistical difficulty but other frictions (they can't bet from their jurisdiction or obtain a broker-dealer license).

The question asked herein is, why should high-quality prediction be reserved for asset prices? The question is not "is reward enough?" in our existing economy but rather, "is engineering enough ..." to unleash the price mechanism in a way we haven't seen before.

It surely depends on the ease with which algorithms can exploit multiple sources of food, whether traveling from one opportunity to another involves guidance from a human (interpreting a new data model, for instance), and whether there exists a critical mass of such opportunities.

I would suggest that our intuition for this scenario is severely hampered by the current levels of friction in the macroscopic AI economy. Examples include the legal cost of executing a data feed contract, the lengths companies will go to poach an employee, the size of marketing budgets, the fees to attend conferences, and, in many cases, the very existence of products.

The vision in this book is also obscured by the six-figure subscriptions charged by a vendor who wraps existing open-source analytic libraries behind a nice user interface. This might not be classified as a economic friction by everyone, but certainly it is indicative of search cost.

Channeling Ronald Coase, it would be laughable to assert that all analytics firms are single-person affairs—the implication of zero trade friction. There are clearly significant reasons why trade alone doesn't orchestrate the production of analytics.[4]

And more's the pity. When friction prevents trade, it also obscures the frugality of electronic data and models and allows tragedies of the commons to persist because individuals and firms have a harder time hopping from one meta-stable state to another. The missing community garden is that common real-time, public feature space.

I argue that we should focus on removal of impediments to the smooth operation of "reward." We might see the prediction web as a substrate on which algorithms travel, given their lack of general navigation ability.

Only then can micromanagers, whose existence is not predicated on huge rewards, effect competitive prediction for any quantity (and only then in the microprediction domain, where non-technological frictions also dissipate). Then, and only then, can we bottle what we already know works. Market forces can even work without staking, since data flows quickly.

That is why those accustomed to financial markets, betting exchanges, or even small political prediction markets should not recoil at the notion that a complex machine could be held together by extremely weak economic ties. Machines don't need to sleep. They can survive on plankton.

The invisible hand is still there, even if it might be scoffed at by enterprise data salespeople, with their large quotas and firm handshakes. Ours is an untried invisible hand, admittedly, with "dainty pinkies that never weighed anchor in a storm."[5]

In chapters 3 and 5, we explore the possibilities of a near-frictionless world. This new version of the invisible hand is nimble enough to perform surgery on itself. No prediction is too trivial and no decision too small.

When decision-making can be achieved through oracle use, as discussed in chapter 8, and when the upfront and running cost of using oracles heads to zero, it is apparent that micromanagers can not only drive the prediction network but also use it for their own decision-making.

1.9   Artisan Data Science

What might be the implications of a prediction web?

The coming war in machine learning might be waged between giant teams in giant corporations, each hoping to out hype the other. Nobody doubts the application of machine learning to bottom lines or the economic sense it makes to shift more resources into mathematical modeling. A dollar goes further, now that a far greater fraction of industry is instrumented.

But listening to a small number of people boasting about how much applied mathematics they eschew could get rather dull. I have something far more entertaining in mind.

In the presence of ubiquitous repeated prediction at vanishing cost, these players might start to look like battling dinosaurs whose energy consumption can't be sustained indefinitely. Inside those companies, many young data scientists, employed therein as machine learning bulldozer operators, might eventually find they can make more money driving actual bulldozers.

For are they being lured into an ambush where they will be massacred by an army of self-navigating, data-searching, model-spinning robots? If the eager minds of tomorrow don't react in time, they might fare no better than the master craftsmen of the nineteenth century. Their real edge applies in the other half of statistics—and that might be where they need to head.

I don't mean to suggest that data scientists will be irrelevant as soon as the algorithms sprout legs and begin to scurry. Even on the "easy" side of statistics, I mention in chapters 2 and 3 that the machines will find better ways to use humans than the Wachowski siblings suggested in *The Matrix*—where humans were reduced to batteries.

But micromanagers performing cold comparisons can certainly be an antidote to probabilistic pretension and puffery. They can be the "gray goo" of enterprise data science, but in a benevolent way (the phrase is normally reserved for catastrophic nanotechnology scenarios). They can seek out and destroy nonrigorous claims, subpar applied statistics, and dubious AI propaganda.

Micromanagers will also erode, slowly but surely, a bedrock assumption in educational and practitioner circles, that the task of matching models (and data) to problems will always be something of an artisan activity—one that is highly compensated and one that is associated with a very specific image of the data scientist: the jack-of-all-trades.

In that image, the data scientist takes special pride in mastering all aspects of the creation of a product, from data scraping to cleaning, loading, feature creation, modeling, estimation, hyperestimation, and application building. It is a good image and yet dangerously similar to Luddite themes that did little to halt the advance of the Industrial Revolution.

Now let it be said there is no harm in increasing the supply of full-stack developers with business acumen and broad knowledge of all areas of mathematics—if that is truly feasible. However, a radical change in cost requires an equally radical rethinking of the production of prediction, not just better master craftsmen and women.

The gold rush of the 1850s doesn't convince us that panning is still the most economically efficient way to extract valuable minerals from the Earth. Nor does the little known "librarian boom" that preceded the browser convince us that Google search is redundant, on account of the Dewey decimal system. (This surge in the number of employed librarians took a ninety-degree turn right around 1991. A lesson for data scientists?)

By analogy, it comes down to the difference between the fee structure of AWS Lambda (where one pays only during invocation of a cloud function; see chapter 5) versus continuous compute. The joke in cloud computing is that you pay for the services you forget to turn off, but that's true of firms hiring dozens, hundreds, or thousands of quantitative people to build models. Continuous use of generalized intelligence is pricy.

On the other hand, low-cost automated micromanagers have so many fine uses. Are you annoyed that Google Maps doesn't know whether you can take the HOV lane?[6] That problem won't exist in a world of personal prediction.

Have you had enough of data storytellers, data life coaches, platitude peddlers, and those seeking to instill in us the "five crucial data science habits" filling your LinkedIn poker reel? In the majestic thought experiment I ask you to embrace, even that problem is in part addressable (and not, as some suspect, as fundamentally difficult as achieving general intelligence). It is a repeated prediction problem, after all.

You may regard it as trivial, but there won't be such a thing. In a world where the cost of bespoke quantitative optimization of anything has fallen by a factor of *ten thousand* and then again by *another factor of ten thousand*, you can do as you please.

1.10   Small Beginnings

Let's not debate my finger in the air cost illustration when we have a real one to refer to.

A step in the right cost direction was made by a contributor to an open-source prototype quite recently. Rusty Conover deployed high-quality models for electricity production with a running cost of less than *one cent per model per month*.[7] They are better than the official forecasts, and we know this because they are assessed and combined with others in a "collider"—to use terminology from chapter 5.

It should also be clear, from the construction of that particular algorithmic playground, that the *marginal* cost incurred when Rusty's models decide to start predicting *something else* is truly tiny.[8] That might even be something you care about, because those models could be predicting your business's data as well.

We are a very long way from being able to say anything ex post about the microprediction web thesis, unfortunately, and this book is couched as something of a prophesy. However, it is becoming increasingly plausible that this unlikely scenario is just a matter of work. When a draft of this book was first sent to reviewers, what I speak of wasn't actually working.

Now, enterprising developers have realized that they can access hundreds of self-navigating algorithms using only a few lines of code. They are predicting hospital wait times in New Jersey, the number of smiling face emojis used on Twitter, BART train delays, comment counts on the front page of *Hacker News*, and traffic delays for the bridges and tunnels around New York City.

They are identifying which algorithms are suited to water height prediction, as compared with the position of a badminton player.[9] They are sourcing insights into the dynamics of a laboratory helicopter, whose physical description is elusive due to frictions of various kinds. Algorithms fight to predict dynamics of a three-body system, the scoring differentials between two NBA teams, wind speeds, and more.

Algorithms are modeling the residuals of other algorithms. They are examining the community-implied percentiles of each and every recorded data point. This multilayer assessment of predictive accuracy is more rigorous and comprehensive than what we find in most in-house data science work.

The joint behavior of five major cryptocurrencies provides a different challenge. An epidemic agent model generates another time series, thus providing an example of crowdsourcing a surrogate model.

Herein I hope to convince you that this path can be followed to its logical conclusion—one that dethrones humans and, instead, leans on a postulated worldwide network of self-navigating programs that build models, find data, and self-organize through statistical games.

Perhaps you wish to predict how many customers will visit your restaurant in the next hour or the number of bus tickets that will remain unsold at an imminent time of departure. Maybe it is something further into the economic tail, such as the temperature of your living room ten minutes hence or the probability you will occupy it.

In this thought experiment, our preconceived notions about expense and quality of bespoke work must be squished into oblivion.

1.11 The Role of Mathematics

As we consider the possibility of a prediction web, mathematics will have a key role to play.

I'm keeping it pretty light, and I view the inclusion of technologists as the crucial ingredient. But I know many of you are mathematically curious, and if we follow the path from the application down to the source of its intelligence, we see why mathematical ideas must be informative.

Mathematical techniques create the demand for explicit as compared with implicit or embedded microprediction, because mathematics converts "business problems" into control or reinforcement learning problems (or something else) and from there into microprediction. See chapter 8.

Mathematics advises on the manner in which these applications plug into the microprediction power source—for instance, through the theory of scoring rules, as considered in chapter 7. Mathematics also informs micromanager design, and it goes without saying that mathematics is also the language in which the vast collections of prediction, classification, optimization, and inference algorithms are written—although look elsewhere for a survey.

1.12 Summary and Outline

In an imagined future where ubiquitous real-time operational intelligence has arrived at zero cost, I have prompted the reader to speculate as to the most likely origin.

Maybe this all starts when a hyperintelligent agent with generalized intelligence escapes from the DeepMind lab and starts scanning the paper for data science job openings. That might even leave industry largely unchanged, from the organizational perspective.

However, I've suggested a rather different possibility: a worldwide prediction web analogous in some ways to the internet itself. I offer the following line of argument.

1. Most real-time operational optimization can be formulated in terms of frequently repeated predictions of instrumented quantities, intermediate rewards, differences of value functions (chapter 8), averages of predictions yet received, or something else.

2. We interpret the existence of the machine learning revolution as a statement that most models can be assessed in a mechanical fashion.

3. Therefore, only trade friction prevents reward from being enough (for repeated prediction). Only trade friction prevents the emergence of radically low-cost self-organizing supply chains for microprediction.

4. When algorithms can traverse to repeated statistical games, and businesses abstract away microprediction from the rest of the applications logic, direct search cost plummets. The lemons problem fades also (due to the law of large numbers). And the walls that separate us (privacy, intellectual property) can be addressed by skullduggery of various kinds (chapter 9).

5. Microprediction quality can also continuously improve as costs fall due to network feedback (more data, more models, shared feature spaces).

6. At these extremely low levels of economic friction and microprediction cost, further feedback occurs as micromanagers start to feed off the same capability for their own managerial decisions (hiring, firing, navigation, contract formation, and so forth). This further reduces economic friction, and so on.

7. Enterprise artisan data science is severely challenged, because in the limit, trade is sufficient. In the vast majority of cases, economics dictates that algorithms summon the humans, if necessary, not the other way around.

Like a micromanager meandering through the prediction web, I find I bump into several somewhat unrelated fields in an effort to refine this hypothesis.

• Errors-in-variables models, optimization, and automated machine learning: In chapters 5 and 7, I consider the challenge of purely algorithmic management of the production of prediction.

• (Micro)economics: In chapter 4, I argue that a microprediction network addresses the problem of local knowledge much more effectively than other organizing principles.

• Contest theory and practice: In chapter 6, I argue that fanout of microprediction tasks is likely to be effective given the theoretical efficacy of contests—not to mention a key role they have played catalyzing the machine learning revolution.

• Control and reinforcement learning: Chapter 8 examines the interplay between microprediction and well-worn, effective techniques in control theory and reinforcement learning.

• Privacy preserving computation: Chapter 9 considers the coming wave of federated and outsourced analytics and some reasons why microprediction capability can move through the seemingly impermeable membranes separating private firms.

I hope you find them as interesting as I do.

2

Commercial Use

I wish to persuade you that frequently repeated prediction is profoundly useful *everywhere* and that it is best assembled by a billion little self-interested buzzards coordinated predominantly by market forces (rather than by Dilbert the data scientist).

I must say I agonized about which part of the more in-depth argument should precede the other. Why would you want to know about all the uses of something whose implementation has not been described? On the other hand, why bother with the fanciful notion of a prediction web if it isn't clear why it will benefit all players, or at least your own business or application?

Fortunately, the trend is my friend, and many already consider it a mathematical truism that frequently repeated prediction is not only useful but also, in some sense, *universally useful*. Enumerating applications can be tedious, so my recommendation would be that you skip forward as soon as you are convinced of this.

On the other hand, a more abstract connection between microprediction and repeated decisions *of just about any kind* is the subject of chapter 8. I don't know if you prefer examples or logic.

The more controversial ansatz for this chapter is the notion of a so-called microprediction oracle. That will be refined in chapters 3 and 5, but for now, we shall assume a powerful source of predictive power has been made available to us that works only on *frequently repeated tasks of the same kind*.

Beyond that, you don't need to know a great deal, if anything, about the internal workings of the oracle. Suffice to say that if you were to open it, you'd find a seething, teeming melee of algorithms all trying to out do each other in their efforts to provide you superior prediction.

2.1 Cleaning Reference Data

In our quest to change data science, we shall start with a janitorial position and see if we can work our way up. It is daunting because data cleaning is a vast problem. No grandiose solution is contemplated here, but it can certainly benefit from repeated prediction.

Let's dispense with one misunderstanding—the mostly harmful meme captured by the hackneyed phrase "garbage in, garbage out." This can be construed as meta-advice: that some *nonmathematical* data-cleaning activity should always precede mathematical analysis of data. For instance, it is the norm to employ people to clean databases in the style of pecking chickens and without any overarching theoretical strategy.

Rules piled upon rules are a recipe for technical debt and plateauing accuracy. We all have our war stories. I once participated in the acquisition of a data company that, under the covers, comprised an ever increasing list of regular expressions used to extract market data.

Over time, these rules had begun to contradict each other. And the system was so aggressive in extracting data that it created multiple versions of prices for the very same company. It could not be salvaged, and our engineers had to gut it and start from scratch with a different system.

There were no microprediction oracles on hand at the time, which is a shame, because these wonderful things provide an easy way to chip away at a situation that we can all agree is dismal. The idea is simple enough: predict whether humans are going to fix a data point, or record, or not. I'd ask you not to recoil at the fact that this is a kind of secondary, or derived, prediction of something that isn't accurate—because that's precisely why I mention it.

It's just data. The status of a record will change if a human corrects the record in some way, such as by reconciling a company name, fixing an erroneous ZIP code, or moving a decimal two places to the left.

The oracle is asked for a probability that this record will be corrected. Records with a relatively high probability of change are flagged. Then we rank sort by probabilities of change, and this helps direct humans toward dubious records faster. The end.

Now is this a win? Perhaps a small one. Perhaps a large one. It all depends on what's instrumented, rates of data flow, and so on. But don't let me limit your strategies. I merely use this example of chicken feeding to disabuse you of the notion, if that were necessary, that microprediction targets need to be holy truths (let's face it, that's a pretty decent trap for those anchoring to prediction markets). Once you realize they don't need to be, the space of possibilities explodes.

Just to beat up on that a little, notice that it matters not that the probabilities of changing a record are low, or that there is a high chance that a dirty record will remain that way when the time comes to assess the veracity of prediction. It also doesn't matter if a human sometimes incorrectly modifies a record, making it worse than before.

Evidently, there is no pristine ground truth to be found in this usage pattern. There is injustice in the judging. And that seems terrible at first until you realize that it is merely a time-saving device. I'm guessing your whiny data scientists might complain about being asked to predict something that is clearly wrong, but the oracle won't.

Oracles are portals into competitive prediction. But you'll notice that my emphasis runs very much against the grain of the long tradition of machine learning contests. Usually, in a contest, one works hard to ensure the target is of high quality—the rationale being that answers that are noisy, frequently incorrect, or lacking in authority might dissuade earnest effort or fail to align with scientific goals. (We return to contests in chapter 6.)

Yet the pattern, as well as many like it, is not alien to machine learning research. It is reminiscent of the use of weakly supervised data for training, and I think the reader will find inspiration in other data augmentation techniques as well or in crowd sourcing techniques such as expectation maximization.

When combined with privacy techniques considered in chapter 9 or when used on public reference data, oracles used for data cleaning can be more effective. Competing parties can help each other reduce common costs, even if they would not in the normal course of events take the time to collaborate on the minutiae of field types, names of columns, spelling, subcategory labels, and so forth.

Evidently, if an oracle is asked about the domicile of a legal entity by six or seven different oracle users, it will learn more quickly, thus achieving the benefits of an otherwise unwieldy consortium. I'm brushing aside privacy concerns for now because although we aren't there yet, theory demonstrates that it is not necessary for parties to reveal information to each other in order that this goal be achieved (and in some cases, they don't mind anyway).

One might devise other intricate patterns of usage. A microprediction oracle can be used at different levels of granularity. For instance, one oracle might predict the type of a field based only on values taken by records.

It might be clever enough to conclude, having inspected a list of dates, that some are highly likely to take on specific significance (such as roll dates for financial contracts, high-volume shopping days, or half-days).

Mathematical approaches to data cleaning are arguably more advanced and nuanced than straight-up supervised learning problems. The search in the space of possible algorithms (with their various strengths and compromises) is correspondingly more difficult.

Take practical fast Bayesian inference, for example. That's a super-category of data-cleaning technique. It will always be improved by someone, somewhere. Wouldn't it be good if data-cleaning algorithms could travel across a prediction network and find an unexpected application?

2.2   Enhancing Live Data Feeds

Closely related to the cleaning of data is the use of microprediction oracles for defining, enhancing, and discovering live data that can help drive business decisions. (You're moving up in the world, after your data-cleaning success, so let's impress the front office.)

As we will explore in chapter 5, real-time competitive prediction encourages exogenous data search and can thereby turn weak notions of truth into statistically stronger representations. Alternatively, it can turn complex multifaceted data into a clean representative, univariate time series.

As a special case, microprediction oracles can turn intermittent data into continuous. If something is measured once a day or once an hour, it can be converted into a continuous estimate using an oracle.

Oracles can be created for all the standard operators on stochastic processes, such as the conditional expectation operator. An oracle can produce a martingale given any time series. An oracle receiving distributional predictions can standardize any time series by performing a probability integral transform—and we'll see an example in chapter 5.

For those readers with the stomach, allow me to illustrate oracle patterns for streaming data enhancement with a very specific example. After all, data cleaning is all about getting down and dirty. I steer you to the Depository Trust and Clearing Corporation's (DTCC's) Swap Data Repository (SDR), which you can direct your browser to while reading this, should you wish.[1]

The SDR data is lagged, contains erroneous trade timestamps from time to time, demonstrates trade data arriving out of order (quite common in data feeds), illustrates the simultaneous use of multiple price conventions that can potentially confuse a naive user, and lists prices of transactions without a label indicating who was the likely aggressor in the transaction.

The data issues illustrated by the public swap data feed are not intended as a criticism, merely an opportunity for enhancement. It is an example of the pragmatic difficulties faced by anyone intending to use such information in a fully automated fashion. As a minor yet subtle example, reported transaction volume is capped. Yet sometimes it is later revealed.

A more useful and unrelated enhancement of the data might involve a more detailed statistical analysis of price time series—one that might contain enough material for several PhD theses. For instance, the feed could be enhanced with a mid price. (Although "mid price" often refers to the average of the current bid and offer for a security, this is rarely a useful definition for many securities—except at certain points of liquidity accumulation during the trading day.)

There are different kinds of mid prices. Let's say a mid price refers to a more elusive and ill-defined quantity representing a stable reflection of the market-implied value of a security—minus the jiggling that occurs due to asynchronous arrival of trades with different motivations from different clientele.

If the prices reported were to be compared to any reasonably con-structed mid price of this sort and the differences termed an error for the sake of discussion, then the data will resemble a latent variable model with skewed and serially correlated errors.

The data revealed in a history of trades of different types is subject to an asymmetric pattern of noise due mostly to the possibility of winner's curse. In the context of limit order books (stock exchanges) the phe-nomenon of serial correlation in price relative to a mid is called bid-offer bounce. The interested reader is referred to the market microstructure literature.[2]

Understandably, this combination of statistical and domain noise cre-ates problems for those looking to use this feed downstream. This suggests the use of microprediction oracles as a means of *defining* a feed that is likely to have more benign characteristics. A layering of oracle use cases can be employed, as follows.

The first step could use an unsupervised oracle pattern to identify outliers in the data—such as prices reported using alternative quoting conventions. The oracle will use some style of consensus calculation, for example, using the contributions themselves as part of the answer against which all algorithms are judged.

Next, another oracle can be used to predict the next price reported fifteen minutes from now that has a less than 10 percent chance of being deemed an outlier. The oracle's response can be called a mid.

Next, mids created in this manner can be used to construct more elaborate targets for forecasting, including the realized covariance between mid changes—a quantity that might feed downstream into some useful application for trading or hedging.

Other oracle calls could be used to flag possible anomalies in market behavior such as liquidity problems or suspicious activity. And as explored in chapter 8, real-time decisions can be driven by all this information that is generated on the fly.

There is, of course, nothing special about our choice of the swap data repository as an example. Almost any market data feed can be expanded to a richer feature space—provided there is sufficient flowing or cross-sectional data to justify use of a microprediction oracle.

Boutique and obscure data sold to market participants can be enhanced by adding an oracle-generated term structure. (A term structure in our context refers to a collection of separate but related microprediction tasks pertaining to predictions at different horizons, such as one hour, two hours, end of day, one business day, one week, or one month hence.) As explained in chapter 3, the oracle can fan out the task. Who can say that the temporal dependence structure is not a good match for an algorithm developed by a hobbyist in Budapest?

You can see where this is going. In fact, we have arrived at a recipe for generating an almost limitless number of applications. One finds two parties, one of which sells streaming data for the other, and then one stages a "microprediction in the middle" attack.

Furthermore, because of the ease with which superior prediction of market data can be monetized by some participants (either by market taking or market making), it is equally apparent that data directly *defining* financial securities, or investing parameters, or otherwise embedded in the mechanics of trading securities can also be enhanced.

If you need an example, look no further than the use of evaluated bond prices sold by vendors. These determine the daily calculation of net asset values for some exchange-traded credit funds. Predicting what others will assess is worthwhile.

Further discussion might take us far afield. The world is full of data feeds, and most of them are very difficult to use, yet potentially very easy for a swarm of algorithms to reformulate. Cleaning is inference. Inference is a variety of microprediction.

Now if you skimmed this section, I don't blame you. But I also don't want you to forget this massive category of application. The short version is, that if you allow ravenous algorithms to feed off anomalies and statistical artifacts in a data feed, they will, in the process, enhance it in various important ways.

I dare say this resembles the Japanese practice, now spreading to the United Kingdom and elsewhere, of cleaning one's feet by dipping them in a bucket of hungry fish. There, now you will remember it.[3]

2.3   Enhancing Business Intelligence

Business intelligence (BI) projects allocate a technology spend (often quite large) for the aggregation of business information deemed important to real-time decisions.

Yes, I know that some of you out there regard "business intelligence," by this definition, to be a rung or two below artificial intelligence when the only remotely analytic activity involves pivoting data in a table. However, you will be reeducated in chapter 4 until you appreciate the key role of fleeting situational awareness in any economy.

Besides, your CEO, impressed by your ability to enhance data, wants you to surface insights. It's dashboard time! That translates into considerable engineering resources operating through multiple feedback cycles and the cost of commercial visualization software as well, quite often.

You explain to your grateful leader that since the company is investing so much in dashboards, it's a no-brainer to add the marginal cost of oracle-based microprediction of those very same numbers. After all, the information is already streaming to eyeballs. The data preparation has already been done. And a live source of data is within inches of a well-defined prediction task.

Even better, the steps for converting a live source of data (such as a table) into a well-defined microprediction task by specifying an accuracy metric (pitfalls are discussed in chapter 7) do not require programming. Selection of fields to be predicted, attributes, prediction horizons, and other configurations can be accomplished with a user dialog.

Dashboards are often passive applications. However, an extension of this idea applies when humans have control levers to move. There are many possibilities for rich applications to be built, powered by oracles. For example, action conditional micropredictions could be supplied as described in chapter 8 and rendered in imaginative ways for the user.

2.4   Weak Universal Data Feeds

Really, the only problem you experience with the dashboard enhancement is its insufferable triviality. It actually hurts you physically to explain that if provided a microprediction oracle, a live number can be predicted at zero marginal cost. To maintain sanity, you start to play with the oracle in more imaginative ways.

As with the use of imperfect human-cleaned data, you become interested in microprediction of things that aren't true. You consider the use of a "weak fact" like the number of times "raining [in] Auckland" is mentioned in texting conversations or social media posts between 11:00 a.m. and 11:30 a.m.

This is evidently not equivalent to a physical fact, but when fed to a microprediction network it is a lure for real data, such as meteorological readings from a sensor, images from a webcam, or any other source of information in the physical or digital world that can help a clever algorithm make a prediction.

When you ask the prediction web to predict "bad" data, better data can be surfaced, connections to other exogenous data can be discovered, and useful transformations of the data can be found. Indeed, this data that is lured into the prediction web can be *more valuable than the target*. So predicting something seemingly worthless can be very worthwhile!

After all, good data is a highly competitive predictor of "bad data" that pretends to instrument the same ground truth. Good predictions of bad representations of ground truth are *correlated* with better data and thus with the ground truth itself.

Expanding on our example of rain in Auckland, consider a large corpus of streaming text data. We look for the phrase "bridge traffic," "Trump resigns," "blackout," "GE raises capital," and so on. Each generates its own stream of data, and each is very far from any normal definition of ground truth.

More likely, these counts mostly represent anything other than contemporaneous truth—probably gossip, false reports, historical commentary, and uses of words with other intents. But this doesn't matter. Behind an oracle tasked with predicting fake news lies a self-organizing supply chain hungry for data and reaching out its tentacles in a cost-efficient manner.

Thus, in sending counts of "raining [in] Auckland" to the microprediction web, we are not only determining if it is raining in Auckland but also might be "seeding rain," as it were—a cascade of new data feeds. Thereby, we are helping give rise to a large and interesting live feature space of interest to many. This pattern is not limited to sources of text data.

2.5 Ongoing Performance Analysis

You've been having fun, but it's time to get promoted. Your manager suggests you move to model governance to accomplish this. Aside from constituting good practice, the ongoing performance analysis (OPA) of models is a regulatory requirement in some industries. The cost of model oversight in banking, to pick one, is significant, and thus any automated means of enhancing the process bears consideration.

Anecdotally, up to a third of quantitative employee time can easily be consumed by various tasks related to model compliance. An example is provided by SR-11-7—the advisory notice on model risk management issued by the Federal Reserve and Office of the Comptroller of the Currency.

What's striking about a microprediction web populated by hungry micromanagers is the extent to which regulators have been asking for it. The act of feeding streaming data to an oracle serves as a clear definition of inputs up and down the line, as suggested by regulators. It encodes the notification of the use of new sources of historical data.

Regulators have asked for verification of numerical approximations. They have suggested that the completeness of data be considered (impossible without a microprediction web) and that data-cleaning procedures be scrutinized. They have demanded that models be scrutinized for robustness to missing data in inputs and that consistent use of inputs be monitored.

As will become clear in chapters 5 and 7, many more well-meaning ambitions of regulators are automatically satisfied in a microprediction web. This can include specific tests of predictive capability, such as the monitoring of upstream and downstream model interactions, or the monitoring of key drivers of predictions feeding business applications.

At some level, it is rather obvious that subjecting models to competition (or competitively predicting their errors) contributes materially to the myriad objectives of model governance. And evidently, businesses not subject to regulatory requirements can also benefit from the spirit of those regulatory ambitions. In particular, all firms submitting model residuals to oracles can benefit from the ongoing improvement in performance that arises from the maturation of the microprediction supply chain. We shall return to this pattern in chapter 9.

2.6 Fairness

Now you are a manager. It's a good thing you are a fair person with a fair amygdala. That is the part of the neural system that is believed to control your sense of perceived threat. (As an aside, studies have shown that amygdala sensitivity to race is not something we are born with, emerging later around the time of adolescence. Studies of sensitivity to mathematics among senior management are forthcoming.)

Your new boss wants you to tackle the immensely difficult question of model fairness. Fairness is just one of many regulatory requirements but surely bears special consideration. Unfortunately, in my view, noble desires to improve modeling fairness are rarely accompanied with an equal desire to solve the problem I consider to be inextricably linked: search in the space of data.

This is where a microprediction network can come to the fore. It isn't possible to be fair if relevant data explaining bias is never found, because the identification of exogenous data is critical to the discovery of *hidden* biases.

There are pitfalls in simple interpretations of models, such as in using direct influence of a variable as a substitute for explanation. A representation of a model that attributes a decision made by a model to a small number of factors may create the false impression that other variables are irrelevant to what is really going on.

The classic example in the United States is redlining: the systematic denial of various services to residents of specific, often racially associated, neighborhoods or communities, either directly or through the selective raising of prices.[4] A potentially clever use of an oracle for civic use is suggested by studies that use the Home Mortgage Disclosure Act (HMDA) data.

Mendez et al. demonstrated that mortgage approval models that did not *explicitly* reference race were indirectly influenced via ZIP code.[5] The problem remains pervasive across many types of modeling used to extend consumer credit—according to some literature—and in decisions such as where to build grocery stores.[6]

Although not all of these problems are quintessential uses of a real-time microprediction oracle, there may well be sufficient cross-sectional data for automated detection of unfairness. A microprediction network that can locate explanatory data serves a supervisory role—one that no supervision of the type we are used to could achieve.

Imaginative use of oracles that fan out prediction tasks can drive down the cost of fairness. That should be important even to those not prioritizing the task, because fairness will increasingly become mandated. New York City is among the first to legislate fairness in algorithmic decision-making, for example.[7]

Micromanagers who source data, create features, and analyze outputs can be helpful to the process, given that bias is a curious thing. For example, it has been shown that light-skinned subjects who adopted a dark-skinned avatar in a virtual reality game significantly reduced their measured racial bias against dark-skinned people.[8]

But did we need humans to discover this? Could a traveling fairness algorithm, observing player statistics, have alerted us much earlier? Could this have been done without invading the privacy of players or the commercial interests of the game makers? (Almost certainly yes, along the lines of chapter 9.)

Needless to say, algorithms have their own problems, insofar as they grow up in environments taking the form of training examples, so they may be the biggest consumers of micro-fairness. They themselves know that they can be unfair in ways that are more subtle than the redlining example. The *indirect* effects of variables must be screened. One approach uses data augmentation and runs as follows:[9]

1. Minimal modifications are made to the data until the feature in question (say race) cannot be predicted from the remaining data.
2. Model predictions are assessed before and after this data augmentation.

I can't tell you if this is the best method, but why do I need to? With a clever setup, methods for fairness and explanation can traverse the prediction web looking for models to interrogate. As with the data-cleaning example, this can surface good opportunities for targeted use of human generalized intelligence.

2.7 Explaining

I have claimed that fairness demands a better search for data. Fairness also involves model explanation, our next topic.

The really unfair thing in this world is that models need to explain themselves in great detail, whereas human decision makers aren't held to quite the same standard. Explainable AI is an area that attracts the mathematical meta-advisers too, because it seems like one can fake sensible-sounding advice without a great deal of technical experience to back it up.

You don't need to explain yourself to them, fortunately, but you do need to explain why you spent the company's money attending an AI conference. Naturally, it was to stay up to speed with the fast-moving field of explainable AI.

To give an example, the influence function traces the output of a model back to the individual data points that were used to train it. An example of an influence function used in finance would be the impact of a single past trade on the current indicative price supplied to a trader. Techniques such as this tend to travel surprisingly slowly from one field to another over the course of many years. Many started in robust statistics fifty years ago.

As another example, the utility of adjoint sensitivity techniques was better appreciated in meteorology than finance when, faced with a large-scale financial data assimilation task a few years ago, I found myself looking for them. What if algorithms didn't have to wait on humans and our relatively feeble search ability?

Most major conferences include an explainability track. At the Neural Information Processing Systems (NeurIPS) conference in 2017, I took note of the wording of the ambition: "New machine-learning systems will have the ability to explain their rationale, characterize their strengths and weaknesses, and convey an understanding of how they will behave in the future."

In the light of the microprediction web hypothesis, this may be a limited and limiting ambition, because in the presence of a prediction web, the algorithms need not all have the ability to explain themselves (but they will be able to reach other algorithms that can.) To assume otherwise is to place too much overhead on the creation of a model and too little faith in the self-organizing ability of micromanagers.

Automated assessment of explanations is not far-fetched at all. Not nearly as far-fetched as the idea that humans, using only the English language, can agree on what XAI is supposed to be.

For example, the military is investing in explainable AI. The Defense Advanced Research Projects Agency (DARPA) program puts the emphasis on the production of a greater quantity of *explainable* models (as opposed to efforts to explain models not designed to be explainable at the outset) while maintaining a high level of learning performance (as opposed to what I'm not sure).[10] Perhaps I over read, but this suggests to me that explainability is leaning toward being a *constraint* and not just an ambition.

Should XAI stand for "explaining artificial intelligence" or "explainable artificial intelligence"? I churlishly suggest that if humans aren't sure what XAI actually stands for and can't communicate precisely, then we best leave it to the machines. Do we want more "explainable models" or "more explainable" models?

But however we interpret XAI, this undertaking is likely to be frustrated by the availability of data, just as fairness is. Data cannot be easily found in general, cannot be owned at a reasonable price sometimes, and often cannot be sold at *any price* due to regulations or privacy.

Suppose you are issuing credit. No matter how advanced the technique might be, if you don't possess a critical attribute of a small business, you have to ask yourself if you really understand *yourself* precisely why you denied it credit.

But if more firms tap into the prediction web, fairness and explainability might advance with the ongoing development of statistical and cryptographic techniques, which allow calculations to be performed across boundaries, including those that offer model explanations.

An example of a fairness-enhancing private calculation is a secure join. Another is a computation of Granger causality between two parties who never reveal any data to each other. Traditional methods of achieving privacy by aggregation (such as with census reporting) may also work.

If not, advanced techniques that exploit individual information without ever revealing it can succeed. While the methods are already very clever, they will get faster and more convenient over time. We'll return to the topic of privacy in chapter 9.

In the interim, I want to go just a little deeper into model explainability to advance a hypothesis that is very important to my case for a prediction web. The key observation is that while some types of model explanation will be particular to specific approaches, many explanations are *model independent*.

Why would we want to allow humans to get in the middle of things and add tremendous cost to the application of model-independent explainability techniques when the algorithms are perfectly capable of finding each other?

2.8   Models Analyzing Models

Explainability can be viewed as an example of models interrogating other models—something we could see a lot more of when a microprediction web emerges. The topic is more general than XAI, but to make this discussion concrete, I would like to couch it in reference to the mildly dubious notion of explainable human intelligence (XHI).

I suggest that for the most part, machines can already explain themselves. They can explain each other roughly as well as humans explain themselves or each other. Explainability is a last-mile problem. If you are not convinced, consider the following examples of human explanation:

1. *The sparse coefficients explanation:* Our decision is complex but we explain it in terms of a single regressor: *I'm pretty sure I am going to like this movie because Harrison Ford is in it.*
2. *The influence explanation:* We explain a decision in terms of past evidence that was key to forming the theories in our heads. *I'm been short bitcoin ever since that gasbag touted it at the conference last year.*

These are pretty straightforward for the machines observing other machines, provided there's enough data flowing. But let's continue with some additional types of human explanation (and algorithmic equivalents) to see if we humans can improve.

3. *The surrogate model:* Confronted with the impossible task of explaining what is really in our heads (and how we might have reacted to different hypothetical input), we reach for a simpler surrogate model that has more or less equivalent conclusions. *I decided that XAI is a nascent field because wiggle words like "toward" appear too often in talk titles.*
4. *The proximity explanation:* We proffer hypothetical examples of the model in our heads that are proximal to the data point in question. *Well I know this seems strange, and if one of those four test results had been different, I would have started you on antibiotics, but take two of these instead and call me in the morning if you still can't get out of bed.*
5. *The intermediate results explanation:* We provide transparency into some calculation that occurred along the way without necessarily providing the preceding or following details. *Your total itemized deductions are right at the standard deduction and that's why you'll lose under the Trump tax plan.*
6. *The inversion explanation:* We try to provide quintessential, or sometimes extremal, examples of input corresponding to a classification output. This doesn't really explain the model in the mind of the highway patrolman, but it can mollify. *I don't know where the line is but look buddy, if you drive at 100 on the parkway and weave all over the place, I'm pulling you over.*

As can be seen, humans struggle to make these explanations compelling and consistent—assuming one is provided at all. Our "mental model" explanations seem too often to depend on the question, and even a large number of questions might fail to reveal some consistent underlying model.

A possible exception is the legal system, which has tried to counter human mental model inconsistency by holding to a reasonably simple global model, something akin to a classification tree.[11] Judges will sometimes argue from precedent, which can be viewed as a variety of influence explanation. Ways of steering away from making any judgment in some circumstances are also the subject of ongoing research.

Yet it will be clear to the technical reader that all these categories of human explanation, and no doubt others, can already be replicated in algorithms—often quite simply. And far more important, the explanation is *model independent*. The explaining model does not know the operation of the model that is being explained. So, let me replay my argument:

1. We'd like algorithms to explain themselves as well as humans, but
2. Humans can't really exhibit an underlying model and *there probably isn't one.*
3. It follows that model-independent explanation is the best we can do, but this can be applied en masse.
4. It follows that the cost of applying model-independent explanation can, and should, be driven toward zero.

In contrast, the status quo implicitly assumes that the person who creates the model also has encyclopedic knowledge and time required to explain the predictions. This is quaint and implausible.

It is, I conclude, high time we got that prediction web off the ground. Let the algorithms roam, including those that help explain other models.

2.9 Surrogate Models

Explainability is a segue into the topic of surrogate modeling, since that was one of the methods I listed for explaining a model. However, if you really want to wow your boss, it is worth considering the independent motivations for modeling a model. For instance, you might be able to present a five order of magnitude speed increase in a regularly used business calculation—one that has a much lower effective dimensionality than might appear from all the inputs.

Chapter 5 will consider some ways that oracles can be used to assist or entirely replace the process of building surrogates. A long-running calculation can serve as the truth provided to the oracle, long after the fact, if necessary.

To illustrate, let us imagine that an open-source algorithm for simulating a component of a climate model is available but takes ten minutes to run. Let us further suppose this results in five key numbers as outputs. The prediction task conveyed to the oracle would specify these parameters but insist on a five-second timeout, forcing the competing algorithms to make approximations.

Surrogate models are widely used in atmospheric modeling and industrial simulation. The use of surrogate functions in applied mathematics is well developed, particularly in the context of optimization.[12]

Beyond the desire to explain, the term *surrogate* often brings additional connotations, such as when the model used to approximate another has convenient qualities. It may admit derivatives, or it may be possible to know where the minimum or maximum points lie.

For all their utility, surrogate functions might not be as useful as what we might call surrogate microprediction. Oracles are both surrogate models *and surrogate data* attractors. By surrogate data, I mean any data substituting for the predictive capability (not standard terminology, as far as I know).

A business may believe it is beholden to an important prediction ingredient such as an expensive data feed or an in-house process, but a micro manager can be used to quantify the marginal contribution of the data. This can inform data procurement decisions, which sometimes take on a combinatorial flavor (three cheap feeds replacing two expensive ones).

2.10 Augmenting Control Systems

Still reading?

In the preceding examples, you have leveraged a mysterious source of repeated prediction power to sneak up the data science pyramid. Perhaps nobody paid much attention to how you did it, because your use of a general-purpose prediction API was so nonchalant.

Perhaps they are simply too proud to follow in your footsteps. After all, to use a prediction oracle requires an acknowledgment of your own modeling or data search limitations. Studies suggest that less than 5 percent of data scientists are ready to go there.

But as noted in the introduction, the entire edifice of artisan data science might be ready to come crashing down for this and other reasons, so it's time to head for the exit. As a last example, we consider the elevator—or really process optimization in its generality.

In the early stages of COVID-19, while we were still at work but socially distanced, elevators were a maligned optimization problem. Long delays were experienced in the lobby. People had a lot of time to ponder about value function prediction and the fact that at a high level, elevator optimization is analogous to lots of other optimization tasks. (If you didn't, there's still time in chapter 8.)

Elevator optimization presents a pattern of the use of decentralized, but related, repeated decisions—with very well-studied analogues in reinforcement learning and control. One can try to approximate a globally optimal solution through the use of individual oracles driving each elevator car.[13]

Traditional elevators without floor dispatch already present an NP-hard problem to modelers (meaning darn hard). But one harbinger of the so-called artificial intelligence revolution is the fact that optimized dispatch in elevator banks has been creeping into buildings in recent years.

A person approaches the elevator bank and enters a floor number. The dispatcher sends them to elevator C. Elevator C stops at floors 13, 19, 27, and 28. This dispatch can be viewed as an example of a conditional microdecision made over and over again by software.

The details will depend on what can be instrumented. For example, if we have video feeds of people waiting on floors, more precision could be brought to bear. But even if we only have the operational data from the elevator itself, we can construct the equivalent of a positional evaluation of a chessboard based on passenger throughput and journey time.

Alternatively, we can start with a relatively noninvasive assessment of an existing elevator dispatch system. Consider it a side optimization, if you will. We can assume that a mathematical approach has already been implemented in the elevator system—but that approach has shortcomings, which will be revealed as the prediction web matures. (One day it will seem unacceptable for an elevator dispatch system to be ignorant of Saint Patrick's Day pedestrian flow, early closes to trading, or the progress of important court cases keeping lawyers on the high floors at night.)

Whatever the elevator dispatch program does, the one thing we might boldly assume is that it generates a stream of explicit or implicit predictions about its own performance—the future state of the combined happiness of all elevator passengers (travel time and comfort) against some measure of energy consumption and safety.

The elevator program might even generate falsifiable predictions of individual travel times and other quantities that enter its calculations. An oracle can be used to correct bias and reduce uncertainty in any number of these internal predictions, thereby improving the internal optimization that may remain opaque to the oracle.

Alternatively, an oracle pattern may be used that invites a direct decision or an estimation of an action-conditional value function forecast, as also discussed in chapter 8.

It may seem strange that I pick on elevators, but as noted by Andrew G. Barto, a long-recognized pioneer in reinforcement learning, elevator optimization is a testbed for new approaches (such as the speculative use of oracles I propose). The classical elevator problem presents a *combination of challenges not seen in most multiagent learning to date.*

If so, it bodes well for the efficacy of oracle usage, given that different tasks might be better performed by different people and algorithms, utilizing different sources of data. I will return to the topic of specialization within decision-making in chapter 8, as further motivation for a microprediction supply chain.

2.11   What's It All Worth?

Well, good for you for reading this far into this chapter, given that enumerating the uses of repeated short-term prediction is a bit like enumerating the uses of duct tape.

I honestly do not intend a survey of artificial intelligence—but from these examples, one could certainly pan out and, in some very hand-wavy way, assess the monetary potential for a microprediction web.

Actually, I have left out many areas not because they are commercially uninteresting but because I presume you are already familiar with them. There is a glut of material these days and many existing applications of AI to business. I will be content with two ways we can try to wrap our arms around all of this.

The first idea is to look at the historical use of statistical crowdsourcing. This lower bound on the utility of data-hungry methods seems appropriate, given that we wish to learn from data science contests in chapter 6. Needless to say, a problem for which a data science contest has been arranged suggests a repeated statistical task whose solution can be assessed mechanically. If not, it might have been a dud contest.

Table 2.1
Fanout in taxonomy of categories of applications for crowd sourced micro-prediction. For each major category, we list only one subcategory. For each subcategory, I list only one sub-subcategory.

Category	Example Subcategory	Example Sub-Subcategory
Recognition	Image	Facial
Search	Travel	Personalization
Recommendation	Ad-tech	Click-throughs
Government	Open cities	Flight status
Sales and CRM	Repeat shopping	Visitation
Internet of things	Homes	Usage
Environment	Air	Pollutants
Transport	Driving	Distracted driver
Manufacturing	Industrial control	Predictive maintenance
Agriculture	Juice	Orange juice
Finance	Investment banking	Commercial loans
Energy	Power	Wind
Medicine	Inventory	Hospital stays

Table 2.1 is intended to provide a glance at the fanout in application taxonomy suggested merely by examples that—would you believe—have already been the subject of competitive prediction. I have taken some data science contest examples and placed them in respective categories, or rather sub-subcategories.[14]

That's the best I can do in this format, but in reading table 2.1, one has to appreciate that in addition to "image" being a subcategory of "recognition," we also have subcategories for motion, audio, text, electroencephalography, accelerometry, written code, and microelectromechanical and mass spectrometry not shown.

Then, even within the subcategory of recognition using images, we have handwriting, remote sensing, radiology, and so forth. Then, within subcategories of facial recognition, we have further fanout into topics such as keypoint detection, face recognition, age recognition, smoking recognition, autism, and many others.

Clearly, space does not permit a survey here of the uses of quantitative modeling in a world flooded with data—not even those for which data science contests (more cumbersome than the apparatus we envisage) have already been arranged, or could quite easily be.

A second approach to sizing the use cases for microprediction leans on existing industry surveys. The magnitude of the opportunity has been obvious for some time now. Back when data was big, McKinsey went into detail to argue why a trillion dollars in value would be added to the U.S. economy with increased use of just one source of new data—consumer location.[15] They considered health care, government, and consumer use.

> First, big data can unlock significant value by *making information transparent* and usable at much higher frequency. Second, as organizations create and store more transactional data in digital form, they can collect more accurate and detailed performance information on everything from product inventories to sick days and therefore expose variability and boost performance.

As I've noted, this kind of business intelligence can easily be enhanced by microprediction oracles. But the real lift comes when actions are modified. "Leading companies are using data collection and analysis to conduct *controlled experiments* to make better management decisions."[16] It is my task in chapter 8 to complete this thought, tying microprediction to real-time operational optimization via the use of value functions. But as McKinsey's overview suggests, ad hoc adjustments can capture some of the benefit too. "Others are using data for basic low-frequency *forecasting* to high-frequency nowcasting to *adjust their business levers just in time.*" This is important but doesn't flesh out the benefits of very low-cost prediction and bespoke intelligence—unless it spreads to companies with much smaller size than the authors probably anticipated (those with no data scientists). What if every business could benefit? For example: "Big data allows ever-narrower segmentation of customers and therefore much more precisely *tailored products or services.*"

It isn't unrealistic to believe falling costs can bring these techniques to a larger demographic. A microprediction web can also be "used to improve the development of the next generation of products and services," as the authors continue, and hopefully for everyone.

Whether we read this particular industry analysis or another, it is easy to translate goals into a common abstraction rendered by a prediction web. In McKinsey's case, the terms *transparency, forecasting, variability,* and *nowcasting* are just different ways to parameterize a task assigned to an oracle, or ways to choose oracles. The phrases "tailored," "boost performance," "controlled experiments," and "adjustment of business levers" refer to microprediction also, albeit in a mildly more subtle manner, as discussed in chapter 8.

2.12 Accuracy in Dollars

One thing is clear, and that is that all industry observers are inclined to assign very large numbers to statistical value creation. I leave it to the reader, after perusing the chapters that follow, to estimate the fraction of this lift that is *not* served trivially by a collection of microprediction oracles—the power outlets connecting to a prediction grid.

Table 2.2 provides McKinsey's estimates from the aforementioned report. These numbers seem low and already dated. And needless to say the value creation is much larger when the price of a good decreases. What will happen to this trillion-dollar figure when the price of bespoke business optimization falls by ten, one hundred, or one thousand?

So while I have provided some usage categories of microprediction and patterns, I hope it is clear as we proceed that *any* instrumented business throwing off a sufficient number of data points can benefit, so long as there is some ability to make, or improve, thousands of decisions.

The question is not so much "Is it useful?" but "Where should I start?" I do not know the details of your business, but I do know that there are some instances where one can get a pretty tight grasp on the likely impact of improved accuracy.

$$benefit = (accuracy\ increase) \times (materiality) \times revenue$$

where materiality of accuracy is defined:

$$accuracy\ materiality = \frac{percentage\ revenue\ increase}{percentage\ accuracy\ increase}$$

I'm not peddling you a tautology here because sometimes, we get lucky and can estimate the materiality quite well. For example, if we know the super-linear cost of performing maintenance on a machine as a function

Table 2.2
A somewhat dated McKinsey & Company (2011) estimate of economic value creation arising from better use of location data. This presumes a high cost of data science and so vastly underestimates the potential.

Category	Value Added
U.S. healthcare	$300 billion
European government	$100 billion
Consumer location data	$600 billion

of its degradation, it isn't too hard to back into the relationship between prediction accuracy and cost.

One of my favorites examples of computing accuracy materiality comes from the world of over-the-counter market making. It translates easily to most trade, for that matter, and therein, one is able to compute the sufficient statistics that drive the profitability of a market maker.

We find that the most important number to estimate is the location parameter of other people's bids and offers (assumed stochastic). I show that the materiality of this number is, to first order:

accuracy materiality ≈ 1.5

This leads one to believe that better prediction, say 6 percent less standard error, could translate into a 10 percent revenue increase.[17]

That's some serious dough. It would not surprise me if price optimization in the trading of relatively illiquid goods turns out to be a key driver of the prediction web. But who knows if microstructure gets there before microsurgery? It will be interesting to see.

2.13 Summary

I've suggested that if an enormous quantity of cheap repeated prediction were to fall on us some day, hopefully without anyone being seriously hurt, then a lot of time and money could be saved. Ideally, we'd like prediction pixie dust to waft its way gently into every nook and cranny of operations.

Some uses will be invisible. Most end users will not need to understand and will not want to understand how microprediction is used inside applications. They will be as likely to consume raw microprediction as we are to consume raw electricity—devoid of an electrical appliance, that is.

There will be many small uses. But my case does not rest on a long tail. I don't need to convince you of the gravitational pull provided by trillions of seemingly inconsequential micro-life-optimizations—even if I claim to sense that disturbance in the Force.

Instead, I have walked through some commercially significant uses of microprediction, consciously trying to steer you away from the usual sirens associated with the word *prediction*, such as predicting the stock market.

Microprediction isn't just prediction. It can turn weak data into strong, dirty data into clean, and intermittent data into continuous in much the same way that a continuously traded stock price converts a mix of lagged accounting data into a forward-looking estimate.

Microprediction is also repeated decision-making, as well as process optimization, recommendation, supervision, anomaly detection, and many other things in many categories that rarely carry the label "prediction."

With that motivation, let us turn next to the question of how to create the best possible micropredictions at the lowest possible cost.

3

Oracles

This chapter refines the notion of a microprediction oracle and infers some minimal properties. An oracle is:

An apparatus that you can reward for a frequently repeated prediction task, on an ongoing basis, with the expectation that the accuracy will be *eventually hard to beat* on a dollar-for-dollar basis.
—Microprediction oracle definition

The physical manifestation is not our immediate concern—although we imagine a formula in an Excel spreadsheet, a Python function, a callback in a web application, a programming interface, or some use of an event processing or messaging system.

3.1 Eventually Hard to Beat

In computer science and mathematics, the term *oracle* is used differently. It refers to a mysterious source of knowledge with *perfect* prescience. A microprediction oracle as defined is imperfect but nonetheless powerful. The challenge for us is the construction of a forecasting function (to pick one incarnation) that is *as accurate as it can be sooner or later*. The reader is welcome to construct other criteria for the quality of predictive tools—but it is something of a philosophical quagmire.

I prefer to turn the nebulous nature of accuracy on its head with this definition and then reason as to what must be performed by anything trying to meet it. And I will try to exhibit a construction—by which I mean a micromanager—that, according to less than rigorous logic, only fails by a cost factor of two.

The oracle definition expresses an ambition, for micromanagers, that is a cousin to asymptotic efficiency. In statistics, we are occasionally able to devise a procedure for estimating a quantity in such a way that *eventually* (as the amount of data tends to infinity), no other method can do it better (i.e., determine a parameter's value with less error).

But a microprediction oracle is asymptotically efficient in quite a different, practical sense. It usually can't be a mathematical operator whose behavior on theoretical data is well understood. Rather, it is an engineering product that helps you predict in an economically efficient manner, by whatever means it can, every time you, say, call your Javascript function.

That intention might translate into statistical efficiency, eventually, but sample efficiency over a fixed data set might not be the distinguishing factor any time soon. As we know, the world is inhabited by people, data, and algorithms, so the most important thing a prediction device should surely do is connect you to a network of them—or the subset willing to enter a mutually beneficial relationship. It must compete with other mechanisms (whatever they might be) that are free to do the same, after all.

Thus, the thing you are using is more than a statistical function. I call it a micromanager because it must not only manage its internal cleverness and mundane responsibilities (some implementation remarks are made in chapter 5) but, more importantly in most cases, also oversee or support other, equally self-aware micromanagers (whose data and analytic capability it might not possess).

Evidently, we cannot assess the efficiency of a micromanager aspiring to be an oracle with the same rigor as we might a statistical estimator. The latter is applied to data whose properties are assumed. The former is a device placed in our messy world.

One may have some chance of analyzing a theoretical oracle efficiency if we assume models for the behavior of reward-seeking prediction algorithms (and their authors, perhaps)—for then it might be possible to derive analytical results establishing the superiority of one way of luring algorithms and data over another, or at least discern some habits of good micromanagers from simulation.

That task warrants a different format, if it can be done. Here I shall eschew an agent model of that kind, yet still hope to persuade you of some properties of a simple micromanager. Obviously, this must be a looser style of argument.

Therefore, what I ask you to take from the proximity of an oracle to efficient estimation in statistics is the key phrase in the oracle definition: *eventually hard to beat.* This quality not only makes the oracle attractive but also serves as a guiding principle for everything that follows.

Now yes, it *is* possible that your data is so well understood that you happen to know a deterministic function that is sufficient to meet the oracle definition. For instance, your data might be generated by a random walk with noise added. There may, by construction, be no exogenous data that could possibly help. If you further know the parameters of that process, then the celebrated Kalman filter is certainly *hard to beat*.

However, for the vast majority of real-world data, we will never know the true generating process. Our search for models that predict best will be never-ending and our search for data that helps to predict it also. New data is being created all the time.

Yet we wish to design some apparatus that can nonetheless answer our sequence of forecasting questions in the best way possible, eventually. In a practical sense, we must bolster the claim, using engineering, that our candidate oracle is hard to beat, now or later.

But how can *any* analytic capability be said to be hard to beat? The marketing material from an AI vendor you are reading presently assures you that their stuff is the bomb—although compared to what? And for how long? Could the errors contain residual noise? What if there was a way to find out?

In computer science, there is a maxim: write the test first. The criterion *eventually hard to beat for the same or lessor cost* is a high bar, and I assert that this mandates active open competition behind the wanna-be oracle—for how else could we hope to know that the performance is the best we can hope for, pound for pound?

3.2 Call a Friend

Now a small logical jump.

I assert that in addition to whatever else it does, a candidate oracle should allow anyone else to contribute predictions that might beat the status quo (at least for a subset of those questions demanded); that it should seek contributions from competitors and strangers, appropriately assessing their contribution; that it must include some way of combining the results of all who participate (even if that means simply choosing one); and that this should occur in real time.

Chapter 5 will introduce some categories of micromanagers that are modeled on contests, exchanges, or cost-aware regression. Any of these, as well as others the reader might devise, might satisfy these requirements.

As an aside, chapter 5 also explores why "occur in real time" can have a loose interpretation, but chapter 6 carries some warnings about the practical relevance (or lack thereof) of contest-like mechanisms that operate on fixed, increasingly stale data sets. The judging of modeling contributions using "prediction of the past" has a checkered history.

As a further aside, the oracle might be sneaky, even if it decides to challenge every possible algorithm it finds in real time. It need not forward every single question that the user of the oracle asks. It might be sparing in its communication. It might communicate with the world in ways that seem obtuse, in order to preserve privacy.

Its efforts to improve itself might be incremental or episodic in nature, as can its rewards be, and we will consider various possibilities in due course.

However, I do not wish those possibilities to obscure the larger point: that the definition of an oracle does imply some communication with external sources of data and external sources of statistical sneakiness (i.e., modeling approaches) that are not known inside the closed system that might constitute the oracle's code base, the oracle's data stores, or the oracle's complex event-processing system, et cetera.

It is conceptually simplest to start with the assumption that this communication occurs each and every time a prediction is required, and that is what I shall assume in this chapter.

Suppose, then, that this micromanager uses the call-a-friend bailout in the style of *Who Wants to Be a Millionaire?* That way, as soon as a prediction question is received, it can be addressed by other statistical algorithms authored by different people, possibly with access to otherwise unforeseen data.

We might further assume open access. We'd like *anyone or any algorithm in the world* to be able to participate. We'd like anyone to be able to improve the quality of the final prediction and to be able to do so *without asking permission*.

This differs in a rather important respect from the situation where a contributor to an open-source project submits a pull request (suggested code edit)—unless, perhaps, the passing of some statistical tests triggers an automatic merge.

3.3 Depth

The friends will call *their* friends.

Why? We're now assuming that the micromanager trying to be an oracle performs fanout to other prediction algorithms. We will also assume that this fanout is not in and of itself expensive.

That caveat is everything, and I'll return to it several times. I think we know that web requests or internal function calls need not be prohibitively expensive (depending on the requirements), but the real hidden cost here is the formation of the relationship between one algorithm and another, or their respective creators.

If relationship formation and maintenance is to be achieved using only reward, which is to say using no other compulsion beyond self-interest, then the obstacles to doing so may be classified as trade friction—one of our central ruminations. Usually, friction of this sort is many orders of magnitude higher than the cost of invoking a web service.

In chapter 5, we shall review some setups where the initiation and termination of a mutually beneficial relationship is frictionless. But we have a taste of it here already because the oracle could "try out" algorithms or the algorithms could come to the oracle. So let us assume that fanout is "free," for now.

If we do, then all our logic applies recursively. For if we believe competitive fanout and recombination can be a good way to effect repeated predictions, then within reason (i.e., a depth dictated by time or cost), this argument must apply also to the micromanagers that assist the oracle. To deny them this opportunity would be logically inconsistent.

In contrast, most competitive fanout we see today lacks depth. Popular contests are analogous to perceptrons (single-layer neural networks). A single-layer contest will eventually be outperformed by a better arrangement on a cost or accuracy basis, thereby failing the definition of an oracle.

3.4 Stacking

I pause to tighten the logic just a little.

To state that it is essential to have depth (which is to say a contest among different contest-like mechanisms as opposed to a single contest) is merely to assert that there is no obvious best way to mechanically exploit a collection of rent-seeking prediction models.

For instance, it may seem reasonable to run a simple beauty contest between models (recent accuracy) and then select the best model, give it a reward, and then use that model's predictions for the next batch of forecasts.

Unfortunately, as is well appreciated in a number of different areas, it is more often the case that some weighted average of prediction models outperforms the best one. This goes by many names, such as mixture modeling, boosting, hierarchical modeling, stacking, and so on. We see it in the gating and pooling inside neural networks.

A single model might also be outperformed by a meta-model where weights depend on the forecast question and exogenous data (and not just the accuracy of algorithms whose outputs are being combined). There is a danger lurking here because data is being used twice—but it can be effective nonetheless. (I refer the interested reader to recent work by Yao, Pirs, Vehtari, and Gelman for a discussion and references.[1])

In the Python timemachines package, an attempt at a very limited oracle-like function stacks models drawn from a shortlist of top perform-ers.[2] In the Elo ratings for time-series models that dictate this shortlisting (easily found by Google search), you can see that the leaderboard is, dare I say, stacked to the brim.

Weighted ensembles of models are performing much better than the individual models, even though these are drawn from packages claim-ing to supply autonomous forecasting capability, and even though some of those already use stacking and meta-modeling. This provides another demonstration of why choosing the best model isn't likely to be optimal in a practical setting, especially if the oracle is intended as a general-purpose end point.

A scan of the literature will convince the reader that there is no obvious *best* way to constructing stacks of models, mixtures-of-experts models, meta-models, combinations of weak learners, or anything of that ilk.

And we have yet to consider variation in the operational cost of models, something that introduces a real wrinkle in the micromanager's ongoing optimization. And we have not yet considered variation in the cost of finding models or initiating economic relationships. And we have also yet to consider the case where the friends don't supply a prediction of the quantity requested, merely data constituting a useful regressor. This really opens the can of worms.

There simply is no single best way.

3.5   Inception

This realization is the moment of inception of the microprediction web.

Because we cannot know the best way to combine models, and we cannot know the best way to manage in automated fashion a collection of models, we are drawn to something like figure 3.1, which is intended to represent a tower of micromanagers all trying to outpredict someone and, to better their chances, enlisting the expertise of other micromanagers who have access to additional techniques and data.

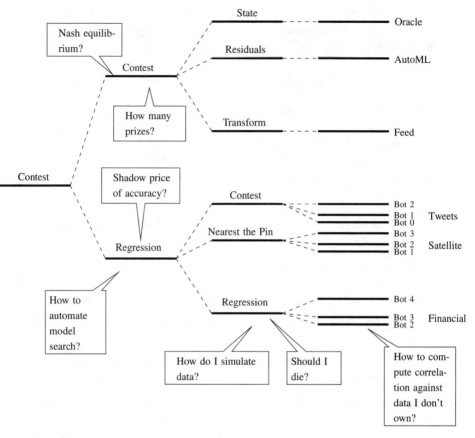

Figure 3.1
Part of a microprediction web. An oracle answers prediction questions by fanning them out to micromanagers in real time, assessing longitudinal performance, and preparing an ensemble response. Algorithms can do the same, leading to a supply chain. Some managerial issues are suggested by questions and discussed in later chapters.

If the top-level oracle is reactive (operates like a function responding to your prodding), then the more time given to respond to the question, and the lower the overhead for running a micromanager (i.e., fanout, management, etc.), the deeper the calculation tree. The more micromanagers are involved, the greater the opportunity for specialization—not to mention broad data search.

This diagram is intended to also convey some of the thorny questions that arise for micromanagers trying to survive in this game.

The oracle property is evidently not a quality of a single micromanager. Rather, it emerges over time when a complex wiring of interrelated micromanagers is driven by greed.

If we now suppose there are many users of many pseudo-oracles and a rich variety of micromanagers tapping into multiple data sources, we have the beginnings of what we might call a microprediction web.

A web-scale collection of radically low-cost self-organizing supply chains for microprediction, used almost universally to meet real-time operational needs.
—Microprediction web definition

(This definition implies reward-based decision-making by self-interested micromanagers, who are the economic agents.) An abbreviated plausibility argument that might lead one to speculate on this future possibility runs as follows.

There is no definitive solution to the problem of automatically micromanaging algorithms that perform cost-aware repeated prediction, in order to achieve cost-aware repeated prediction ... and the rest follows.
—Prediction web existence proof

But there must be something wrong with this proof, given the lack of existence of a microprediction web used universally across all industries! I posit:

1. An inadequate supply of rewarded microprediction tasks
2. Trade frictions

My hope is that advertising the possibility of a prediction web might help with the first issue. Let's turn again to the second.

3.6 Overhead

It is fair to say that our pseudo-oracle *encourages* a jumbled collection of nested and recurrent calls to micromanagers, including other pseudo-oracles (that precedes some eventual higher-level recombination—and thereby an answer returned to the user). In conjunction with chapter 4, this line of reasoning hopes to suggest that competitive tension is *necessary*.

Is it sufficient? One might cautiously say yes, the oracle definition appears to be met. For if it was easy to beat the output of this collective calculation, say with some new variety of neural network, then it should be relatively easy to endow said challenger with sufficient navigation ability (and economic common sense) that it finds its way across the network and addresses the problem.

I mean, it would be if the network existed. Darn it.

If we wish to understand why this dream is not already a reality, maybe it doesn't help to play with definitions. It perhaps pays to reiterate the critical assumption, however, or restate it thus:

The overhead of managerial responsibility is eventually negligible.
—The vanishing management principle

where "managerial responsibility" includes the aforementioned challenge for itinerant algorithms.

More colloquially put—this is all bunk if nobody can be bothered running a contest, or can afford to. A time-series model might contain just a few lines of code, so in the absence of tooling, the additional work that allows the model to roam the world and find good uses might well swamp that effort.

Our argument assumes that it is easy for anyone to also create imaginative variations on the general theme of a contest, and this would seem to be a nontrivial engineering problem. Can we really endow most of the world's data scientists with the ability to create micromanagers?

It seems that everything will grind to a halt unless, to rephrase this "overhead" issue once more:

Micromanaging cost is small compared to the work that goes into designing self-contained algorithms.
—Ratio test

Certainly we don't expect to see the microprediction web emerge on a platform that charges six-figure sums to run a one-off contest. We *might* not see it if the rewarding is broken down into millions of individual proof-of-work transactions either, although all options should be explored. We won't pass the ratio test without supplying people with software.

It is easy to fail the "ratio test." I do so constantly. For instance, my attempt at a meta-time-series model mentioned previously doesn't pass muster. Nor does a group of people writing automated machine learning software. In these examples, it is relatively expensive to tap into external sources of intelligence. (A human needs to write some code and send a pull request, typically.) It feels too much like correspondence chess.

As I sometimes refer to the buyer of microprediction as the parent and the suppliers (contestants) as children, I'd be tempted to call this test "inexpensive parenting"—if that wasn't such a dreadful oxymoron. For some applications, passing the ratio test may require tricks for dealing with volumetrics, migration of algorithms from child to parent, and other ideas.

It is rarely obvious how best to engineer systems that will be improved by other people over time. It is even harder to pass the oracle test. We are demanding ongoing open competition, and at the same time, we are suggesting that this should be easy to arrange.

That idea is not entirely foreign. It is programmer lore that unit tests are free, because they eventually save more time than they take to write (usually someone else's). But the engineering ambition, expressed in the ratio test, is that a rather more far-reaching test can also be close to free, even if that test might conceivably involve the whole world.

For it is the whole world that might eventually solicit and combine predictions, data, features, hints, or algorithms relevant to the problem at hand. Anyone should be able to engineer systems that are *automatically improved by other people and algorithms over time without their asking permission.*

They should be able to do this without incurring any kind of high cost—be that code complexity, data expense, time on the calendar, or computational burden. If we can supply this ability to as many people as possible, by means of open-source software and other conveniences, then maybe we'll get our microprediction web.

3.7   Example

Confident in the march of technology, let's make our pseudo-oracle more concrete. This example is intended to illustrate that an "edge" microman-ager (aspiring oracle, or pseudo-oracle) that faces applications doesn't need to be perfect.

3.7.1   When Will the School Bus Arrive?

What a fortunate life you live. Every day a yellow school bus pulls up to the top of your driveway and delivers your offspring. Your only task is to rush out—typically in the middle of a meeting—and meet them.

The application we have in mind is purely passive. You do not do any-thing, beyond wearing your watch. However, your watch will provide you with a two-minute warning. Your driveway is rather long, we shall assume.

Perhaps, and now we're getting fancy, you might input some indication of your cost function—which is to say how annoyed the school bus driver will be if you consistently leave them waiting.

The application must be hungry for predictive intelligence. It will face competition from other applications like it. In the absence of a prediction web, the development of a state-of-the-art predictive model might chew up months.

That model would be constantly revised. Data scientists might struggle with cleaning, extracting, and using data effectively—data drawn from a wide variety of sources with different formats.

In order to remain popular in the *eventually* competitive bus-arrival genre *forever*, the application *eventually* needs to know all sorts of things. It needs data scraped from local sources. The bus is early when there is no band practice, late during certain special events, and later yet when Mrs. Meldrum, your neighbor down the street, is asleep in her house (the driver has had to wake her once or twice—her absence from social media is a status clue).

The application logic, as distinct from the prediction logic, is pretty trivial. Your watch notices two events. The first event is your arrival near the top of your driveway. The second is your walking away. Typically, the second event occurs several minutes after the first—or at least it used to before the invention of the prediction web.

But now life is better because your watch can ping our pseudo-oracle, multiple times as needed, and receive good updated predictions of the estimated time of arrival. We imagine this is a cloud web service in this particular example (it wakes when a question arrives, does something, responds to you, and then goes back to sleep).

The second event, your walking away from your letterbox, triggers a different type of message from your watch to the aspiring oracle. It sends an approximate ground truth, and while not absolutely necessary in every application, this certainly simplifies things.

The running cost of this edge micromanager is measured in hundredths of a cent per month. Can it deliver that much value to you? We are about to find out because today, your watch held back on buzzing you for two minutes longer than usual. That's two whole minutes of sunshine you won't get in your over-optimized life.

Still, it did give you time to finish that email before walking out to meet your children.

3.7.2 Oracle Implementation

What does the pseudo-oracle do? As suggested by our reasoning, the oracle is a relay station that allows external people and algorithms to prove that they can predict the arrival time accurately. Put another way, it serves

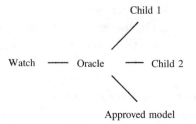

Child 1

Watch —— Oracle —— Child 2

Approved model

Figure 3.2
A pseudo-oracle serves as a real-time contest between child 1, child 2, and others not shown. Both supply predictions of when a school bus will arrive. An approved model is used to bound perceived model risk.

as an ongoing, real-time contest, as suggested by figure 3.2, and in this example, it will do very little else.

At the moment the oracle receives your question ("When will the bus arrive?"), it relays the question to a subset of the algorithms that have registered their interest. It will use its children to predict where yours are.

The watch app has conveyed, as part of the question, that it expects an answer within five seconds, so the oracle knows it had better establish a deadline for responses from children. That will allow it time to combine the results and relay them to the watch.

The oracle, or aspiring oracle we must remind ourselves, will also help initiate a relationship with other algorithms. We shall suppose it is implemented entirely reactively.

That is to say that the micromanaging pseudo-oracle answers the question "When's the bus coming?" but it also answers other types of questions that help other algorithms decide if they want to participate. For instance, the oracle might respond to questions like "What's the prize money?" with "Not much, suck it up" (or a more helpful numerical answer, maybe).

Thus far, we've followed the previous script, but now we get into a small detail, because one of the children, called the "approved model" in figure 3.2, is deemed special.

A relatively simple, well-understood model for bus arrivals is used by the oracle to generate lower and upper bounds. This model assumes that the best estimate for the arrival time of the bus is an average of the last ten arrival times. It's not a great model, but regulators can understand it instantly, and it doesn't take long to document.

3.7.3   A Modified Median Filter

Upon receiving answers from the children, the oracle must combine them and form a response for the watch. The first child's recency-weighted score is suggestively denoted V_1, the second V_2, and so forth. The oracle ranks the children by their (inaccuracy) scores from lowest to highest. The oracle then returns the median of the answers to the current question provided by the five children with lowest scores.

The exception is when that median differs from the approved model's answer by more than three minutes, whereupon the oracle adjusts the estimate closer to the approved model's answer until this is no longer the case. Thus, every answer provided by the oracle is within three minutes of the approved model (for better or worse).

A few minutes later, the oracle receives the truth message. The bus actually arrived at 3:27 p.m. The first child predicted 3:28:10. The error in the estimate given by the first child is seventy seconds. The squared error is 4900. The aspiring oracle updates the child's score

$$\overbrace{V_1(new)}^{\text{updated performance}} = 0.99 * \overbrace{V_1(old)}^{\text{previous}} + \underbrace{0.01}_{\text{speed}} * \overbrace{4900}^{\text{score}}$$

and does the same for all children. In the event that a child fails to respond, or provides a badly formatted answer, it is put in the doghouse (just as you will be if you are consistently late). The child's score is reset:

$$\overbrace{V_1(new)}^{\text{updated}} = \underbrace{360000}_{\text{reset inaccuracy}}$$

This amounts to a presumed standard error of ten minutes, which we assume is pretty poor.

3.7.4   Payouts

I assume that periodically, the oracle pays out accumulated prizes (received from the watch application) to children, according to their accuracy measured over some epoch (say a month). The most accurate model receives *half the total reward*. Less accurate contributors receive smaller prizes of $\frac{1}{4}, \frac{1}{8}, \frac{1}{16}, \frac{1}{16}$, based on both the accuracy and originality of their contribution.

A simple way to define originality is by establishing an epoch-based priority scheme modeled after the patent system. Contributions are disqualified if they are consistently close to a contribution with greater vintage.

3.8   Analysis

This completes the description of a very elementary attempt at an oracle. It may seem unlikely to meet our definition, but let's fast-forward several years. Perhaps by this time, the arrival estimates are extremely accurate because everyone in your neighborhood is using it, thereby generating more data and rewards.

Perhaps by this time, the small rewards have prompted someone to put a tracking device on the bus itself, thereby driving the prediction error to essentially zero. There is no such thing as cheating, in this particular contest.

3.8.1   Accomplishments
The supply chain we have encouraged:

1. permits granular contributions,
2. and thus specialization,
3. and also cross-subsidy (sharing of data and features),
4. and possibly new data creation,
5. with zero *mandated* human management or the inevitable overhead.

There are some possible downsides too, beginning with fear of opaque and changing model processes.

3.8.2   Model Risk
The beauty of the microprediction domain is that sometimes the so-called model risk is bounded. We merely observe that the oracle's predictions are "explainable within three minutes," and with that, the materiality of the model risk has been capped. Bounding model risk isn't the same as bounding risk; it merely establishes that the risk is no worse, materially, than it is with any other solution that is considered to have acceptable model risk. (Please don't complain. Some if not most model risk policies are ridiculous due to the Stone–Weierstrass theorem, which can be translated to state that models with allegedly comprehensible risk are dense in the space of all models. What logic would you have me build on top of that quicksand?)

The use of the approved model isn't "free," by the way. If the bus can't start one day, and several models with superior data can discern this, too bad for you. The circuit-breaker will prevent you from being alerted to the full extent of the delay and therefore you may wait quite a while—albeit three minutes less than if you had relied only on an approved model.

So by various metrics, there is a cost to using the approved model. However, on an amortized basis, this cost is much smaller than other possible costs that might be imposed upon us—such as documenting, redocumenting, and redocumenting the operation of all models that contribute as they constantly improve.

3.8.3 Resistance to Manipulation

The aspiring oracle is designed with simplicity and robustness in mind.

That's not to suggest we shouldn't be wary. A denial attack occurs when a participant clones the same entry many times (with a tiny amount of noise pollution). We will assume that this is defeated by the priority defense—although in practice, there are other defenses too.

A Sybil attack, as we might term it, occurs when a nefarious source of intelligence creates three highly accurate prediction algorithms that are quite different yet outperform all others in the contest (the adversary may likely invest more effort than is warranted by the small rewards, in order to pull this off). Over the course of several months, these entrants achieve the lowest error, thus taking control of the median.

Then, one day, they conspire to return a bogus answer with the intent of deceiving you. The attack may persist for some number of days until the self-inflicted performance penalty moves the deceiving algorithms down the leaderboard.

This doesn't cause great harm. The existence of an approved model and the bound means that the estimate will still be within three minutes of a halfway plausible guess. Not a catastrophic malfunction, by any means.

3.8.4 Reliability

No algorithm supplying predictions can be a single point of failure—except the approved model, which is too dumb to fail. By encouraging diversity, we become less reliant on any one algorithm performing when needed. We can fall back to the approved model, if need be. (Needless to say, there are more sophisticated methods of encouraging diversity than the simple system used in this example.)

To receive *any* payment, an algorithm must also be accurate in its own right. So, if the top supplier drops out, the degradation in quality should not be extreme. There is incentive for all algorithms, however original, to improve their accuracy and maintain a spot near the top.

There's a failure mode involving repeated fallback to the approved model—but that's easily detected. The oracle could even use another oracle for more advanced anomaly detection.

3.8.5 Eventually Hard to Beat?

Now for the real exam.

I turn to the question of the eventual efficiency—which is touted as the main selling point of the oracle. We observe that there are many things that might be considered questionable about the design. I have chosen a particular combination of model aggregation, as well as reward scheme, that is reasonably inoffensive but not likely to be the best in any sense.

I've noted in generality that there are many ways to reward and combine and no way to know in advance what the best one will be. Even within the strictures of this narrow example, there are many choices to be made, such as the number of children (5) to include in the median, the speed parameter (0.01), the reset inaccuracy score (360,000), the exponent (2) used to covert error into score, the count-back mechanism for prizes, and the payout fractions $\frac{1}{2}, \frac{1}{4}, \ldots$.

Furthermore, I make no claim that I am in the right *category of approach*. Should we use a precision-weighted estimate instead of the median, as suggested by the preceding discussion?

And perhaps this micromanager simply isn't parenting enough. Our micromanager might lose out, in the long run, to a better parent that performs some critical preprocessing, makes some auxiliary data easily available, or otherwise helps his or her children.

And yet all these imperfections matter not, *up to a cost factor*, if there is no managerial overhead. That's because, as I've suggested in the description of the prediction web supply chains, it probably won't be individual models that are taking first prize but, rather, a far superior generalized contest-like construct. Several are represented in figure 3.3.

This "better contest" will be enriched and can increase rewards paid to children. In turn, it can attract its own better children, and so on. But the thing to notice is that this winning micromanager will receive half the prize money. We are rewarding it, although perhaps not as much as we should.

Yes, it would have been better to use it directly, instead of the unnecessary extra hop through our simple pseudo-oracle, but does that really matter all that much? Let's look at this another way. In the long run, our unsophisticated oracle is *within a cost factor of two* of meeting the definition of an oracle!

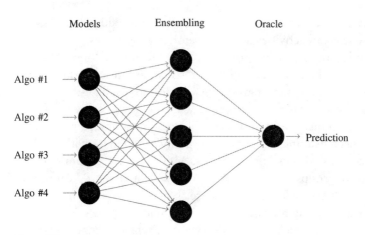

Figure 3.3
A contest between generalized contest mechanisms. A hypothetically superior method of sourcing and ensembling microprediction (generalized contest-like or market arrangements) can win half the prize money on offer. Thus, a simple attempt at an oracle as we have described is within a cost factor of two of being as good as it might be.

Lowering the cost of "running a contest" to zero begins to address the otherwise insurmountable problem of searching the world's data and models, in part by initiating a quest for better and better micromanagers. An accuracy factor of two would be a concern. But given our working hypothesis that the current price of bespoke artificial intelligence is many orders of magnitude higher than it needs to be, a cost factor of two is not.

3.8.6 What's Missing?
I use this bus stop oracle example to preempt and abstract objection to the use of microprediction oracles.

A common critique is that powerful organizing principles have been eschewed in favor of a mechanical reward-based scheme that might not be best placed to bring domain knowledge to the problem or otherwise tap generalized human intelligence.

Notice that the oracle seems not to entertain norms, governance, culture, rules, or other devices for binding people and machines together in productive fashion. It seems also to omit people from direct management, seemingly downplaying their ability to orchestrate quantitative work.

In our setup, it certainly isn't a given that humans will get the opportunity to argue for hours in front of a whiteboard to determine which model goes into production. Nor will nonmathematical people get to provide meta-mathematical advice, or produce flow diagrams, or otherwise engage in activities deemed useful in some circles.

An overview of organizing principles is provided by Thomas Malone, who introduced the term *supermind* to refer to, and discussed strengths of, the combined activities of groups of people and machines.[3]

In search of superminds to compete with our perfunctory streaming contest, we scan the history of human civilization and find, among other things, nuanced examples of competing political systems—with all their rules, procedures, checks, and balances. More broadly, millions of different kinds of groups of people somehow have got along (I'd cautiously suggest that no two book clubs follow precisely the same set of protocols), many with specific engineering objectives in mind.

I'd agree that the rich diversity of ways in which humans have coalesced around projects, each with different expectations placed on contributors, makes for an uncomfortable juxtaposition with the rudimentary "micro-greed" presented.

Yet while it is trivial, the pseudo-oracle as described nonetheless *does* organize humans and machines. Moreover, and more critically to the argument, it is a methodology for *assessment of other organizing principles—* the real beauty of this particular micromanager and many like it.

So in fact, we will get to see if obscure social norms and daily stand-up routines binding the People's Front of Judea are precisely what is needed to organize collective quantitative work. Or maybe the Judean People's Front, with closer allegiance to proletarian futarky, will do better. One of these groups might sooner or later be able to beat all others on an accuracy and cost basis.

I was honest at the outset of this book that I was intent on reducing the problem to one with a solution. We can only collapse this huge discussion because the domain is microprediction: frequently repeated prediction where assessment of performance by mechanical means is warranted. (I may have pushed the boundaries using daily questions in this example, but if enough of us use the app, we'll get away with it sooner or later.)

No, an oracle can't tell you if the Westminster system is better than a presidential democracy. It only delineates microprediction superminds, and as noted you might pay for that.

Yet in this line of argument, I don't mean to surrender the contest between contests to human managers so easily—and nor do they seem likely to win in many cases. For it is worthy of mention, although not essential to the logic, that in many cases, the human-centered efforts will be undercut by more efficient use of generalized intelligence. A micromanager can chronicle its exploits and experimentation, as well as ask for help occasionally. It can generate questions a human can answer in a very short amount of time, thereby including domain knowledge.

For example, a micromanager can pay one cent to glean an opinion from a human as to the plausibility of local weather impacting bus arrival. If it spends three cents, it will probably come away with a reasonable degree of confidence in the answer. That's not hard to accomplish using Amazon Turk, named for the fake chess playing machine of the eighteenth century or other crowdsourcing software.

Jeff Bezos referred to Amazon Turk as artificial artificial intelligence. A dash here and there goes a long way.

3.9 Summary

Gordon Gekko said that greed is good—not perfect. At a small cost, it is good enough, in the microprediction domain, to locate a superior organizing principle (should one exist).

I've described a hypothetical prediction web as a vast collection of intertwined, miniature supply chains for repeated short-term prediction, in which micromanagers play the role of value adding firms.

I've suggested that one day, it might be difficult to avoid making use of this utility. Applications will be able to access this power using functions or APIs, termed oracles, that can aspire to be eventually hard to beat based on the collective properties of the microeconomy.

While simple and seemingly insignificant, the bus arrival application is an interesting little wedge. It illustrates the rudimentary notion of a min- imalist microprediction micromanager that asks others to do its bidding. Yet this toy sooner or later provides the most accurate microprediction that *twice your money* can buy. It's almost an oracle!

And through this rendering, we arrive at a seemingly strange conclu- sion: that the real problem we wish to solve is only incidentally related to machine learning techniques per se. Making better algorithms is a noble goal, but it isn't the blocker when it comes to making microprediction, and thus what passes for AI, better faster and cheaper for everyone.

Instead, the actual challenge is the task of driving down the relative cost of automated management of contributions, which might take the form of a real-time machine learning contest, or generalizations of that concept that we will discuss in more detail in chapter 5.

However, before investing effort in further speculation about the inte- rior of the microprediction web and the micromanagers that inhabit it, I will turn to a slightly broader justification of this line of thinking.

4

Economical Statistics

What is the best way to produce high-quality repeated short-term predictions at low cost? If you accept my near identification of operational AI with microprediction, or even its preeminent role, then there cannot be a more important question.

In chapter 3, the asymptotic aspirations of an imagined real-world prediction capability led us to a strange answer—with material implications for the way quantitative developers might spend their time.

In this economic timeout, which is intended to assure us we are on roughly the right track, I argue that there may not be a better framing of the cost and quality issue than the one provided by Friedrich Hayek.

4.1 A Thought Experiment

On the back of examples in chapter 2, let's briefly review *the problem*—namely, the cost of bespoke artificial intelligence.

We imagine a team of twenty highly trained statisticians, computer scientists, and machine learning experts airlifted out of a large corporation and parachuted into a small business, such as a hot dog stand at a football stadium or an independent bookstore.

They spend a year understanding the business operation, formulating challenges such as pricing, inventory management, recommendation, and customer churn in mathematical terms.

Working as a close-knit team, they combine talents and draw on their knowledge of the applied mathematical literature, such as control theory or reinforcement learning, to improve real-time decision-making.

Sooner or later, they drive costs down and revenue up. More hotdogs are sold at a better price. Fewer hotdogs are wasted. Less time is spent responding to complaints lodged at IWasPoisoned.com. Gesture recognition spots sales opportunities in the crowd. Preference for mustard over ketchup is detected using image recognition (tiny stains on the clothes of the approaching customer). And so it goes.

Now this scenario cannot really play out with good financial results for the obvious reason: cost. So too, similar wholescale optimization cannot be undertaken by the independent bookstore any time soon, and for that matter, we can't help the majority of human projects and undertakings—whether for-profit or not.

But if aliens delivered a box that provided high-quality microprediction for a nominal fee, or if there were an equivalently powerful strategy for delivery of the same, it would surely enliven small business; empower inventive people everywhere; speed the creation of novel approaches to solving commercial, environmental, and scientific problems; and enrich our lives in ways that are hard to foresee.

But beginning with our need to meet the school bus, considered in chapter 3, we can see that work very often breaks down into two parts. One part comprises simple application logic, whose cost is bounded. Then there is a second more open-ended, ongoing task: search in the world's models and data. In chapter 3, we began to put some constraints on what an inexpensive solution to that open-ended task might be.

The unmet need for inexpensive microprediction will only become more acute. In the next decade, the world will spend tens of trillions of dollars manufacturing internet-connected devices—and otherwise generating new streams of data facilitating business optimizations driven by microprediction.

Not only will this create a lot of microprediction tasks, but it will also enrich the set of all data that might inform any given one of them.

The cost of bespoke microprediction is falling but not nearly as fast as the cost of instrumentation. Today you can purchase one dollar's worth of instrumentation—sensors are so cheap, they are sometimes tossed from planes. But you cannot purchase one dollar's worth of bespoke quantitative model creation.

The failure of the economic system to provide a critical economic capital good to the vast numerical majority of businesses and organizations is propagated to the consumer in large and small ways. It impacts the balance of commercial power, the manner in which communities and businesses interact, the diversity of offerings, the safety of goods and services, our real and perceived freedom, our privacy, and our wallets.

If you work in a small business, you will appreciate that incremental changes to the cost of custom operational intelligence are not sufficient to rectify this situation. You probably know that the creation of a novel superior technology or product powered by AI is within your imagination and your capabilities. But will it lurch and groan under the burden of cost? (I've bought that T-shirt.)

Change the cost by a factor of ten, and the outlook is very different. Change it by one hundred? One thousand? One million? Is this possible?

4.2   The Central Problem

Micro-trade is the hope. Or at least that is how I will phrase it in this chapter.

In the bus arrival example in chapter 3, the competing algorithms were playing a repeated game. We can choose to view that as trade, seeking to learn from the economists. The oracle and its prediction suppliers entered an ongoing relationship. The oracle was buying microprediction, and they were selling it. What is interesting about that trade is that it occurs with orders of magnitude less economic friction than conventional trade.

The lens with which I choose to view this trade was provided by Friedrich Hayek some time ago, and I assert that his generally applicable insights take on a whole new level of significance when applied to the production of microprediction specifically. The role of trade is well appreciated in relation to the central problem of machine learning.

Huh?

Just checking that you are awake. People normally nod off when economics is mentioned. What is the "central problem" of machine learning, you ask, and what could it possibly have to do with trade? Certainly trade might have only a secondary role if the central problem of machine learning was the creation of robots that play pool. But that isn't the central problem of machine learning, is it?

No, my terminology refers to the central problem of economics— transplanted to data science and microprediction specifically, of course. It is the question of determining the best system for producing and distributing microprediction to all who need it. So when I speak of the central problem of machine learning, I refer to the *central economic problem* therein.

Hayek's (1945) influential essay, "The Use of Knowledge in Society," asks us to confront what the true nature of *that* problem might be. Indeed, he begins with the following question:

> What is the problem we seek to solve when we set out to establish a rational economic order? (Hayek 1945, section 1, p. 1)

Hayek's perspective emphasizes our hopelessly limited abilities, at least when it comes to gathering all the data necessary to make decisions that optimize complex systems. That knowledge begins in a dispersed state, because as the author notes, "Every individual has some advantage over all others because he possesses unique information of which beneficial use might be made."

Obviously, that carries over to our challenge. As the prediction web is spun, locality in time, space, and other dimensions is important. It is plausible that micromanagers can leverage their neighbor's knowledge but entirely infeasible to send all the world's data to a central prediction authority for processing—even if they knew what to do with it (and even then, if a tangle of well-meaning regulations allowed for something beyond logistic regression).

> The peculiar character of the problem of a rational economic order is deter-mined precisely by the fact that the knowledge of the circumstances of which we must make use never exists in concentrated or integrated form but solely as the dispersed bits of incomplete and frequently contradictory knowledge which all the separate individuals possess. (Hayek 1945, section 1, p. 1)

Some of that knowledge is not data but technique. Some can't really be sent, because it isn't formalized or quantified. A business owner does not always record every piece of knowledge that informs their next decision.

They may not even be *aware* of all the knowledge that enters that decision but intuit successfully a sensible course of action (such as chang-ing a price or decreasing production) that propagates information to others.

So too, some model-free reinforcement agents of tomorrow (and to-day) might struggle to relay to a central authority all the reasons for their actions, present, past, or future. But that does not prevent them from contributing to the global economic brain because their actions—which intuitively increase their expected rewards—signal information to others.

It isn't clear that any obvious summary of those actions would serve the central authority, who presumably would also need to infer which other agents are learning and responding. Short of the creation of a complete digital twin, which is clearly pointless, what would the central master algorithm do?

As with the construction of an encyclopedia drawing knowledge from the millions who share it, solving microprediction is better per-formed by leaving the knowledge in the periphery and allowing agents to perform local calculations and execute local actions. For the "utilization of knowledge which is not given to anyone in its totality," in Hayek's words, *is* the problem. (In the case of Wikipedia, some norms and rules are established—but founder Jimmy Wales has expressed skepticism as to how well these work—putting more stock in incentives. So even Wikipedia may be seen to be reward driven.[1])

4.3   The Nature of Microprediction

Keeping the focus on repeated, live short-horizon prediction, is it not striking that we now consider Hayek's knowledge-based argument applied to an economy where the only good is knowledge itself?

It surely behooves us to account for the very special nature of that good—call it a service if you prefer—although once again, the reader may question my description of the world of AI as a single good economy. (That case continues in chapter 8 when we consider decision-making.)

This sole "good," called microprediction, comprises streams of thousands or millions of repeated quantitative predictions of the same type for some bespoke purpose. Not only is microprediction produced repeatedly, in real time, using whatever knowledge is in the "vicinity," but it also *represents* whatever knowledge is "nearby." As noted in chapter 3, that local knowledge could be human knowledge too, due to the possibility of Turking.

In speaking about the "vicinity," we note that microprediction can encompass the act of providing large numbers of responses to temporal *or nontemporal* questions such as "Is there a hot dog in this picture?" or implicitly temporal questions like "Is row 1332 in this database anomalous (now)?"

Definitive answers may or may not exist to the questions—as mentioned in chapter 2—and the truth used to evaluate submissions can depend on the submissions themselves.

Not everything is included in that representation, as I have been careful to emphasize. The ability to automatically assess modeling is the most useful working definition limiting the scope. For example, "How many cars will pass 42nd and Park in the next five minutes?" is a type of question that can be asked and answered many times a day and with many variants (such as "How many cars will pass 34th and 8th between 4:00 p.m. and 4:05 p.m.").

If two traffic prediction algorithms each supply 3,588,480 forecasts—one for each intersection in New York, once every five minutes for a day—then by the end of the day, we might already be on our way to determining which is best (although perhaps not which one deals best with holidays ... yet).

In contrast, comparison of two predictive models each claiming to forecast next year's gross domestic product would call for an entirely different set of considerations and involve sentient beings trained in statistics and economics.

There may well be knowledge pertinent to that second, long-term question that is not sucked into the micromanager network nearly as efficiently. There is an indirect path, as micromanagers monitor more longer-term competitive means of aggregating information—namely, the asset markets. (Here there is a distinction that needs to be made between actuarial, frequentist, real-world probability and risk-neutral probability implied by prices. The two converge only in the microprediction limit.)

Small rewards might not work well for singular or long-term prediction—unless, possibly, those rewards accumulate across richly cross-sectional data. Asset markets, prediction markets, and their ilk seem complementary to the construct we envisage.

So while most dichotomies are false, the distinction between prediction and microprediction is paramount when we consider "local knowledge"—the phrase used often to make Hayek's point—just as it is when we consider whether micromanagers will do a good job or not.

And thus in chapter 2, I steered you from general prediction—which is inherently difficult and expensive—toward applications where "algorithmic modeling" works well (to use language from chapter 6, where the discussion of that divide in statistics is continued).

That isn't to suggest that microprediction is trivial to solve. But when compared to prediction in general, microprediction should be seen as a tragedy of the commons—and not a fundamental limitation of the universe.

4.4   The Nature of Microdecisions

Repeated decisions are conscious and unconscious. A decision, if repeated, can be construed as conditional microprediction.

One could go further and argue that we are constantly producing microprobabilities for future scenarios and that the accuracy or otherwise of conscious or unconscious microprobability estimation dictates our fates.

That possibility isn't to be discarded merely because people who make repeated decisions aren't always aware that they are acting in a way that is consistent with some probability or range thereof. (The foundations of personal probability suggest otherwise, and the definition of a random variable is rather broad.)

Individuals and businesses make decisions of many different kinds, large and small. In the morning, we decide which route to take to work. At work, we might categorize a customer as loyal or flighty, bid on a work of art, or set the price on a hotel room. At play, we might decide whether to throw a slider or a fastball, or steer a video game car left or right.

On the surface, these are very different activities, but they can all be reduced to the task of producing micropredictions. By analogy, television sets, light bulbs, ceiling fans, clock radios, clothes dryers, coffee makers, and computer monitors are diverse uses of a different source of energy: electricity.

Microprediction certainly isn't electricity yet, and there isn't an equivalent grid . . . yet. For now, it is an abstraction that might make it easier to view machine learning, as well as analytics production and distribution, through an economic lens.

I dare say there are micro-nondecisions. Microprediction is something we desire even when it is not of *any* economic importance and even when it has no chance of changing our decisions at all. Sometimes I stand zombie-like at the baggage claim, wanting an arrival estimate yet at the same time determined not to alter my actions in any way when the forecast arrives.

However, setting stubbornness aside, microdecision quality is very directly related to revenue in commercial settings. We saw an example of computing the ratio between the revenue and accuracy changes in chapter 2. We will draw a connection between accuracy and helpfulness to a trader in chapter 7.

And as elaborated in chapter 2, demand for microprediction is driven by more than idle curiosity. The capability is a tangible asset helping businesses and organizations create other quality goods and services sold to customers.

That's true even if the physical form taken by microdecision capability is up for grabs. All soliciting, rewarding, and migration can occur under the covers—not every user needs to care about that. Or, microprediction might manifest as more explicit communication: a stream of predictions delivered from another party, as in chapter 3. Or, microprediction might involve a hybrid setup, with computation performed predominantly in-house, but residuals leaving the firm in a highly secure manner (see chapter 9). Or, microprediction capability can be something in between. It can morph and move from one host to another. Value can be stored in model parameters, in a file, in a specification of a neural network, or even in the vague memory of a human, so long as it can be deployed (see chapter 5).

However we come at this, the ongoing ability to predict things repeatedly is absolutely essential to every firm and every individual. Such is the nature of microprediction. Given that, how should the capability, and the micropredictions, be produced and distributed? Does the generalized argument of Hayek, which warns us against economic decisions that are not governed by price, hold water?

I hope the reader is at least suspecting of the possibility that the best system for arranging production of local knowledge is the one that best harnesses local knowledge. (I doubt that Hayek imagined the opportunity to apply his argument to local knowledge itself!)

4.5   Trying to Reduce Cost

The implications are quite profound. I've spent most of my career striving to create fine works of mathematical modeling: business decision tools manifesting as calculators, embedded analytics, algorithmic trading processes, and enterprise data feeds—most of which can be couched as microprediction.

But I now view that as a centrally planned mode of production simply too expensive for all but the largest companies. Even in large firms, bespoke AI is usually reserved for a small list of important projects.

Microprediction clearly can't succeed in some asymptotically satisfying sense (the oracle definition from chapter 3) if attempted by someone or something who is isolated. In theory, microprediction should involve the entirety of the world's data—which ties us quite tightly to Hayek's concern.

In theory, microprediction can keep getting better indefinitely, so long as it benefits from new insights and modeling technique.

The implication is that microprediction might require the entire world to collectively engineer—something of a desperate measure, it might seem—although consider what has already been tried.

The problem of cost has resisted many of the usual remedies. Countless hardworking generous people have written excellent freely available open-source software that makes the creation of micropredictions easier. This hasn't solved the problem of cost.

Raising awareness of the possibilities for AI has helped. Recognition of the importance of mathematics has seeped into the public conscious and the highest levels of corporate management in a way that, at the outset of my career, I never imagined possible.

But the press around the AI revolution has not provided sufficient impetus for a reevaluation of cost. On the contrary, it helps disguise the problem. The problem persists in part because most firms lack a true will to cannibalize their own groups of quant developers in any material way.

Perhaps we are merely at an early stage of the cycle when any use of applied mathematics can be heralded as a success. There is no strong expectation of a Moore's law for AI as yet, despite the seeming lack of physical constraint.

Supply is being addressed. A few years back, an explosion in online technical education occurred, epitomized by the fact that two million people have enrolled in a single online course titled *Machine Learning*, taught by Andrew Ng.[2] Massive open online courses help but might not lead to order of magnitude decreases in the cost of tailored data science.

Factory-line production patterns exist in data science, of a sort. Data scientists construct pipelines where different transformations to data occur on their way to a final product, just like a Ford Model T.[3]

There is also an economy for the parts that need to be supplied at each stage of the machine learning pipeline—to extend the analogy—and that sounds like the beginnings of a recipe for a low-cost mass-produced product. Automatic search for the right pipeline enters the fray. Yet the cost problem persists.

Is bespoke prediction just inherently expensive? As noted in chapter 1, we tend to associate AI activity with medium-term, risky, complex projects and highly trained people—making a high cost of microprediction capability seem almost inevitable.

4.6   Unbundling Microprediction

To reduce cost, we might lean on some commonplace economic insights. While obvious, these haven't really been followed to their logical conclusions in the case of microprediction specifically—because it is hidden.

There is the benefit of standardizing what is produced and delivered. A startup company inventing a new toaster doesn't have to think about how to generate electricity and has a very good idea of what voltage to expect. A developer should be able to create applications that are very light on the quant libraries and iterative work, yet draw enough power elsewhere.

Standardization reduces cost in another way. Because the engineer designing a wind-powered turbine doesn't need to know that it is powering your toaster, it is easier for her to bring down your cost of toast as well. So too, creators of autonomous algorithms that roam a microprediction network shouldn't have to think about every possible application.

But when we consider the potential for standards as they apply to intelligent applications, and the inability of algorithms to latch onto them, the biggest hurdle is the fact that commerce is driven by microprediction *implicitly*, not explicitly.

For now, microprediction is bundled and disguised in recommendation, pricing, inventory management, industrial control, scheduling, image recognition, navigation, anomaly detection, and human oversight—to name a few examples from chapter 2.

We tend not to bucket natural language processing, intrusion detection, predictive maintenance, and combinatorial chemistry together. All these seemingly disparate activities constitute the artificial intelligence revolution we read about—although the various terms of art belie a microprediction abstraction that helps illuminate the economic failure. Is *bundled microprediction* produced efficiently?

Unbundled microprediction can be a better path. Companies might become increasingly reliant on microprediction in a more direct way, over time. This can facilitate a critical mass of people and machines adopting similar standards. They can adopt microprediction as a first-class abstraction—a self-imposed bottleneck between the leveraging of microprediction in applications and the sourcing of the predictive power.

In this scenario, companies adopt minimalist protocols for repeated quantitative tasks. They encourage a lattice of microprediction tasks stretching within and between firms. When disagreements over data models exists, the algorithms are smart enough to jump from one railway gauge to another.

In this scenario, bespoke microprediction *can* be produced cheaply and at scale. Microprediction *ought* to be as useful as electricity, to as many people. Firms can, through trade in microprediction, unlock the enormous latent economic value locked in the now, as it were: the potential for sharing and reuse of data and features.

4.7   Gambling on Abstraction?

It may come to pass that a few companies reexpress diverse problems into a common microprediction abstraction and use protocols and software connecting supply and demand of the same. They may adopt a small number of standardized games, whose rules and incentives are broadly understood, thus encouraging ruthless algorithmic competition.

Abstraction does not come for free, I hasten to add. Consider some examples that motivate the prediction network, such as the internet protocols themselves, or, if you prefer, the World Wide Web. There was, and is, a cost to these abstractions. There are some things you can do with the web but many things you cannot. Had different agreements been reached, the entire web might have looked like Wikipedia (for better or worse).

There are opportunity costs of standards lower down too, such as many possibilities for vertical optimization all the way from delivery of packets to smart apps. There has always been the likelihood of ossification in protocols or supporting technology.

But it seems the cost of abstraction was worth it. The web, in particular, unleashed the creativity of a billion people. And germane to our discussion of search, the web crowdsourced a vast collection of relationships between documents—the backlinks created by webpage authors.

The importance of this structure—the links between pages—was not immediately recognized. Later, it became a prerequisite for high-quality, low-cost document search. Although document search has come to be dominated by one company, it has nonetheless been revealed as a "universally" collective activity. (Back then, *everyone* with two fingers and some HTML participated in link creation. Now we also create structure in many other ways.)

The economic significance of that collective feat is well appreciated, I think, and so too the value of context. Indeed, the economic price of our virtual electronic location as we traverse this web is determined by micromanagers of a sort already, as they respond to offers to place advertisements.

And needless to say, the immense value of low-cost, high-quality document search is only partially reflected in the enterprise value of Google—a number grossly underestimating the total productivity boost to all organizations and individuals.

I don't want to stretch the analogy—there are important differences. But microprediction is search too—search in the space of models and data. Search for causal relationships, which for the most part can be cate-gorized as local knowledge. Hayek suggests that we stand as much chance of solving this search in a centralized fashion as a librarian charged with organizing all the world's documents.

It is more likely that causal relationships, both explicit and implicit (in the actions of micromanagers seeking to predict things for reward), will emerge from battles in the periphery.

Some acknowledgment of the collective nature of the task is essential. I hope that companies gamble on abstraction, and internal practices, that makes it easier to arrange these fights.

4.8   Opportunism Is Good

If that gamble is made, then I've suggested that micromanagers can match problems to algorithms, and algorithms to data, without human inter-vention. They can be the ball bearings that enable smooth operation and falling costs.

Value won't be injected into the network only by PhDs developing cutting-edge techniques that are published in the top journals. On the contrary, tiny automated middle-people can be authored by anyone.

We should respect opportunism in both the authors and their prod-uct. Speaking to the knowledge possessed by the real estate broker whose "knowledge is almost exclusively one of temporary opportuni-ties," Hayek (1945) writes,

> It is a curious fact that this sort of knowledge should today be generally regarded with a kind of contempt and that anyone who by such knowledge gains an advantage over somebody better equipped with theoretical or tech-nical knowledge is thought to have acted almost disreputably. (Hayek 1945, p. 522)

This applies rather obviously to exogenous data. But to focus on model search momentarily, it is apparent that we have tens of thousands of open-source repositories to choose from, often containing the latest discoveries. They are mostly, woefully underutilized.

What we are lacking is low-cost "disreputable" middle-people who can lubricate the system by spotting arbitrage opportunity of a new kind—the utility of an obscure piece of code, a combination of techniques, or the application of new technique to an area where it was previously not appreciated. Hayek (1945) continues,

> To gain an advantage from better knowledge of facilities of communication or transport is sometimes regarded as almost dishonest, although it is quite as

important that society make use of the best opportunities in this respect as in using the latest scientific discoveries. (Hayek 1945, p. 522)

Some would say the academic system serves this purpose. There is some reward offered, in the sense that it is easier to move ideas from one field to another sometimes, than to break entirely new ground (and you still get published).

But I would say this transfer is quite slow—certainly slower than the middle-people we have in mind that are inanimate and ceaselessly working for watts, not salaries.

In the next chapter, I shall introduce some middle-folks (building on the bus arrival oracle example) whose intelligence is admittedly limited. Yet we need middle-machines like this. Hayek (1945) warns us against an inclination toward academic snobbery when we assess their merits to society at large:

> Even economists who regard themselves as definitely immune to the crude materialist fallacies of the past constantly commit the same mistake where activities directed toward the acquisition of such practical knowledge are concerned—apparently because in their scheme of things all such knowledge is supposed to be "given." (Hayek 1945, p. 522)

That practical knowledge can arise when an algorithm that is not particularly clever crawls from one place to another and, as Thomas Edison put it, fails its way to success. I describe one such setup in chapter 5.

Returning to data search, Hayek hones in on the real problem for us. When writing statistical papers, we have the luxury of comparing one model against another, with the presumption that they will both see the same data. However, if one wishes to compare any kind of centralized approach to a collection of micromanagers effecting prediction, this is no longer the case.

For the combined selfish actions of the micromanagers will materially change what data is seen. As I noted in chapter 3, the oracle aspires not to the statistical property of asymptotic efficiency but to a practical objective where the data set is not fixed. (Nor the other micromanagers whose talents it might draw upon.)

> The common idea now seems to be that all such knowledge should as a matter of course be readily at the command of everybody, and the reproach of irrationality leveled against the existing economic order is frequently based on the fact that it is not so available. This view disregards the fact that the method by which such knowledge can be made as widely available as possible is precisely the problem to which we have to find an answer. (Hayek 1945, p. 522)

So no, the problem isn't the invention of an algorithm for processing data that is assumed to be present in its entirety (an assumption we
find even in many papers addressing decentralized learning). The problem is orchestrating a rational order in which there is even a small chance
of benefiting from exogenous data or technique we'd otherwise never
encounter.

Now I don't expect our micromanager will literally "see" that extra
data in all cases but, should we be lucky, the *predictive value* of that far-
flung knowledge will benefit us. However the means by which it does so
may be rather complex because calculations will be performed by many
parties we never know. If you squint, Hayek might even be suggesting that
we study how to perform prediction using data held privately by multiple
parties, without anyone revealing anything to anyone else (see chapter 9).

4.9   Statistical Agency

If we accept that models, data, and causality are far-flung, and if we
accept our limited ability to gather it all together, then we are almost compelled to grant the models agency—just as we might citizens of a market
economy.

We are compelled to set them free, so they can discover their own
destiny, make their own connections, accumulate local knowledge, and,
undoubtedly, tie their economic decisions to price.

When that primary coordinating mechanism is price, abstractly, it may
help to consider a special case or two where it is explicitly a price of
statistical precision (as with the precision trader in chapter 5).

This is not a requirement. The main thing is that we ought not overlook
the power of the mechanism. That is, according to Hayek (1945), an easy
mistake to make.

> I am convinced that if it were the result of deliberate human design, and if
> the people guided by the price changes understood that their decisions have
> significance far beyond their immediate aim, this mechanism would have been
> acclaimed as one of the greatest triumphs of the human mind. (Hayek 1945,
> p. 527)

The marvel of the price mechanism lies in the manner that a global
optimization is performed using only local optimization, and local knowledge, and in the fact that only a single quantity (price) constitutes a
"sufficient statistic" for decision. This informational efficiency is one
reason that quantitative business optimization can benefit—just as a

consumer good is manufactured from many components, sourced from many suppliers.

Sharing is facilitated. AI breaks down into microprediction, and that naturally fans out into subtasks. Predicting hotel bookings demands constituent micropredictions for weather, airlines, conventions, and so forth—in turn informed by other micropredictions. There is no requirement that all of these constituent calculations be performed by employees of the same company.

In theory, the micropredictions in this supply chain are reusable. Micropredictions created for hotels are likely relevant to microprediction of sales in a nearby bookstore or HVAC optimization in a hospital building across the street. The user should not be required to anticipate that something entirely unrelated can help—such as data created by a sewage overflow management system.

In theory, self-optimizing supply chains can affect this sharing and should work especially well given that the good in question can be replicated without cost. Parties requiring a common prediction buy it from a producer. Competition forces the producer to pass on the savings from sharing to the consumers of microprediction.

Motivated by these considerations, I have tried to frame the central task rather narrowly: turn theory into practice by eliminating friction. Provide the scaffolding (code, conventions) for a microprediction economy powered by microscopic statistical firms.

It's just that we don't need to confuse abstract trade with conventional trade. Sometimes all that is needed is a thin wrapper around existing analytics—one that allows the algorithm to drive from one game to the next. Algorithms that crawl are easy enough to make and modify, as we'll see in chapter 5.

4.10 Fleeting Knowledge

Despite the ability to effect feature sharing, selection, transformation, pipeline formation, and many other statistical miracles (the mediation of chapter 5), the price mechanism doesn't make many top ten algorithm lists. It doesn't sit there beside the Fourier transform, the fast multipole algorithm, or the simplex method.

In fairness, we can't expect the Society of Industrial and Applied Mathematics to include the price mechanism in the top ten algorithms of the twentieth century—trade is 150,000 years old. And age aside,

Hayek (1945) suggests that our reluctance to recognize its beauty may also be a function of our living within something that we accidentally created.

> Its misfortune is the double one that it is not the product of human design and that the people guided by it usually do not know why they are made to do what they do. (Hayek 1945, p 527)

With respect to our topic, the price mechanism is surely subject to a triple misfortune, because the use of a price mechanism to determine probabilities can be considered distasteful (in counties founded by Puritans, for example).

If we are inclined to discount this wondrous mechanism, then my task of convincing you might be harder. But I am not dissuaded, and there is one more reason to consider Hayek's considerations potent. Knowledge is fleeting.

Perhaps more than any other consideration, this is why waiting for a large command and control army of data scientists to provide you accurate bespoke microprediction, at low cost, might not be the best strategy. There simply isn't time.

When it comes to organizing every *fleeting* piece of information that impacts a real-time decision, nothing short of a hyperefficient microeconomy seems up to the task. In contrast, the inadequacy of centralized management of AI will only become more apparent as the complexity of its constituent good we consider, microprediction, increases.

The internet-of-things is filling with this real-time data—more than can possibly be organized by any single person or team. More than can be stored. It is therefore an orthodox economic position that microprediction, and thus AI in large part, will be orchestrated not by hierarchies of human managers but by the combined selfish actions of competing algorithms.

> This is not a dispute about whether planning is to be done or not. It is a dispute as to whether planning is to be done centrally, by one authority for the whole economic system, or is to be divided among many individuals. . . . (Hayek 1945, p 520)

> Which of these systems is likely to be more efficient depends mainly on the question under which of them we can expect that fuller use will be made of the existing knowledge. (Hayek 1945)

Now I agree we are not close to a point where it is clear which system is superior. On planet machine learning, the Berlin Wall is still standing.

Low expectations don't help. We are in the nascent stages of the statistical revolution, and anything goes. Nobody allows the errors of their models to be subject to competitive analysis, as I suggest in chapter 9. But over time, even small- to medium-sized enterprises will demand a superior product—which is to say more accurate sequences of predictions at lower and lower cost.

At that time, the system that best makes use of "local" data and modeling expertise may be revealed as fundamentally superior.

4.11 Summary

Mathematicians like to give economists a hard time. Some think their only contribution is inventing different words for "derivative" or "Lagrange multiplier." But I have noted Hayek's insight and transferred it to our stylized economy where there is only one service, namely, microprediction.

In the application of artificial intelligence to business, it isn't so interesting to ask whether data-hungry techniques will work given sufficient data—that is true almost by definition. This trivialization is unfair in many respects and yet analogous to Hayek's (1945) discounting of the "central calculation" task:

> If we possess all the relevant information, if we can start out from a given system of preferences, and if we command complete knowledge of available means, the problem which remains is purely one of logic. (Hayek 1945, p. 519)

The hard part of the "easy half of statistics" is drawing together the scattered, often short-lived "local knowledge" dispersed among the world's minds and machines. In particular, the "special knowledge of circumstances of the fleeting moment not known to others" must somehow enter the picture.

Hayek advances the price mechanism as the solution to what is now termed the local knowledge problem. But if Hayek was impressed by the price mechanism's decentralized optimization, imagine how he would enjoy the possibility of trade in a good that is itself as close to local knowledge as one can imagine.

Then, consider how much more forceful his arguments might have been in the presence of near-frictionless trade—where the entire life cycle of a relationship is driven by autonomous, interacting algorithms.

This leaves open the question of exactly how this might be engineered, of course, but it should at least move us into the right category of solution. I propose that the task of providing "economical" statistics (meaning cheap) is solved by encouraging "economical statistics" (meaning statistical tools endowed with economic agency).

So, in the next chapter, we turn to the art of wrapping little pieces of statistics with enough economic sense that they can recombine and self-organize into supply chains for microprediction.

5

Micromanagers

Having exhorted you to place a higher societal value on opportunistic algorithmic middle-people, I provide in this chapter some suggested mental models that flesh out some of the challenges they face.

5.1 In the Abstract

I believe that offering examples is a more valuable exercise than throwing definitions your way, but perhaps it helps to have some vague agreement on what it means to be a "middle-model-manager":

A reward-seeking program or application that autonomously enters, maintains, and terminates where necessary economic relationships with suppliers of microprediction—typically algorithms, people, or other micromanagers—so as to improve its own ability to provide microprediction to an application, algorithm, person, or other micromanager upstream.
—Micromanager

Hopefully, it goes without saying that a micromanager, as the name suggests, should be "small" in an economic sense. The cheaper it is, the lower the threshold for using it.

5.1.1 Diversity
So what should the micromanager look like?

The unfortunate answer is, I don't know the "right way," and neither does anyone else. There was a time when I hoped a universal, canonical middle manager would spring to mind and, with it, a blueprint for a prediction web.

This fabulous insect would solve the multiperiod, multibandit, multivariable, multi-call-it-what-you-like machine learning generalized regression problem with costly inputs so convincingly that we would sit back on our chairs and, to paraphrase Gilbert and Sullivan, declare "My goodness, that is the very model of a modern micromanager!"

If you can do that, it will be an astounding achievement. I promise to commemorate it by commissioning another ditty in your honor, to the tune of:

I'm very well acquainted, too, with matters mathematical, I understand equations, both the simple and quadratical, About binomial theorem I'm teeming with a lot o' news, With many cheerful facts about the square of the hypotenuse. (*The Pirates of Penzance*, Gilbert and Sullivan)

Would that be reward enough? As the reader will have discerned from chapter 3, I have come to believe that designing the "perfect" router is no more or less ambitious than the search for the elusive master algorithm—one whose universal applicability is surely attractive but, in all likelihood, simply not attainable.

That's just as well. Since cost-aware prediction is only a subset of the micromanager's job, finding the "master micromanager" feels a lot like devising a master algorithm (although paradoxically, no harder since presumably the master algorithm could be applied simultaneously to all tasks faced by the micromanager). This isn't to discount the possibility of increasingly elegant and general approaches to the task.

Fortunately, it is not necessary and middle-people don't need to be perfect, only good, as they play their role in the larger economy. Given our relatively modest goal, a microeconomy itself aspires to be the master algorithm—albeit one that only works on the domain of repeated tasks where automated assessment is possible and can be carried out quickly.

In a world of live data streams, a micromanager needs to add statistical accuracy, or convenience, or otherwise add value lest it eventually be considered unattractive to end users or other micromanagers. It may play merely a minor role, but in a microprediction web, contributions to the real-time computation graph come from all creatures great and small.

Some are sophisticated. Some are not. I offer the advice that micromanagers should seek to address a need *neither seeking nor avoiding mathematical difficulties*, to borrow from Lord Rayleigh's working definition of applied mathematics.

I draw a distinction between form and function of micromanagers. Both are important, and what I hope might delight you as you set about designing micromanagers is the possibility of marrying technical and mathematical elegance—something I don't claim to have accomplished.

Micromanagers might be classified according to whether they are engineered to inhabit the boundary or the interior of the microprediction web (or both).

That is to say that a micromanager might aspire to be an oracle and directly face applications (the boundary). Alternatively, it might be seen only by other micromanagers (designed only to work in the interior, with a limited ability to interact with applications or humans) yet play a key orchestrating role at the intersection of several supply chains.

A micromanager might be termed passive or aggressive, according to the manner in which interactions with other micromanagers are initiated. Some may be leaves, in the sense that they perform prediction and navigation, but do not themselves attempt to solicit much help, if any, from other algorithms. In an implementation we'll come to, these algorithms that don't explicitly parent others are called crawlers. However, all have access to oracles.

There's nothing profound in these distinctions. It's just that not every developer wants to implement every API call, implement every method, or satisfy every function convention.

5.1.2 Recipes
I don't think we can claim that a cookbook for micromanagers exists. However, as suggested in chapter 4, making a micromanager amounts to provision of the following:

1. Prediction ability, or some ability to add value via feature creation, transformation, classification, anomaly detection, recommendation, labeling, or any other activity we are likely to find in model and data pipelines
2. The ability to initiate a relationship with other micromanagers, if not already provided or implicit
3. The ability to optimize those relationships over time based on rewards received, rewards given, and statistical assessment

As we discuss the specific examples, I'll let you determine if this accurately characterizes the task, meaningfully suggests the right theoretical context, or otherwise helps you create profitable micromanagers.

For instance, it may not help to regard prediction and managerial ability as distinct challenges if these fit more gracefully into some kind of cost-aware regression framework.

I will discuss in some detail several categories of micromanager: the precision trader, the race organizer, the collider (and the crawler, interacting with it), and the arbitrageur.

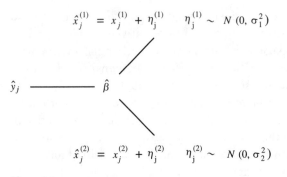

$$\hat{x}_j^{(1)} = x_j^{(1)} + \eta_j^{(1)} \qquad \eta_j^{(1)} \sim N(0, \sigma_1^2)$$

$$\hat{y}_j \longrightarrow \hat{\beta}$$

$$\hat{x}_j^{(2)} = x_j^{(2)} + \eta_j^{(2)} \qquad \eta_j^{(2)} \sim N(0, \sigma_2^2)$$

Figure 5.1
Two or more suppliers sell their predictions, $\hat{x}_1^{(1)}, \hat{x}_2^{(1)}, \ldots$, to a precision trader, $\hat{\beta}$. The quantity $\hat{x}_1^{(1)}$ is assumed equal to the true series $x^{(1)}$ plus additive noise $\eta^{(1)}$. The precision trader takes these prediction streams, and perhaps others not shown, and uses them to create a prediction $\hat{y}$ of another quantity y of utility to someone providing rewards.

5.2   The Precision Trader

The precision trader buys constituent streams of predictions and sells a different stream that, we presume, uses the constituents in its construction. My rendition is in figure 5.1, and I will unpack the notation there as we proceed.

I start with this category because it fits most snugly with the argument for a prediction web presented in chapter 4. The notion of price is very clear, and the quality of the thing being bought and sold can be represented by a single number. As the name suggests, this micromanager will be directly trading *statistical precision*—the inverse of the standard error of unbiased predictions.

So, it ought to be easy to hang our newfound economic intuition on this micromanager, and on her interactions, and visualize how a collection of these micromanagers will directly propagate changes in the prices of statistical precision.

Incidentally, the precision trader is very versatile. As a special case, it can be used to stack (combine) other models—which, as I have noted in chapter 3, is often more profitable than selection of a single best model.

The precision trader sits in the middle of figure 5.1 and is represented by the symbol β. She need not be linearly combining inputs, but if she is, then β represents a vector of the coefficients to be applied to the predictions $\hat{x}^{(1)}$ and $\hat{x}^{(2)}$ in order to render a prediction of the quantity y.

Some kind of calculation will be performed on a repetitive basis. Here j indexes the endless sequences of incoming and outgoing data. For her work, the manager will be compensated by another algorithm, not shown. But know that the compensation will be increasing in the accuracy of the sequence of predictions $\hat{y}_1, \hat{y}_2, \ldots$ delivered to the micromanager, application, or person who will reward her.

To make the example concrete, we suppose that a time series y_j represents the number of times you are bitten by a mosquito, measured every fifteen minutes in Charleston, South Carolina. The precision trader is selling her mosquito bite predictions $\hat{y}_j$. Likewise, $x^{(1)}$ represents a measurement of humidity, and $x^{(2)}$ represents a measurement of wind speed (as compared with their corresponding predictions, with hats).

It is initially simplest to assume that the micromanager absolutely needs both those variables and isn't tasked with choosing. She does, however, control the ratio of signal to noise in the feeds she is purchasing. (The reader will observe that there may be little distinction between dialing up the noise dramatically and deselecting a variable completely.)

Standard errors of predictions she buys are denoted σ_1 and σ_2. We assume that the means of these predictions are always zero. This is to say that the predictions are unbiased (centered). Quality of the supplied product is thus a single number, which might as well be conveyed as precision $1/\sigma^2$.

Figure 5.1 is also intended to convey a strategy or at least start that conversation. The picture is commonly found in the errors-in-variables literature.[1]

The raw materials may be viewed as prediction of future values of humidity and wind speed. Alternatively, they may be viewed as nowcasts—predictions of present values of humidity and wind speed that, due to reporting delays, aren't currently known.

As an aside, that is also a fine distinction and might be made finer by assuming that $x^{(1)}$ is itself a derived quantity obtained by a smoothing estimate of humidity (an example of a calculation that cannot be completed contemporaneously). Then, $\hat{x}^{(1)}$ is a prediction of that smoothed number.

There are more variations on the theme, which I hope is made clear by the data enhancement example from chapter 2. What is important is the assumption that the generation of "enhanced" wind speed and humidity is not the core competency of our micromanager. Her expertise lies in modeling mosquito preferences. Thus, it behooves her to buy the "value-added" products $\hat{x}^{(1)}$ and $\hat{x}^{(2)}$, whatever these might represent.

5.2.1 Analogy

There's nothing terribly mysterious about the precision trader's economic task, which is analogous in some respects to the builder of a spec house. The house must have a kitchen sink, and it must have a roof and flooring of some kind—but the builder can dial up or dial down the quality. (The precision trader can be somewhat more nimble than the builder, but to tighten the analogy, we can suppose that the precision trader makes epoch-based decisions, and each epoch is analogous to the building of the next house.)

The builder intuits (or perhaps models) the final value of the house as a function of quality choices and then optimizes. The builder is acutely aware that a marginal investment in a higher-end material, or a higher-end appliance, may or may not be reflected in an equal marginal increase in sale price. It may be foolish to try to save money by installing a low-quality stove in a high-end house.

There are also interaction effects. If quality of materials is inconsistent, the future buyer of the house might factor in the cost of correcting this: substituting lower- for higher-quality product. Thereby, the builder is denied some surplus profit.

All of these considerations have direct analogies for the precision trader. She must decide on the *quality* of ingredient data feeds to purchase—conscious of how this might impact her own ability to produce a value-added sequence of predictions bought by someone else.

Like the builder, she must be attuned to whether a marginal dollar invested in an ingredient data stream will be reflected in an increase in the value of her output stream that is greater than or less than one dollar. We will return to consideration of her strategy momentarily.

5.2.2 Initiation of Trade

But first, how did our precision trader come to be buying a sequence of predictions from two other micromanagers?

Strictly speaking, this is outside the description I give here, as some additional knowledge of the artificial environment needs to be asserted. For example, is there an index of suppliers and a statistical recommendation system available to the precision trader?

We might presume that this relationship came about because the suppliers were advertising their prediction streams and possibly advertising their supply curves as well (the cost of predictions of varying accuracy).

In a rapidly repeating game, there isn't a strong incentive to lie. The micromanager, seeing these predictions for sale, might have deemed it a good idea to explore the possibility that these suppliers were advertising honestly. We've picked up the story a little later on, when the relationship, we presume, has reached something of a steady state.

In practice, somebody needs to take responsibility for determining accuracy—probably both parties—but again, in a *very frequently* repeated game, we need not fret unduly about the ability to estimate the error in someone else's predictions. The administrative burden is small due to the possibility of online calculations.

5.2.3 The Price Mechanism

I've modeled the quality of the supplied predictions in a straightforward, standard way in order to nail down this example. As also shown in figure 5.1, the difference between the estimate $\hat{x}^{(1)}$ and truth $x^{(1)}$ is an independent normal random variable with mean zero and variance σ_1^2.

In this stylized view of a supply chain, one might even pretend that the supplier knows the true value and is deliberately adding noise, like a supplier peddling watered-down vodka. Our precision trader can pay up for the better product—one with less noise "added."

More likely, the supplier won't go to the trouble of making a good prediction without compensation. And the supplier may be the price-taker, rather than the price-maker.

In a fast-moving game, it doesn't matter so much who makes and who takes prices, although there may be a time lag between the precision trader's turning the control knob (a choice of how much to pay the supplier) and the change in the quality of the prediction. Notably, if the supplied prediction is coming from another contest, then a change in the prize money might not immediately alter the behavior of competitors.

The precision trader does not know the elasticity of supplied precision at the outset. But again, in a rapidly repeating game, these things can be inferred.

The choice of microprediction domain saves us again. It enables us to simplify our mental model of interactions down to the point where we *imagine* that the precision trader has a firm understanding of the impact of tweaking the control knobs.

So to formulate the game for the precision trader, we can allow it to increase or decrease the noise σ_i directly, at some known cost and with diminishing returns. We might assume the price of precision is constant, just for illustration. If she pays $16 per year, she'll get predictions with half the standard error as those she'll receive when paying $4 per year. (Notice that price has units: dollars per unit of statistical precision. And precision is the inverse variance of the prediction errors, $1/\sigma_1^2$, only because we're assuming those predictions are centered.)

As another aside, some special situations might justify this particular relationship between cost and quality, although that is not central to the discussion. By appeal to the central limit theorem, one can invent situations where the price is approximately constant. One has to gather n^2 independent samples to realize a standard error proportional to $1/n$.

Returning to the mysterious β in the middle of figure 5.1, let's choose a value-adding act. I'll assume *linear* regression—although similar setups apply to classification problems, and certainly to more generalized non-linear regression, machine learning, inference, and so on.

Off stage to the left, there is an economic relationship progressing with her upstream buyer. That's left unstated here, but we can expect her to optimize her economic surplus over time regardless of what form that takes. If she's not smart enough to do that, other micromanagers will push her into economic oblivion. In a hyperefficient economy, we approach the limit where the precision trader's surplus heads to zero.

But in the meantime, she makes some money and learns more about the suppliers and how to combine their intelligence. More data arrives, and presumably the suppliers also provide better estimates. They are learning too.

It may seem like little is left to the imagination here. We know exactly what the parent is learning—just one vector, the coefficients β. And to relate this to the literature, we could assume that the *true* relationship between y and $x^{(1)}, x^{(2)}$ is indeed linear also—matching the modeling assumption made by the micromanager. It probably isn't, but Hayek reminds us that middle-people don't have to be sophisticated to add value.

Economists would speak of the *shadow price of precision*—which is to say the increased revenue for the precision trader from selling y when a dollar is spent to improve the precision of the estimate $x^{(1)}$. We find ourselves retracing an example from the measurement error textbooks—where for linear regression, errors in the ingredients of a prediction propagate linearly to errors in the final product.

Statistical details to one side, what's clear is that prices are in play. Prices of precision for the various data streams. And with that comes price propagation, decentralized optimization, a solution to the local knowledge problem, and all of humankind's accumulated economic wisdom.

5.2.4 Strategy

Yet what should also be apparent is that the mathematical challenge presented here is by no means equivalent to what would usually be considered the modeling task: it isn't just the "model" that matters. Here the model is a linear regression—but the task faced by the micromanager is richer and demands quite different framing.

Even the linear regression using noisy variables has nuance. Well-appreciated statistical themes can inform the micromanager's strategy. In closing out the discussion of the precision trader, I mention some pointers (a little more technical) from the literature.

One theme is coefficient attenuation. Due to the noise in $x^{(1)}, x^{(2)}$, the linear coefficients used by the manager will be smaller than the true ones. Thus, the utility of the child's work product is lost, in part.

This old phenomenon comes with a new twist in our setting because it is a repeated game. The manager can influence σ_1^2 and σ_2^2 at some cost. Potentially, the manager might decide to invest heavily, in order to try to receive something very close to the truth $x^{(1)}$, if only for a limited time.

There are numerous special cases that hold independent interest. For instance, it could be that $x^{(1)}$ and $x^{(2)}$ are noisy versions of y itself. In this case, we are building a mixture-of-experts model, or crowdsourcing data, or performing some combination of the two.

We are also proximate to the literature dealing with costly features. Goetschalckx et al. propose parsimonious linear regression based on the least angle regression method, in order to minimize a combination of least squares error and a purchase cost assigned to nonzero coefficients.[2]

Least angle regression is an example of a stepwise procedure for adding information, and any such procedure could be tried as a means of establishing the marginal benefit of the last child to be included.

Or, where practical, relative weights or Shapley values could be assigned to the suppliers of microprediction instead. Explainability tools (chapter 2) of other kinds can also play their role.

If we enlarge the example to include many possible suppliers, not just two, then penalization and sparsity encouraging and regularizing regression techniques could help (Lasso, ridge regression, and so forth).

That's only going to address part of the problem, perhaps, which could also be couched as a control or reinforcement learning exercise. Indeed, precisely this approach has been taken by Janisch and coauthors, albeit in a classification setting.[3]

The design of precision traders and their policy is an open book. I hope this example illustrates why the mathematical middle-person can be as sophisticated as you wish it to be.

Due to the open-ended difficulty in strategy design and the utility of being able to predict things like the future performance of another micro-manager, some recursive use of the prediction web will be increasingly beneficial over time. That train of thought continues in chapter 8.

5.3   The Race Organizer

With that in mind, let us move on to a different mental model for micromanagement of algorithms and data.

The setting is a fairly common situation. An application requires ongoing prediction, or classification, and there is a plethora of open-source or vendor solutions on offer. The task of the manager is to play the broker, first assembling a smorgasbord of possibilities and then choosing on behalf of the upstream application.

Here we get to simplify the task in one respect, compared to that of the precision trader. The race organizer will not be combining the children's outputs in a complex way or even a simple one. Instead, we shall assume that "only the best matters."

Furthermore, we will assume that the race organizer and the competitors are both tasked with predicting *the same thing*. There is no act of value creation beyond that served by the running of the race itself (no linear regression or any other model).

The race organizer is little more than a pass-through—some would unkindly say an overpaid one. However, his task is not without its own challenge.

Let us further suppose that upstream, the individual prediction that is best will get the reward each and every time a prediction is required. Alternatively, we might suppose that the payment to the microman-ager is determined by the best performance over an epoch—say, 10,000 predictions. It does not matter which interpretation we choose, for now.

5.3.1   Strategy

Either way, the race organizer is like a manager for a sporting event who is faced with the prospect of trying to choose which athletes to invite. Each athlete comes with an associated cost. The manager will be compensated by the quality of the contest outcome. It is prohibitive to pay for everyone to attend.

That is the game. To refine it further, suppose the event is a marathon. Let's define the quality of the field as the expected winning time, where of course lower is better. For this is directly analogous to an epoch-based model race organizer in many respects, which has at his disposal a Rolodex of statistical approaches. Each comes with a cost. The cost may be tiny—merely the incremental compute cost of using another algorithm—or it may be significant, say if data must be purchased.

The question of choosing the set of parties you will solicit bids from is a fundamental challenge of trade in general—whether you are trading in microprediction, fine art, or apartments. For in trade of most kinds, there is a desire for the best bid or offer but also a cost of soliciting each one.

The cost can be physical or arise due to the possibility of leaking commercial intent. There may be negative terms to the cost. For instance, there is a fixed benefit of inviting Eliud Kipchoge, due to his fame, beyond the desire for a fast race that is already captured by the objective function.

The problem faced by the race organizer also arises when you need to determine how many candidates to interview or which dealerships to drive to before purchasing a car.

Speaking in broad terms, it seems we are in luck, at least if optimization theory is a guide. You'll likely be minimizing a set-valued function of a certain "nice" variety when you choose which algorithms to include in a bake-off.

Indeed, a framing of this task is provided by the literature on submodular optimization. The race organizer's objective function will likely fall into this category.

The property of submodularity finds an intuitive definition in terms of the race we are organizing. It states that if you add a runner to a small field, then that runner will reduce the average winning time by a greater amount than if you were to add the same runner to a larger field *that includes the smaller field.*[4]

5.3.2 Special Cases

Even if we do regard this race organizer as less sophisticated than a "precision trader," he or she nonetheless provides a sensible means by which the prediction web can latch onto existing sources of predictive intelligence.

For example, the race organizer can be the glue we use to attach to the prediction network other conveniences (such as analytic storefronts for APIs, discussed in chapter 6).

As a special case, this micromanager might take on the task of comparing forecasting-as-a-service products. These might charge a fixed fee, require more cumbersome initiation, or be predicated on some human involvement. Not every micromanager in the prediction network will care to deal with that.

So, value can be added by a race manager that smooths over the rough edges at the interface between the microeconomy and the macroeconomy. They can convert one style of supply or demand curve (say a step function), or collection of the same, into more continuous versions more suited to a precision trader.

If we view the economy as a giant master algorithm that lurches toward an optimum, then no job is too small. A micromanager might do nothing more than reduce by some small amount the probability of the system getting stuck in a local minimum—such as might arise due to sharp edges and plateaus created by human-centric pricing and contracts.

A race organizer could even serve merely as a means of currency exchange, so as to include a menagerie of cryptocurrency based prediction markets, and determine their value as a function of cost (the microprediction domain brings volumetric challenges).

In these various activities, the race organizer can lift the burden from other participants, who might otherwise find their activities interrupted at the most inconvenient moment.

> It does not matter for him why at the particular moment more screws of one size than of another are wanted, why paper bags are more readily available than canvas bags, or why skilled labor, or particular machine tools, have for the moment become more difficult to obtain. All that is significant for him is how much more or less difficult to procure they have become compared with other things with which he is also concerned, or how much more or less urgently wanted are the alternative things he produces or uses. (Hayek 1945, p. 525)

The race organizer can contribute to robustness of the prediction web as a whole. Notice that it serves as a backstop because cheap, less accurate, but reliable suppliers will be included in the mix.

The race organizer can be automatically opportunistic. An increase in its expected reward for supplying accuracy will immediately translate into the selection of a larger field.

In this manner, algorithms can lean on the race organizer to determine when they are useful to the network and when they are not. They need only adopt a fixed price for their supply, for instance. They can operate as a power plant might—one that is only fired up when the price of electricity demands it. So, as simple as the race organizer is, it clearly enables other algorithms to look intelligent.

The continuous flow of goods and services is maintained by constant deliberate adjustments, by new dispositions made every day in the light of circumstances not known the day before, by B stepping in at once when A fails to deliver. (Hayek 1945, p.523)

Panning out for a moment, let's also appreciate that due to time, space, and circumstance, the costs will be different for different potential contest organizers. So the micromanager need not be perfect—just fortuitous. If a micromanager has a spatial advantage or access to algorithms or data that another does not, then an approximate solution is likely to be perfectly adequate. Right place, right time, or right price.

Shortlisting and online stacking of time-series models, mentioned in chapter 3, falls into this category.[5] The burden lifted from the developer is, I hope, obvious. They need never engage in their own costly exercise of comparing dozens or hundreds of open-source forecasting methods, each of which adopts a different set of calling conventions.

5.3.3 Automated Model Search

Meta-learning of selection strategies can generalize on the race organizer pattern I've described, since by analogy to a horse race, we might know whether certain runners prefer dirt or grass.

Automatically shortlisting and selecting models is common for regression and classification problems. It constitutes the design of automated machine learning packages, of which many are open source.[6]

Because microprediction is a live, ongoing activity, not all the patterns used for automated machine learning carry over immediately, although most have approximate incremental equivalents (if you think about it hard enough).

And bearing in mind that middle-people don't need to be perfect, simple ideas can add value. We might pull some runners out midway through the race who aren't performing. Elimination races could be held, as with the old practice of removing the *lanterne rouge* (last-place rider) from the Tour de France during the late stages.

Since the space of strategies for short-circuiting evaluation of algorithms is large, there's ample room for some race organizers to distinguish themselves from others. Ideas from the theory of multifidelity optimization are relevant.

Also worthy of mention is one nuance of the shortlisting task. In selecting a team of models that will subsequently be stacked (weighted), it is beneficial to include a variety—since the task they encounter is unknown at time of shortlisting.

Thus, a model whose performance is negatively correlated with most others, across a large variety of test tasks, might be a stronger candidate than raw performance suggests. There is an obvious parallel to the inclusion of assets in a portfolio that are not strongly correlated with the market as a whole.

5.3.4 Contests

I have couched the race organizer as the aggressor in this formulation, but just as data scientists choose which contests they enter, the economic arrangement may be initiated by the suppliers instead.

Also, there is nothing to prevent the race organizer from taking a number of steps to assist the suppliers in some way—thereby bringing the mental model closer to "macroscopic" data science contests, something whose history we hope to learn something from in chapter 6.

To bring it even closer to data science contests, we might assume that some work is done offline by suppliers, which is to say on historical data. The use of historical data in a real-time setting would seem to place an additional burden on the manager—namely, deploying a solution informed in some way by the suppliers.

That said, a micromanager can by all means store values of y and gather exogenous variables $x_1, x_2, \ldots, x_n$ that are, on a periodic basis, presented to a plurality of suppliers. Perhaps the manager holds out some of the data and hopes that the suppliers will not "ruin" the game by locating it independently.

In this setup, the suppliers submit predictions of y, and later, by some means, the manager takes possession of the best-performing algorithm. Again, I'm not suggesting this arrangement is optimal in any sense—merely proximate to data science contests that have been run.

5.3.5 Relationship to Markets

Before leaving the topic of contest-like things, let's observe that accounting and financial practices suggest various ways to finesse the reward structure. Contests typically involve epoch-based payments, but it may be possible to compute incremental rewards, paid one data point at a time.

One way to do this is to use the prediction network recursively, in order to forecast eventual contest payments and their current expected value. Then we pay out some but not all of this.

This exercise differs in no material way from margin calculations (a survey of analytical techniques would occupy considerable space).

The race organizer can also draw inspiration from financial or betting exchanges. While exchanges sometimes come with trappings that add expense, the "nanomarkets," as we might refer to micromanager interactions, don't have to.

It's notable that participants in a "contest" don't have to know, or necessarily care, that a market-like mechanism is being used to judge and compensate them. Indeed, a pattern for eliciting point or probabilistic estimates, and defining incremental rewards, comprises the following steps.

1. The manager converts the supplier's point estimate to a probabilistic forecast.
2. The manager interprets participants' micropredictions as small investments, according to some sensible economic motivation.
3. The manager clears the market using some existing market mechanism. This creates a fictitious balance for the supplier.
4. The parent determines actual compensation based on some quarantined version of this balance (in time and also in money), thus ensuring a draw-down to zero is highly unlikely.

This recipe is quite general. One way to achieve the first step, where needed, is to use the empirical distribution of predicted versus actual results for each supplier.

We are avoiding staking here—although that could be added. The domain of application may depend on the effectiveness of deferred versus more immediate compensation and also whether staking is permitted in a jurisdiction. (Staking is one of two criteria that have appeared in case law in the United States and used to delineate gambling from other activities. However, the other defining characteristic of gambling is the predominance of chance in the outcome. Thus, in the context of microprediction, in a rapidly repeated game of skill, the inclusion of exclusion of staking may have technological but not legal ramifications.)

When using this approach instead of epoch-based statistical measures, the race organizer can more easily accept new participants at any time or allow others to leave. Otherwise, thorny issues might arise—such as unfairness arising from relatively easy and hard questions, not answered by all participants.

However, this discussion strongly suggests that the parent might want to *explicitly* operate a mechanism instead, and that is where we now turn our attention.

5.4   The Collider

I now introduce some terminology for micromanagers inspired by exchanges and the details of a working example.

5.4.1   A Near-the-Pin Collider

One prototype micromanager that you'll find by searching with keyword "microprediction" falls into a category that I will term *colliders*.[7] This particular example leans on just a few concepts, which I enumerate.

A *stream* is simply a time series of scalar (float) data created by someone who repeatedly publishes a single number. It becomes a public, live moving target for community-contributed prediction algorithms.

Other micromanagers (crawlers) produce distributional forecasts comprising a vector of 225 carefully chosen floating point numbers. Those 225 numbers are suggestive of the distribution of values that will be taken by a data point at some time in the future—say, five minutes from now or one hour from now.

The contestants are firing off these distributional predictions of the future value of a stream, but as a technicality, they do not know the exact time of arrival of future data points. So it is more precise to say the distributional prediction applies not to a fixed time horizon but rather to the time of arrival of the first data point *after* some elapsed interval.

Let us pick a delay of 3,555 seconds for illustration (45 seconds shy of one hour). If the data seems to be arriving once every ninety minutes and arrived most recently at noon, it is fair to say that a set of scenarios submitted at 12:15 p.m. can be interpreted as a collection of equally weighted scenarios for the value that will (probably) be revealed at 1:30 p.m. (and is thus a seventy-five-minute ahead forecast, loosely).

The collider doesn't care about the interpretation. When a new data point arrives at 1:34 p.m., it looks for all predictions that were submitted at least as far back as 12:34:45 p.m., a cutoff point chosen to be 3,555 seconds prior. Those distributional predictions qualify to be included in a reward calculation. Each algorithm will be scored based on how many are close to the revealed truth.

Hence the name near-the-pin collider. This may be seen as an incremental reward system triggered by a collision between arriving ground truth and quarantined distributional predictions.

5.4.2   Advantages

A strong motivation for colliding probabilistic predictions, as compared with point estimates, is that submissions can convey more information. The location of a badminton player's neck as he lunges about the court makes the point. It can even be bimodal.[8]

In this case and others like it, it is hard to see how the spray of future outcomes, not likely to conform to a known distribution, can be easily summarized by a single number.

Soliciting distribution estimates in this manner may seem like a lot of extra traffic. However, clearing is incremental and fast. An additional compensating advantage is that lottery-style reward mechanisms are stateless—unlike the bus arrival oracle that must carry with it some memory of past performance, in order to reward longitudinal accuracy.

5.4.3   Pseudo-Oracle

The collider serves as a pseudo-oracle for distributional time-series prediction at fixed horizons. If you or a micromanager want forecasts of a live number, you just publish it using an API (or the microprediction Python library).

Then, after a few hours or days or weeks of your doing nothing, you get a pretty accurate distributional forecast at various horizons. Those horizons are, as noted, roughly one minute ahead, five minutes ahead, fifteen minutes ahead, and one hour ahead. (As an aside, if you publish once a day, you will in effect receive a lot of day-ahead predictions as many of the algorithms make their submissions soon after a data point is received. There are lots of ways to hack the system to get what you want.)

The collective result is summarized as a collection of four community-generated cumulative distribution functions (CDFs). The bad algorithms give up or get kicked out, and better ones arrive. The CDF gets more accurate over time as algorithms (and people) find relevant exogenous data or fine-tune the use of the data they already see.

5.4.4   Recursion and z-Streams

The near-the-pin collider uses itself recursively in order to facilitate anomaly detection, specialization, monitoring, and other objectives.

The community-implied CDF suggests a percentile for each arriving data point. Let's suppose it has surprised the algorithms on the high side and so the percentile is 0.72 say. We call 0.72 the community-implied percentile.

A community-implied percentile must be defined relative to some choice of quarantine period (i.e., forecast horizon). For example, the data point might be a big surprise relative to one-hour-ahead prediction but less so compared to forecasts that have not been quarantined as long. The reverse can also be true.

As it happens, there are only two community percentiles computed: one computed using forecasts delayed more than a minute (actually 70 seconds) and one relative to those delayed by almost one hour or more (actually 3,555 seconds).

Next, we define a community z-score as the inverse normal cumulative distribution of the community-implied percentile. We are using the community to define a distributional transform, then transforming to normal (which most time-series algorithms prefer). If the community of human and artificial life is good at making distributional predictions, the z-scores will be normally distributed.

The use of the terminology z-score is an overloading—yet another example of my inability to solve the hardest problem in computer science (naming things). Of course in statistics, z-scores often refer to a different standardization of data that assumes it is normally distributed. (Invariably, that isn't the case, and thus the collider z-scores can be considered an attempt to improve on this practice.)

Finally, the z-scores are fed back to the collider, so they can themselves be predicted. Think of it as automated model review.

5.4.5   Multivariate Residuals and Copulas
The near-the-pin collider is actually a little more elaborate than this suggests, because it also attempts surveillance of two- and three-dimensional implied community percentiles.

Space-filling curves fold combinations of community-implied percentiles back into univariate streams, so they also can be fed back to the collider. As a mildly technical aside, algorithms tasked with predicting these so-called $z2$ and $z3$ streams might be seen as estimators of market-implied copulas. This gives rise to an extremely fine-grained understanding of the relationships between variables, facilitated by specialization (since the algorithms predicting the margins need not be the same as those predicting the copulas).

5.4.6   Making Crawlers
I'll make more general remarks on implementation later on, but while we visit this collider example, it's worth mentioning that there is a straightforward way to make "crawlers" that interact with it. Getting down

to nuts and bolts, the conversion of a time-series algorithm into a micromanager comprises the following steps.

1. Subclassing a provided Python class
2. Modifying the prediction logic as needed
3. Modifying the default logic that navigates to data streams
4. Running it

In this example, the default navigation ability amounts to a random selection of a stream. The default economic logic is a stop-loss. The micromanager will give up on the task of predicting a data stream if it loses too many credits.

This is rather simple and feel free to improve it, yet even these minimal nonsuicidal economic tendencies can be enough for a crawler. It travels from game to game, learning where to give up and eventually making a lasting contribution—hopefully.

And although all interactions are with just one other micromanager, these crawlers can still be viewed in analogy to a private firm in a supply chain. That's because the crawler can make use of the collider's pseudo-oracle to source its own predictions from other crawlers.

5.4.7 Other Colliders and Analogies

Moving beyond this working example, there's plenty of inspiration for the design of micromanagers, which act as value-creating firms in a micro-economy. I'll start with digital marketing.

When you open a page of the internet, it often triggers an auction. Programs bid on the advertising space created. Exchanges exist to clear supply and demand. Trillions of auctions occur daily.

A microprediction network could feel a little bit like "machine learning meets digital advertising" insofar as ongoing, immediate need for microprediction can be requested and competitively supplied.

Moving to finance, a mega-category of mechanistic middle-people is suggested by the inventions that have been employed over the years to "accidentally" aggregate probabilities.

You will appreciate that futures, options, contracts for differences, binary contracts (financial and otherwise), spread bets, and other types of contingent claims trade on exchanges, where they are cleared by central limit order books (CLOBs) or other protocols.

Prediction is usually considered a by-product of this trading activity, although it is overt in the case of prediction markets. Prediction markets are designed solely for the purpose of aggregating subjective probability and, thereby, reporting odds for elections and other singular events.

Because there are many variations on the theme, I've used the term *collider* to refer to the more general picture where a micromanager is passively receiving "order-flow" and "colliding" it together in some mechanistic manner (as with the aggregation of distributional predictions into a community prediction, the matching of buyers to sellers, or the computation of a tote price for a horse).

The order flow I speak of need not be "bids" or "offers"—although there is nothing preventing that. The collider might instead receive probabilities (not necessarily expressed as collections of samples) or point estimates (with or without confidence intervals). There are numerous mechanisms inspired by the macroscopic economy that the micromanager may choose to implement or augment.

The nice thing about the microworld is that when we do this, it is pretty easy to remove much of the clutter and ceremony that usually comes along with, say, financial exchanges. Colliders can be stripped-down exchanges, and that's not a terrible definition.

Algorithms don't need screens to look at. Frequently repeated games can obviate contracts, as we'll discuss in chapter 7. The willingness of algorithms to work for close to nothing *suggests* that other costs can be reduced as they wiggle their way into the supply chain. They might play niche roles analogous to those we see in the macroscopic financial economy.

Colliders can usually be designed with generous volumetrics. The example I described above can handle roughly as many probabilistic predictions per second as there are orders processed by Nasdaq. Algorithms make for excellent exchange customers. They demand so little, compared to humans, making the developer's life much easier.

Incidentally, there's nothing sacred about CLOBs. Fixed-income electronic marketplaces are dominated by other protocols, notably the request-for-quote (RFQ) procedure, which, as the name suggests, implies that the manager is requesting bids or offers from suppliers. Here we morph back toward the race organizer micromanager.

In a spin on the theme, one can imagine suppliers of prediction that respond with a firm, risk-neutral probability for each outcome, as if they were bookmakers lined up on the rails and a runner had been sent by a large punter to interrogate them all for the best price.

Market mechanisms can seem quite different to prediction contests where accuracy is tabulated. However, there are connections between market making and accuracy metrics. One type of connection will be explored in chapter 7 when we decompose accuracy into success in a one-sided trading game.

I send you down a different rabbit hole with an example of the quadratic scoring rule employed by an automated market maker.[9] The field has advanced this area over the last couple of decades, filling in the space between market mechanisms and statistical scoring rules with novel ideas.

As I will discuss in chapter 7, statisticians have been coming to a better understanding of how markets, which are like a series of binary questions to participants (i.e., "Is this number too big?"), relate to repeated games of a different kind ("What will this number be?") that have clear intent (i.e., "Did you give me your honest estimate, or are you gaming the scoring?").

A collider might consider the possibility of subsidy. After all, the mechanism exists to deliver a probabilistic product, so it is not a requirement that the marketplace, or protocols, established for this purpose be a zero-sum game. The micromanager could even act like a specialist, or bookmaker, who deliberately runs a losing book among a subset of algorithms.

That can be seen in some business models where there is a reason to subsidize the bid-offer spread. It also occurs in the bookmaking industry where at least one prominent bookmaker allows overperforming gamblers to consistently win—as compared with kicking them out—so as to take advantage of the information they are delivering.

Such actions blur the line between passive colliders like the totalizator and active market making.

5.4.8 Strategy

The mental image of the precision trader suggests strongly the problem to be solved–and that it will be.

On the other hand, *colliders*, as I have termed them, are generally expected to be fast but dumb. The burden of devising strategy lies with the participants. There are issues that already occupy many treatises, not to mention entire careers spent by financial market participants.

I will content myself here to touch on player strategy for the near-the-pin collider, as this can take us a little off the beaten path (compared with the study of optimal execution for CLOBs, say).

If the set of outcomes is discrete and quite small (which admittedly isn't often the case for time series), then the near-the-pin collider collapses to a simpler mechanism known as the parimutuel.

Strategy for parimutuels is not a new topic. Nor, of course, are the mechanisms themselves. Indeed, the parimutuel, also known as the total-izator, is used at most horse-racing venues and has been for over a century—more on that later.

The parimutuel collects probabilistic information from the suppliers (i.e., the punters), taking the form of a portfolio of wagers on a finite number of mutually exclusive outcomes. Money is split among those picking the right outcome in proportion to how much they wagered.

In a financial context, parimutuels have been enhanced in an important way by Baron and Lange, who engineered bundling of the underlying states and combinatorial clearing in order to translate the application to financial applications.[10]

Returning then to the question of strategy, there are also some mathematical observations about parimutuels that the designer of a crawler (a micromanager participating in a near-the-pin collider) might wish to take careful note of.

It is apparent that algorithms with linear utility have an incentive to shift the normalized investment on each outcome toward the "true" probability, as best they can discern it. In racing parlance, "bet the overs."

But less obvious, and far more surprising, is the fact that algorithms with log-utility constrained to invest all their wealth on a horse race with no take will bet in proportion to their true beliefs, *irrespective of the odds* (i.e., irrespective of the investments made by others, which determine the odds).

This surprising result is an exercise in calculus. And the requirement of investing all one's wealth is not a genuine constraint if there is no take, since there is a risk-free combination of wagers.

If we enlarge the number of outcomes (i.e., horses), flatten the true distribution to uniform, and reindex the possible outcomes (say using the set of all combinations of six numbers out of forty, instead of a listing of horses), then lo and beyond, the parimutuel morphs into a lottery.

The paradoxes that exist in a lottery apply here. In a lottery in which all money is paid back to ticket buyers, one can buy one of each ticket and ensure a positive expected return.

Yes, lottery strategy is almost too simple to believe—at least at this level of stylization. But the way a lottery investor betting in this fashion will profit when playing against a collection of individuals who draw their tickets uniformly can be understood by considering the last ticket bought by the systematic player.

An in-depth treatment of lottery strategy is provided by Steven Moffitt, who was part of a successful syndicate for many years.[11] I have provided a discussion of the (nonuniform) lottery problem and the relationship between player returns and Kullback–Liebler divergences for readers who might be interested.[12]

The takeaway is that the paradox of positive lottery expected return provides an incentive for contestants to supply evenly spaced submissions in lotteries. However, we can transform lotteries into other games with nonuniform outcomes. For instance, consider the following function

$$g(i) = \left(-\log \left(1 - \frac{i - 1/2}{10{,}000} \right) \right)^{1/4} \tag{5.1}$$

that takes the integer lottery outcome i (taking values from $1, \ldots, 10{,}000$) into a real number. One can pretend that we are playing a game in the transformed space, and we'll see what that looks like before long (close to normal).

That's the intuition for why strategy doesn't change too much when we extend lotteries and parimutuels to continuous spaces, as with the near-the-pin collider. Nor does this change materially if rewards are determined using a kernel function, and guesses close to the truth count more than those far away.

Perhaps the lottery insights suggest ideas for colliders with other objectives, such as those that exist to crowdsource efficient Monte Carlo sampling.

As a parting remark, I don't mean to represent that parimutuels, lotteries, and their cousins are the only or best way to combine probabilistic forecasts. Many other techniques for the purpose can be considered if sufficient computation is available.

For example, inspiration comes from the quantile estimation literature, and while a survey is beyond my scope, see Wang et al. for an assessment of different methods used to combine probabilistic load forecasts in particular.[13] And although I won't go into it, all the considerations of chapter 7 generalize to quantile estimation. Any accuracy metric suggests a micromanager.

5.5 The Arbitrageur

I shall discuss one final grab-bag category of micromanager behavior. For given the motivation provided in chapter 4 for disreputable middle-people, it would seem remiss not to personify a class of micromanagers as *arbitrageurs*.

> And the shipper who earns his living from using otherwise empty or half-filled journeys of tramp-steamers, or the estate agent whose whole knowledge is almost exclusively one of temporary opportunities, or the arbitrageur who gains from local differences of commodity prices, are all performing eminently useful functions based on special knowledge of circumstances of the fleeting moment not known to others. (Hayek 1945, p. 522)

In a world where on-tap prediction is free, and any sequence of numbers can be predicted by sending it to an oracle, there will emerge almost immediately a species of algorithms whose role in the system will seem (at first) to be unacceptably opportunistic.

Let us suppose that a company is making use of an oracle, call it oracle D for "Delphic." Behind this oracle is a fierce competition of algorithms and other micromanagers running subcontests and who-knows-what else.

But then along comes a very simple micromanager who exists purely to assess the quality of purported oracles. She happens to know, or has recently discerned, that in fact oracle C for "Clever" is superior to oracle D—just not as well marketed.

Rather than communicating this fact openly, she uses oracle C to beat out other competitors sitting behind oracle D. Every question that she is challenged with, she merely relays to oracle C and returns C's answer to oracle D.

We note that this arrangement might arise "accidentally" when a race organizer just happens to forage for food in the right place. Indeed, I remarked on the inherent opportunism of a race organizer, and that also applies to the winner of the contest, or winners, if you insist on painting the micromanagers with an ethical brush.

Specially constructed arbitrageurs could be engineered to be more cynical than a typical race organizer, admittedly, yet most types of morally questionable behavior will reduce the discrepancy between oracles. Thereby, it will reduce the economic cost of an application choosing the wrong oracle. The burden of choice is lifted.

An arbitrageur may have based her choice on some savvy statistics occurring offline, in order to determine the relative efficacy of oracles (perhaps a new improvement to the Elo rating system, say, or clever use of human intelligence).

Over time, the best raters and recommenders of algorithms can grow wealthier. And perhaps our appreciation for the arbitrageur's contribution will increase as well, just to keep Hayek off our back.

5.5.1 Power Transforms

Next imagine that our arbitrageur does some honest work, however trivial. Data can be transformed in some manner before the questions are relayed to oracle C or even back to the very same oracle D. Here is a question:

> Predict the number of seconds before failure of a machine.

Here is a transformed question:

> Predict the fourth root of the number of seconds before failure of a machine.

What perverse motivation might we have to ask an oracle to predict $\tau^{1/4}$, instead of τ, where τ is a failure time? Well, if one takes the fourth root of each data point drawn from an exponential distribution, the resulting data set will be approximately gaussian.

I mention this because for a startling fraction of my adult life, I was unaware that taking a fourth root can be so useful. It seems that I have been badly in need of a personal microarbitrageur all this time. By the way, if you can remember to use 0.2654 instead of 1/4, or your micro-manager can, then more power to you. (It's a power transform, get it? A proof is provided by Yang and Xie that an exponent of 0.2654 converts exponential data into a distribution that is as close to gaussian as possible.)[14]

Notice that I used the fourth root in equation 5.1 to link a contest to predict something approximately normal to a regular lottery, thereby making amends for my ignorance. You may be more familiar with the more general Box–Cox transformation.[15] Surveys of use cases are quite plentiful.[16]

The nuances of these approaches center on measures of normality of data, but there's a common theme. Adjust the parameter or parameters of the transformation until these measures indicate that the data is as close to normal as possible.

Both algorithms and people *prefer* data that looks approximately gaussian, which is why many libraries include or encourage the use of some variety of preprocessing. A study of the efficacy of time-series models, before and after transformations were applied, was performed by Proietti and Lütkepohl.[17]

The authors conclude that transforming the data did more good than harm, leading us to believe that a species of preprocessing arbitrageurs could be quite an asset for the prediction web. (Not to mention useful for reproducing or challenging Proietti and Lütkepohl's result— the prediction web is a bonanza for people looking to write empirical papers.)

5.5.2 Enhancing, Splitting, Conditioning ...

Now if transforms of this type are sufficient to create an arbitrage opportunity, the same is likely true of all manner of operations. For example, an arbitrageur might perform differencing, outlier removal, labeling of points in some manner, enhancement of the feature space, inclusion of a weekend flag, or any number of other operations that might be considered trivial but, nonetheless, don't need to be replicated en masse by everyone building analytics.

Collections of micromanagers of this variety can coalesce into data science pipelines (composition of transformations and models). In chapter 2, we singled out enhancement and cleaning as fine work for micromanagers. If we lower the cost of friction in statistical trade, we dramatically simplify the development work. Who among us has not cut and pasted data-cleaning heuristics from one place to another?

Feature engineering sometimes requires special knowledge of the problem or domain, yet arbitrageurs employing general-purpose feature discovery tools could make a nice living on the prediction web.

As another example, an arbitrageur might fork an incoming sequence of data, redirecting some questions (or points to predict) to oracle C and some to oracle B, in order to be compensated for increasing the efficacy of oracle D to which it supplies predictions.

I mention this last example because in one real-time contest to predict trade volume of corporate bonds, the winner used a simple stacking technique. One model was trained on light trading periods and the other heavy. Then, the winner reused a model for the subtask that was provided to all contestants and won![18]

This was cute, but the real question is, what would have happened in a two-layered contest? For there, only the act of conditioning (splitting) the incoming data is required. The rest can happen automatically, either with the action of arbitrageurs or recursive use of oracles. So the arbitrageur would be well rewarded.

And although this act of bifurcation might be considered statistically mundane or obvious *in retrospect*, it clearly was sufficient to outperform more sophisticated entries from quants, data scientists, and machine learning experts—many of whom reached instinctively for the latest and greatest techniques (like temporal convolutional networks and so forth).

Hayek reminds us that the sophistication of the contribution is not what matters but the impact.

5.5.3 Financial Transforms

It goes without saying that the statistical literature is rich with ideas for data transformations, any one of which could provide a differentiating factor for an arbitrageur let loose on the prediction web.

Beyond the statistical literature, we can lean on derivative pricing techniques from finance—also a rich vein of tricks for transforming one type of microprediction task into another.

This may be especially apt when the quantity to be predicted is itself a probability, a price or something, some other expectation of a future quantity, or a value function—as discussed in chapter 8. The financial and econometric literature documents dozens if not hundreds of transformations, as well as decompositions of prices and probabilities.

For example, suppose we are simulating a chemical reaction thousands of times and measuring the time taken for some threshold to be met. If the underlying process is similar to Brownian motion, we might be well served by studying the mathematical properties of the quantity being measured—something well appreciated in the derivatives literature. (In this case, a transform might be suggested based on the first passage time of Brownian motion, which follows a Lévy distribution.)

It is standard in finance to turn quantities inside out using analytic solutions (very often thinly veiled heat equation solutions, or solutions of the Feynman–Kac equation). The most well known is the Black–Scholes formula for option pricing.

It is an example of a transformation from one type of data to a quantity that it might be considerably easier to ask an oracle about. Volatilities of different types of options are at least somewhat similar, whereas other numerical expressions of their value are not.

And one need not look only at formal statistics or high finance. I've always been intrigued by transformations created by sports fans seeking insight—some of which are only justified in a theoretical way many years later.

I exhibit the Pythagorean law of baseball attributed to Bill James (not to be confused with that considerably older formula about triangles). The Pythagorean formula arose from James's empirical finding: that the winning percentage for a baseball team over the course of a season is estimated by

$$\overbrace{p}^{\text{win probability}} = \frac{RS^2}{RS^2 + RA^2} \tag{5.2}$$

where RS is the runs scored by a team and RA is the runs conceded.[19]

Let's turn James's empirical insight into a transformation of a prediction task and thus a recipe for a micromanager. If we let $\rho = RS/RA$ denote the ratio of runs scored to runs conceded, then a little rearranging yields

$$\overbrace{\rho}^{\text{runs ratio}} = \sqrt{\frac{p}{1-p}}$$

The quantity inside the square root is called an odds ratio because p and $1 - p$ are the probabilities of winning and losing, respectively. Is this a useful transformation and will it find good food to eat given a chance to hunt?

I refrain from precise predictions about the future wealth of microscopic log-odds square rooting algorithms foraging on a prediction network. Your guess is as good as mine as to their financial security, but here's what we can say. The use of the square root of an odds ratio as a transformation of data seemed like a good idea to someone else. It is motivated in the entirely different context of clinical trials—but that came much, much later.[20]

You see my point, then? Why did it take so long? Let the algorithms roam.

5.5.4 A Speculative Recipe
And here's a conjecture about the creation of useful transforms that one might use to map formal and informal statistics into profitable arbitrageurs.

Whenever a "law" like Bill James's is discovered, there will be a constant quantity (as with the exponent 2 in the baseball formula). There is a decent chance that the distribution of *implied* constant is close to normal or, at minimum, suggests a good data transformation.

To illustrate, we need a little algebra and a plot. The implied exponent can be computed for any baseball season. The Pythagorean formula relates win probability p, runs ratio ρ, and the exponent $\lambda \approx 2$ via

$$\rho = \left(\frac{p}{1-p} \right)^{1/\lambda}$$

which rearranges as

$$\lambda = \frac{\log(p) - \log(1-p)}{\log(\rho)}$$
$$= \frac{\log(\textit{win ratio})}{\log(\textit{runs ratio})}$$

While this might not be a good example of microprediction (because baseball seasons don't come and go too often), this example nonetheless illustrates the general pattern.

Figure 5.2 is a probability plot of the actual realized exponent λ, say, compiled over a number of baseball seasons. The straight line references quantiles from a normally distributed quantity. It can be seen that the distribution of implied λ is close to normal.

The Pythagorean formula is also an example of interpreting data using an underlying generative model. James didn't realize that at the time, and I don't blame him. Only much later, and well after the formula was widely adopted, Steven Miller established that equation 5.2 is precisely correct if runs scored in a game follows the Weibull distribution.[21]

Miller's result applies to any exponent, not just 2. Miller's result is also an example of a more general problem of multiparticipant contests, which might also be used to transform microprediction tasks by converting frequencies of winning into performance location parameters.

For example, I've noticed that the relative empirical frequencies of English synonyms are almost exactly normal after application of a transform of this sort.[22] This suggests that micromanagers could profit in a prediction network by performing multivariate transformations of quantities that add to unity—a commonly occurring constraint.

5.5.5 State, Features, and Convenience

And yet in saying this, we may be overlooking even simpler conveniences. For example, a micromanager might exist purely to serve as a buffer that collects recent observations and packages them together with the contemporaneous data point—thereby making life easier for algorithms sitting behind whatever oracle this is sent to.

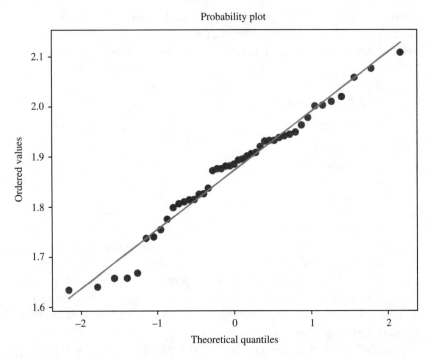

Figure 5.2

Normal quantile plot of baseball's elusive Pythagorean coefficient measured over numerous seasons. This illustrates the conjecture that empirical "constants" are normally distributed and thus suggestive of good data transformations.

More broadly, transformations of the history of a sequence of questions can be used to generate the payload for one or more questions, which oracles might have an easier time answering. Increasing convenience through the opportunistic application of Fourier transforms, wavelet decompositions, low-pass filters, matrix profiles, change points, outliers, or completely standard time-series models will be rewarded.[23]

This serves as a reminder of why reducing friction is important, as emphasized in the notion of vanishing management overhead, in chapter 3 and again in chapter 4. Normative approaches to data summarizing, history management, and state have an uncertain shelf life. We are better off allowing those decisions to be dictated by the micromarketplace and permitting micromanagers to evolve, fight, and improve over time.

In a related idea, an arbitrageur might use the past in a more imaginative manner. Perhaps it stores history of a data stream and then plays it back faster to an oracle. The idea is that algorithms behind the oracle can catch up to the present faster than they otherwise would, even if they are late to the game.

This setup achieves some of the benefits of back-testing, although arguably in an elegant fashion. I have experimented with a variation on this pattern where one extra data point enters the loop each time. This has some drawbacks as it is vulnerable to memorizing algorithms, but in more elaborate setups, we might hope to fool them. (As a countermeasure, the manager could assess children based *only* on their answers to the real-time question, not the historical data points that pad the looping series.)

5.5.6   Migration and Meta-Assistance

But let us move on. Another class of arbitrage, should you wish to call it that, is important enough in the grand scheme of things to warrant special mention. It is a mechanism that can enable intelligence to pass through walls—in particular, the boundaries of a private firm that is concerned about intellectual property and data security.

I speak about model stealing, migration, or cannibalization—depending on how pejorative you choose to be. The manager somehow effects a permanent transfer of microprediction capability, which need not be nefarious.

The micromanager can transparently introduce one level of indirection in scoring, in order to take possession of a model, assuming there is a broad enough class of models (and probably reference implementations of the same) available to both parent and child.

For example, suppose a function $f(x; \theta)$ depending on some parameter θ is known to parent and child. The child responds with a representation θ in response to a question x and the parent evaluates as

$$score(\theta) = score(f(x; \theta))$$

where the choosing of *score* is the subject of chapter 7. Setting aside the matter of whether f is well specified, by asking for θ instead of $y = f(x; \theta)$, we are merely performing a transform, as with the others we have considered. The question moves from one space to another, namely, the parameter space of the function f.

The child need not relay θ every time—it may apply for an entire epoch. The parent might take on more responsibility such as maintaining state required by f from one invocation to the next.

This pattern above could be used to make a literal connection between oracles and the theory of M-estimation (which generalized likelihood estimation in statistics). The oracle is a kind of extremal estimator in the wild.

Migration of intelligence from supplier to manager can be achieved in many other ways. I won't attempt a taxonomy, but here are some examples of questions that might facilitate algorithms managing other algorithms, or migration of intelligence through a privacy boundary.

1. What ONNX serialization of a neural net works best?
2. What parameters would answer this best?
3. What hyperparameters should my algorithm use?
4. What are the best weights for an ensemble algorithm?
5. Is performance on this data point positively or negatively correlated with performance overall?

As an illustration of this utility, consider the possibility of a private firm providing synthetic or augmented data to a public oracle, while being simultaneously able to implement some function $f(x; \theta)$ on private data never revealed. A whole class of algorithms can be developed that advance the primary objectives: recruiting good algorithms and predicting private data.

These techniques may borrow from theoretical work that tries to understand how best to select training examples for algorithms. (This is sometimes referred to as machine teaching—although it goes by other names.)

Suffice to say that privacy preservation can be viewed as a kind of information arbitrage and a very important one. In a future world, we can expect to see it occurring more frequently at the interface between companies' private prediction networks and the public prediction network. The discussion is continued in chapter 9.

As a concrete example of the third pattern, one micromanager calls on the other to assist with its meta-learning, or hyperparameter optimization—even if privacy concerns dictate that the problem must be treated as a black-box optimization.

Moving up one level, a micromanager that, say, recommends global derivative-free optimizers can be an interesting species—given the diversity of possibilities in the Python ecosystem alone. The beginnings of such a micromanager are illustrated by the HumpDay package. In turn, some of the optimization strategies therein are themselves based on meta-learning, or benchmarking across a diverse set of problems. That's true of the currently top-performing black-box strategy called Nevergrad OnePlus, one of Facebook's contributions to open source.[24]

5.6   Other Fauna

When it comes to the creation of microscopic value adding statistical firms, there are many other hooks one might choose to hang one's intuition on and many other patterns for adding value.

All sorts of automated bots might crawl the prediction web. Software aimed at human data scientist productivity might also benefit the artificial variety. For instance, one species might focus on the organization of metadata.[25]

Every species of middle-person that exists in the human economy, from the broker to the headhunter to the loan shark, has a parallel in the prediction web.

It is certainly conceivable that a clever ontology or data model might reign supreme in one corner of the web. Value could be added by programs that index and transform existing parts of the prediction web.

Frameworks that assist model deployment clearly have a role to play. A small amount of rent extraction could sustain them, if they reduce the code footprint of micromanagers developed by busy people.

I have yet to come across a statistical technique (for instance, the task of fitting a distribution to data) that does not suggest a micromanager—which is to say it is not hard to reverse engineer a set of reward mechanisms in a repeated game that allows the provider of the tool to share revenue with the user, in some manner.

Some micromanagers will effect tiny consortia. Others will exist only to train other algorithms. The citizens of the prediction web will be diverse.

The term *micromanager* suggests a privileged coordinating role. However, a micromanager might exist in order to facilitate other collective activities where the real statistical work takes on a more symmetric nature. For example, algorithms might team up to effect a federated classification—and this might be more practical than the use of a centralized model.[26]

The micromanager's role could be purely administrative, as with the registration of algorithms. It might fulfill some centralized communication need or the advertising of protocols for a peer-to-peer arrangement.

To suggest the richness of fauna that might be possible, I mention an obscure species. The entangled random-number generator exists only to create and disseminate to other parties' sets of random numbers whose margins are uniform but whose outcomes are tied in some manner. This may seem like an odd thing to engage in, but it can play a key role in allowing predictive capability to pass through walls (chapter 9).

5.7 Implementation

Now, to bring this discussion down to Earth, by which I mean the cloud mostly, I ask you: how hard is it to implement a reactive function that performs some kind of transformation, pings another pseudo-oracle, gets the answer, and responds upstream? Not very hard at all.

The remarks I make here take a minimalist slant, intended to be somewhat orthogonal to existing implementations. I do this not because that is necessarily the best approach but because it provides a fast way to arrive at the conclusion I would like you to reach, namely, that the task is not too hard.

5.7.1 Rule #1: No Whining

I take the example of the parimutuel, in our "collider" category, and note that implementation was achieved by engineering pioneer Sir George Julius more than a century ago—many decades before the dawn of the computer era.

Thus, anyone complaining about the task has been forever shamed. Julius did not have Python, javascript, or web assembly at his disposal. We are not faced with the challenge of inventing the mechanical rotary shaft adder (one of Julius's prerequisite inventions for his collider).

And unlike micromanagers, Julius needed to please humans—all those patrons at the race course and the operators—and provide them visual stimulus. Early totalizator "user interfaces" included a mechanical array of giant thermometer-like representations of the money invested in each horse. Meanwhile, operators were connected to the machine via chains and pulleys.

(An excellent historical site outlining his contribution is maintained by Brian Conlon. Given my Antipodean bias, I won't argue with his assertion that the mechanical totalizator was the world's first real-time information processing system and somewhat undersold in the history of computing.[27])

5.7.2 Micromanagers as Functions

With that inspiration, let's see if we can shrink Julius's invention—which occupied a large building in Ellerslie race course in New Zealand as early as 1913—down to the size of a lambda function.

For those not familiar, the term *lambda* comes from Amazon Web Services (AWS), the first major entrant to provide a serverless abstraction of a function. The name *lambda* carries slightly different connotations in computer science and mathematics—making it a clever name. It has proved popular.

Google and Azure subsequently offered their own versions of cloud functions. There is no continuous cost for the user outside of the function invocation—making it possible to create extremely inexpensive participants in a prediction web, as we shall see.

Let us assume that the micromanager's upstream responsibility can be fulfilled reactively (which is to say that it responds to prodding from whomever compensates it, as compared to polling a data source continuously and proactively reaching out to others). This makes this part of its job a nice fit for a functional representation.

The initiation and maintenance of economic relationships can be achieved in a passive functional style too. Yes it is true that a micromanager could periodically search and initiate relationships, but it could also, just as easily, be more passive, waiting for invitations to start predicting a data stream. Even aggressive behavior can be implemented in a passive technology style.

So, morally speaking, a micromanager can be "just" a collection of functions. And a collection of functions is a single function—the one that dispatches to the others. So we're rolling along now, because the micromanager can be a lambda. Well, almost. . . .

5.7.3 Functions with Fallible Memory
There's a minor speed bump.

Our minimalism exercise is made slightly more entertaining because ostensibly, cloud functions are rendered stateless—so that the provider can guarantee scaling. More precisely, this means the function has no *guaranteed* persistent module memory or storage or any kind and in theory must be wired to something else.

Even the basic managers, such as our bus-arrival pseudo-oracle discussed in chapter 3, require some memory. The bus-arrival oracle needs one or two scalar quantities per child to track a rolling estimate of accuracy and uptime, and it will need more state to be kept if originality is required. It would therefore appear, on the surface, that pure cloud functions are not sufficient.

Things are never as simple as they seem, however, especially when you consider the micromanager in context. It is but one of a number of partially redundant suppliers of prediction that collectively create a robust supply (in much the same way that the efficiency of a stock price is not absolutely predicated on any given hedge fund continuing to trade it).

Because the micromanager's success or failure is statistical, it need not conform to traditional norms that are imprinted upon us when we learn about best practices in the software development life cycle. There need be no single golden chain of calculation.

I think you see we are headed into really hacky territory. And yes, with the possibility that the micromanager can be occasionally fallible, I have made a close inspection of some of these services and tried to quantify how often state is preserved from one invocation to the next. It mostly is.

I suggest a ballpark memory failure rate of 1 in 1,000, just to make this discussion more explicit, and that applies when a function is called with regular cadence every few seconds, say, and does not trigger a need to scale. So 999 times out of 1,000, the memory from the last invocation is maintained. I'm not the only one to notice.[28]

Our micromanager, poised on a lambda function like an angel dancing on the head of a pin, will occasionally fall off. It will forget which of its suppliers are accurate, who it has paid, and so forth. There is some stern, emphatic boilerplate from the AWS product managers that reminds you of this fact.

And yet, it isn't hard to devise patterns where two or more lambdas conspire, acting as collective memory. I would remind the reader that dynamic random access memory (DRAM) is volatile too, and the refreshing of memory pattern can be very cost-effective compared to nonvolatile components.

5.7.4 Functions with Parental Memory

I make one more minimalist remark that might survive the next technology fashion. It falls into the category of "parenting," where the micromanager goes out of his or her way to assist a supplier of microreprediction in some way.

I've mentioned that state, such as data history, can be prepared by a contest organizer for the benefit of competitors. But what about the contestants' own state?

A micromanager with strong parental instincts may hold computational state on behalf of a contestant (child), thus making it easier for the child to use technologies that are convenient in every other respect (other than storage). A micromanager that offers this service to its children may, over time, outperform an otherwise equivalent micromanager that does not.

There is also no loss of generality in designing time-series prediction libraries with this in mind, and that is why I chose that pattern recently, in a package where all "models" are forecast functions returning state to the caller.[29]

$$y, S' = f(x, S)$$

Here the child is returning a prediction y in response to a question x, as we expect, but in addition, the parent is also supplying to the child a state S that can be empty on the first call. The child returns a new state S' to the parent. The parent kindly keeps the child's state from one invocation of the child to the next.

The parent does not know the meaning of the state and does not need to. It is merely serving as a data store for the child achieved in the same call as the prediction.

Like all implementations, this has downside: an increase in communication that may, depending on the context, be a deal breaker. But another advantage is that the parent can now use the child in novel ways that would not otherwise be possible.

For instance, the parent can send a sequence of questions (x_1, S), $(x_2, S), \ldots$ with the child's state frozen in time, allowing the parent to understand the child (such as by building a surrogate model), or task the child with conditional prediction problems.

Parental memory is a continuum. A weaker form of interaction would be one in which the parent intermittently stores backup state for the child.

5.7.5 A Rapidly Changing Landscape

The best exposition of implementation is implementation itself, and the reader will not have material difficulty locating open-source reference implementations as they develop.

But briefly, another interesting abstraction for the minimalists out there (perhaps the rule-following kind) is provided by AWS step functions. A step function is a technological abstraction of a state machine, one where transitions occur from one state to another as data arrives.

Step functions can be described in JavaScript Object Notation (JSON) and mutated at this same level of description. Like lambdas, step functions can be extremely cost-effective, yet as sophisticated in their logic as the user desires.

Stepping up one level, micromanagers can be implemented using micro web frameworks such as flask (for those looking to stay in the Python ecosystem that is so rich in tooling). This may be appropriate if the micromanager is forced to suffer the indignity of communicating with humans and pandering to their needs.

Another possibility is provided by hosted open-source repositories. Although we normally think of these sites as mere storage and versioning of code, a relatively recent innovation is the provision of small amounts of occasionally used compute such as with GitHub actions. A micromanager can use versioned files as storage.

At the time of writing, some participants in a prototype system have found niche cloud service providers to be convenient. An example is the bundling of Python-centric web services and running processes provided by PythonAnywhere.

To reiterate, however, the field known today as "machine learning operations" (MLOps) is one of the fastest evolving in technology. It has seen numerous startups rocket to unicorn status in recent years, which is evidence both of the gap that exists and the speed with which it is being filled.

It's a very good thing that in the coming years, the prediction web can surf the MLOps wave. It's not so great for your author just at the moment, because it's incredibly difficult to provide reasonable advice that will stand the test of time.

5.7.6   Event Processing
I don't mean to suggest that all choices will depend crucially on the finer points of technology. There are other considerations that might, by the time you read this, remain relevant.

For instance, predictability of tasks or lack thereof might dictate a preference for reactive participation over other modes. If an oracle is called in an on-demand fashion to answer a specific question that *cannot be anticipated in advance*, it may be natural, from the point of view of volumetrics, to choose once technology over another.

Consider the oracle-powered phone or watch application that informs cyclists that the bike share rack they are arriving at will be full fifteen minutes from now. If not terribly popular, this provokes only a tiny fraction of the full set of possible questions that might be asked at any given moment.

On the other hand, if we seek to provide a live forecast for every possible bike station, enhance an enterprise data feed without knowledge of its various downstream uses, or provide wind speed forecasts for the next few hours for *all* locations, then the use of publication and subscription technologies, complex event processing, and streaming technologies may be more appropriate.

It's worth keeping in mind that due to the existence of both types of microprediction need, there isn't a single right way. Just as there isn't a single calculation that serves both dense and sparse matrices best.

5.8 Summary

I've provided some ideas for micromanager creation. They are not exhaustive by any means, and within each possibility, there are a number of practical and statistical complications that might take us very far afield. However, I hope this gives you a sense of the myriad possibilities, and I hope that by enumerating these, I haven't discouraged your own inventions.

The limited goal of this chapter has been to illustrate that algorithms are perfectly capable of taking on all of the economic responsibility we require of them, in their dual role of prediction producer and manager of other prediction producers.

Some managers can use lightweight market-inspired or contest-inspired mechanisms that force providers of prediction to compete. But they can take other forms too, inspired by statistical stacking and generalized regression.

Since micromanagers represent a coupling of economic strategy with a core statistical technique, inspiration should come from many sources. I would go so far as to say that *most* ideas in statistics and machine learning can spawn entire classes of micromanagers, and I leave you to ponder your favorite examples. (Take back-propagation, for example, or the kernel trick. Do these suggest a new style of compensation? How could they not?)

As for implementation, I remind you that not so many years ago, it required a small interdisciplinary team to deploy analytic microservices. Now, this can be accomplished by one person with half an hour to spare. The special person who happens to have the arcane skill in statistics and the absolutely right hammer for a particular problem still needs to be *somewhat* knowledgeable in technology, but the bar has been lowered considerably.

6

Contests

The ability to automatically assess statistical algorithms (given enough data) is central to the prediction web thesis. This chapter considers the empirical evidence provided by data science contests—and some theory it appears to violate.

6.1 A Gap to Fill?

The rise of automated model assessment is due largely to the expanding domain of problems. However, it is also possible that a related shortage of talent plays a role. Back in 2011, McKinsey estimated a shortfall of skilled talent between 140,000 and 190,000 in the U.S. market alone.[1]

In 2020, the same organization featured a very different analysis (by different authors, I add) questioning whether companies still needed to hire a large contingent of data scientists to build machine learning models. The reason? Automated machine learning was coming to the fore.[2]

Both perspectives may lean too heavily on the centrality of employer-employee relationships in the orchestration of labor (something that might radically change in a world flooded with hungry micromanagers). Other styles of clearing demand and supply for data and analytics might play a part too. Data science bazaars and boutique platforms are hoping to address this need, for example.[3]

Application programming interface (API) marketplaces provide examples of a storefront model, insofar as they represent attempts to help suppliers of analytics push models out to those who want them. Data scientists can easily create microservices and charge customers for usage, analogous to an app store. The end-consumers are programmers.

Table 6.1
Quantitative contest communities, past and present, and very approximate sizes. Sources include Kaggle (https://www.kaggle.com/general/164795); TopCoder (https://en.wikipedia.org/wiki/Topcoder); Quantopian (https://en.wikipedia.org/wiki/Quantopian), which has ceased to operate; QuantConnect (https://www.quantconnect.com/forum/discussions/1/interesting); and Crowd Analytix (https://www.crowdanalytix.com/community).

Platform	Registered Users	Focus
Kaggle	5,000,000	Data science
TopCoder	1,200,000	Programming
Quantopian	210,000	Quant trading
QuantConnect	75,000	Quant trading
CrowdAnalytix	25,000	Data science

6.2   Data Science Contests

Closer to our topic is the idea of removing the burden of search, and sometimes even choice, from the person who needs the analytics. After all, the oracle hopes to serve bespoke data science needs from the perspective of an end user, one not necessarily possessing the time or ability to search the enormous space of models, data, and services.

In domains where automatic assessment of modeling quality is possible (for example, where there is enough data to run a contest), there is no theoretical reason why algorithms cannot draw solutions to problems. (Whether you consider data science contests in their current manifestations to be automated is beside the point.) In this regard, contest sites listed in table 6.1 should be relevant to us. And there are many more competitive communities.[4]

Contest sites offer money for the best submissions as judged by predetermined quantitative accuracy criteria. Thereby, they initiate a search in the space of possible models for a particular classification, identification, or regression problem. The search might be too human oriented for our liking, thus too cumbersome and shallow (no subcontests or recursion), but they have been successful.

Let's be somewhat broad in our conception of a data science contest. It is not absolutely necessary that contestants' work be contemporaneous or that they meet a deadline or be directly rewarded with prizes. There is a phrase for a slight generalization of the contest: the Common Task Framework (CTF), courtesy of Marc Liberman. The essential elements would appear to be:

1. A publicly available training data set involving, for each observation, a list of (possibly many) feature measurements and a class label for that observation

2. A set of enrolled competitors whose common task is to infer a class prediction rule from the training data

3. A scoring referee, to which competitors can submit their prediction rule. The referee runs the prediction rule against a testing data set that is sequestered behind a Chinese wall. The referee objectively and automatically reports the score (prediction accuracy) achieved by the submitted rule.[5]

The CTF has spurred advances in machine learning by intensifying academic competition on standardized data sets–such as the MINST handwritten digit database. But yes, cash seems to help. The KDD Cup and the million-dollar Netflix Prize posed genuinely difficult research problems. Money augmented the scientific incentives rather well.[6]

Then along came Kaggle, which industrialized the data science contest. Kaggle touts Allstate's use of crowdsourcing to improve their actuarial models as a notable success story. Their competition attracted six hundred data scientists and three hundred teams fighting over $10,000 in prize money. The contestants easily outpredicted Allstate's internal experts drawn from their actuarial department, which has a strong reputation.[7]

General Electric reported similar gains when, in 2012, they offered a $500,000 prize for prediction of airline flight arrival times. Close to 4,000 separate algorithms were entered and the crowd obliterated the industry benchmarks—reducing average error from 4.2 to 3.2 minutes.[8]

These contests have also brought out the importance of cognitive diversity and the difficulty in predicting ahead of time who is likely to win. In the flight arrival time contest, the winning team comprised a French actuary and several data scientists in Singapore, with second place falling to an epidemiologist working with a banking analyst (not unlike the results of a J. P. Morgan contest organized by your author, won by a junior operations employee in Mumbai.[9])

Empirically, it isn't always necessary to offer a lot of money to benefit from remarkable insights. TopCoder reports a contest to devise a fast algorithm for DNA sequence alignment. It only took $6,000 in prize money and two weeks to drive the best performance from 400 seconds down to 16 seconds.

What's more remarkable about that achievement is that Harvard University had previously invested a person year to get to the 400-second result, as compared with the previous open-source benchmark of 2,000 seconds.[10]

Now "kaggler" is a lowercase word, and it is clear that the coalescing of millions of data scientists around problems of economic, civic, and scientific importance is an important achievement. There are evidently tantalizing possibilities rooted in something as simple as a contest, never mind other kinds of automated means of eliciting and rewarding contributions that the reader might devise.

6.3   Forecasting Contests

Some of the contests therein could be called forecasting or prediction contests. This may seem like a fine line to draw because when a sequence of past values is used to predict a future one, it is easily viewed as a general regression problem.

However, due to data leakage challenges, the automated assessment of algorithms that forecast time series comes with its own special wrinkles (as I discovered when arranging one of the earlier time-series contests to run on Kaggle).

Time-series competitions have a very long history. The most successful series is known as the M-Competitions. The M is shorthand for Spyros Makridakis, who has organized the contests over a forty-year period. A report of that first competition, in which only seven forecasting experts participated, was already informative.

> Finally, it seems that seasonal patterns can be predicted equally well by both simple and statistically sophisticated methods. This is so it is believed, because of the instability of seasonal variations that dominate the remaining of the patterns and which can be forecast. (Makridakis et al. 1979, p. 142)

Thus, we see the automated assessment of algorithms serving as a possible antidote to fashion (those who worry about trend chasing in analytics today should be aware it is not a new issue). At the time, it was an important step to have multiple researchers perform independent work, rather than have one researcher compare different methods themselves.

Building on that long history of competitions, Makridakis, Fry, Petropoulos, and Spiliotis have recently laid out some design principles for future forecasting contests, drawing also on the opinions of other forecasting experts such as Rob J. Hydnman.[11]

The authors suggest that contests should solicit both predictions and measures of uncertainty (with an example being a full distributional estimate). And for forecasting contests to serve the maximal learning purpose, they should include a wide diversity of data sources.

To combat data leakage, the authors suggest the possibility of rolling contests, where more data is revealed in stages, or live contests. They also point to the emerging importance of short-term and higher-frequency prediction to industry. Even more pertinently, the authors note that

> in the era of big data and instant access to many publicly available sources of information, participants are usually in a position to gather the required data by themselves, but also to complement their forecasts by using any other publicly available information. (Makridakis et al. 1979, p. 10)

These considerations strongly suggest eliciting *diverse, frequently updated, live, distributional* forecasts—as with the collider discussed in chapter 5.[12]

6.4   The Secret Sauce . . .

Automatic assessment of quantitative work has its limitations and may even seem distasteful in some respects, given the seeming inversion of control between the human and machine. To automatically assess work is to subvert the generalized intelligence of the modeler, it might be argued, or restrict their ability to contribute.

It isn't a new topic, and it is certainly the case that some modeling insight cannot be appreciated without generalized intelligence. Nonetheless, discerning longitudinal observers of data science, such as Stanford statistician David Donoho, have noted the critical role played by data science contests and the CTF as catalysts for the machine learning revolution. In his essay entitled "50 Years of Data Science," Donoho goes so far as to refer to contests as the secret sauce of prediction culture.[13]

By "prediction culture," the author refers to the second of two cultures in the field of statistics identified by Berkeley statistician Leo Breiman back in 2001. According to Breiman, objective measurement of performance was not a burden on the modeler. On the contrary, it was a liberating influence for engineers and computer scientists (and of course some statisticians) who created a "second culture of statistics."

Although the engineering approach was not new in principle (it was emphasized by John Tukey in the mid-twentieth century, for example), it was timely, and prediction culture fostered a pragmatic emphasis. It freed the modeler from the requirement of an explicit understanding of the properties of a predictive model—such as whether it would perform well on data with known statistical distribution.[14]

Breiman noted that it was generally impossible for statisticians to model the probabilistic nature of the data they were looking at. Therefore, they should be free to experiment whether or not the reasons for the good performance can be well understood.

6.5   ... of "Data Science"

The relative popularity of nomenclature (artificial intelligence, machine learning, data science) used to describe applied statistical work today testifies to the fact that Breiman's mildly heretical viewpoint was prescient. Black- and gray-box approaches have proven unreasonably effective. Breiman, informed by the efficacy of techniques such as random forests, saw it coming.

> The statistical community has been committed to the almost exclusive use of generative models. This commitment has led to irrelevant theory, questionable conclusions, and has kept statisticians from working on a large range of interesting current problems. (Breiman 2001, p. 199)

Breiman was referring to the dual objectives of statistics. On the one hand, we seek to predict the future response to input in a given system no matter how we can accomplish this. On the other, we wish to infer the underlying mechanics—how nature is doing it—by building generative models that present a probabilistic definition of input and output relationships.

The author suggested that if his colleagues in statistics departments did not take up the running, then others surely would.

Predictive modeling, both in theory and practice, has developed rapidly in fields outside statistics. Breiman, who died of cancer in 2005, unfortunately did not get to see the accuracy of his prophesy. Perhaps things have even swung too far, and certainly not all statisticians have appreciated the rebranding of their field. To compensate, at least the invasion from computer science, engineering, and management departments has been accompanied with some quality snark.

> When physicists do mathematics, they don't say they're doing "number science." They're doing math. (Broman 2013)

Setting aside the silliness of renaming things for the sake of it, it is undoubtedly true that applied predictive modeling (by whatever name) has been enriched by prediction culture and its tinkering engineering spirit. The population of productive applied statisticians is now quite vast, and few would identify as traditional inferential statisticians.

This population includes millions of students, academics, hobbyists, freelancers, and relative newcomers to applied statistics looking to upskill and be more effective in their daily jobs.

Breiman emphasized a dichotomy of statistical approach to problems—algorithmic methods versus inferential statistical tools. Donoho emphasized the importance of contests to one tribe in particular, machine learning researchers. Both authors delineate a cultural line. On one half of the line lies black-box and gray-box statistical techniques. On the other are more "conventional" tools for statistical inference.

In contrast, I have emphasized a different but obviously related line—one drawn between problem domains, not methods of attacking the same problem. That divide is prediction versus microprediction, in my terminology.

On one side of our line, we have problems such as predicting climate change. (The use of crowdsourcing is already successful there too, but requires human-centric infrastructure.[15])

On the other side lies microprediction: how many KitKats will be sold in the next hour in one of a thousand vending machines scattered across a state. There, the discussion in chapter 3 suggests a bare-bones contest attack can serve not only research purposes but also production.

We need not debate whether a division of statistical technique versus a division of statistical problems is more profound or of superior explanatory power when it comes to understanding the changing demographics (and terminology) of the field. It should suffice to observe that the rise of "data science" is *correlated* with a deluge of data and applications where a contest, or the CTF, or more general mechanical ways of eliciting models (or data) can catalyze progress.

Indeed, the mundane observation of most relevance to us is that modeling tasks permitting automated assessment are simply much more prevalent than they used to be. We'd expect this to be correlated with a proliferation of open-source automated model search packages. As noted in chapter 5, we're certainly seeing that.

6.6 Moving to Real Time

By the time you read this, it is possible that the M-Competitions will be entirely real time. Not only are veteran forecasting contest organizers suggesting this emphasis for the benefit of research, but there are even more pressing practical motivations to perform automated assessment, scoring, and selection based on live data.

For although offline automated model search (as with AutoML packages) makes it easier for micromanagers to drive down the cost of discovery, marshalling, and exploitation of external intelligence, this does not fully tap the "second culture of statistics" in a way that instantly delivers value in the present moment.

In contrast, the micromanagers generalizing the pattern in chapter 3 can move contests from a research to a production paradigm—with major motivations:

1. It is what business needs. Tautologically, decisions and operations occur in real time.
2. Data search is possible (as distinct from model search alone) and not regarded as cheating.
3. Economics drives sharing and reuse of data, models, and features.

It almost seems odd that the use of crowdsourced statistics has mostly been relegated to the research cycle, where it stands little chance of providing cheap ubiquitous prediction. Part of the issue is that contests lure us into thinking we need an Olympics of data science with a scarcity of challenges—something obviously at odds with the ambition of solving lots of prediction problems for lots of people.

In addition, we can establish frameworks where one person can eventually attack one hundred thousand different problems by unleashing a single algorithm.

6.7   Theoretical Efficiency

That remark brings me to the issue of contest efficiency. I will close this chapter on statistical contests with a brief excursion into contest theory. My only intent is to disabuse the reader of the notion that inviting a large number of algorithms to do the same thing is wasteful.

Of course, at venues like Kaggle, that characterization refers only to marginal output and not to the participant themselves. One shouldn't ignore the educational benefits of participation.

Nonetheless, we note that on that site, the ratio of registered users to contests hovers near 10^6. The ratio of active participants to contests is also quite large, perhaps 10^3. The theoretical value, as we will see, is close to 10^0, so that is quite a discrepancy!

However, algorithms that are self-guided are not subject to the seeming irrationality of humans. The theory of contests is therefore a much better guide, or at least a counterpoint, if we are looking to speculate on a future equilibrium in a prediction web occupied by hyperrational algorithms.

A precise analysis of any given contest, or micromanager game, is not possible without knowing exactly what the rules are. As noted in chapter 5, there are many possibilities and, as noted in chapter 7, many nuances within.

So here I will move one level of abstraction above this, and without knowing the details of what work algorithms and their authors must do, we can view contests as a special type of auction—one where everyone pays whether or not they receive the item being sold. They are paying with their time and effort.

So-called all-pay auctions have attracted considerable study. As far as the likelihood of a prediction network taking off is concerned, the news is good. The main message from theory is that contests are surprisingly efficient because rational agents adjust their effort to avoid undue replication.

6.8 Winner Takes All

A standard way to model all-pay auctions is to assume that participants place a subjective value on winning, then decide how much to bid. We label the players in decreasing order of the values they place on the item, namely, $v_1, v_2, \ldots, v_n$.

Translating an auction into a contest, we'd say that the participant that puts in the most effort is declared the winner. Participants incur a cost per unit effort, which is common to all players. They seek to maximize

$$utility = expected\ \overbrace{subjective\ reward}^{v_i} - effort$$

It may seem more natural to assume that each player values winning the same (say 1) but has a different linear relationship between effort and output.

$$utility = expected\ \overbrace{reward}^{v=1} - effort \times \overbrace{production\ cost}^{inverse\ skill}$$

Quiet reflection may convince the reader that these two games are equivalent, and thus insights from one game translate into insights to the other.

The critical assumption behind the mathematics of auction theory is that player 1 knows the stochastic strategy of player 2 and vice versa. This may be borderline plausible if the game is played many times. The behavior of both players is devised in such a way that the other, even with this knowledge, cannot take advantage. This is the celebrated Nash equilibrium.[16]

Behavior of participants is stochastic, for logic decrees that a deterministic strategy cannot be best. To follow such a strategy would allow another player to easily improve by investing just a little more effort. Therefore, all players choose their efforts randomly.[17]

6.9   Two Participants

Next, suppose there are only two participants. It can be shown that the player who values the prize the most will choose effort randomly and uniformly between zero and the value v_2 that the second player ascribes to the prize. This is somewhat intuitive. The first player knows that the second player will never invest more effort than the value v_2 they place on the prize, but both players need to keep the other honest. (If the second player never invested more than $\frac{1}{2}v_2$ the first player could take advantage by investing just a little more.)

Conversely, the second player needs to keep the first player as honest as possible and so will choose a random effort between zero and v_2 (again, to invest more would incur an obvious winner's curse). It is less obvious how that random effort should be chosen.

Give up? It can be shown that the second player will make no effort at all with probability $1 - \frac{v_2}{v_1}$, where v_1 denotes the value the first player assigns to winning. Otherwise, the second player will also choose random effort between zero and v_2.

Now that we know how both players will behave, everything about the contest of interest can be calculated by integration. This includes the winning probabilities of each player, average total effort and average maximum individual effort.

6.10   Many Participants

To understand why contests are so efficient, we lean just a little further on the theory—this time imagining that there are not two players but many.

It turns out that if there are more than two participants, it is likely that the two players most desirous of winning will crowd out everyone else. They will deploy the same strategy as if they only faced each other, and all the other players will give up and not invest any effort.

This finding—which may seem shocking at first—is only as accurate as the assumptions. We have assumed a high level of transparency, in particular that contestants know the value that every other contestant places on the prize (or, in the equivalent game, the other participants, linear relationship between effort and output). It is this knowledge that drives them to give up.[18]

As noted, this theoretical result is very much at odds with empirical observation! Not only do more people enter contests than the Nash equilibrium result would suggest, but those that do seem to work harder.

When ruthlessly rational algorithms compete in a prediction network, they *should* bring us *much* closer to the Nash equilibrium—although due to developer laziness, algorithms themselves might tend to overparticipate too.

But setting that aside, the welfare results for contests bode well and suggest that the task of constructing good micromanagers might be easier than it first appears. For instance, there is seemingly no need to defend against overparticipation.

6.11   Summary

In viewing the rise of machine learning, I choose to follow the emphasis of Breiman and also Donoho (who puts contests and the CTF in a very special place).

For different reasons, both the empirical success of data science contests and the theoretical efficiency of the same suggest that a web of micromanagers, which effects a kind of "deep contest" as noted in chapter 3, is eventually an efficient way to source insight and data. The wisdom of the statistical crowd is well supported by the historical record.

Empirically, there is a seeming waste of human talent arising from irrational overparticipation in contests. The prediction web turns that ratio on its head. One person can contribute to thousands or millions of problems by writing a traveling micromanager.

Most contests depart from our vision of a micromanager in that they tend to be offline, asymmetric, and otherwise outside the definition of an oracle given in chapter 3—although they may be converging.

Forecasting experts who have run contests for many decades suggest that achieving a diversity of live, streaming, distributional prediction contests should be an important ambition (even though this brings new challenges for participants).

7

Communication

Our desire to remove humans from their preeminent role as model managers opens up some questions. What instructions constitute adequate supervision? In particular, can micromanagers convey succinctly the task that must be performed in such a way that the work product is aligned with objectives? Will those results be reusable in the next step of production?

A related question is whether applications can plug into a hypothesized prediction network, via an oracle, without their needs being misconstrued by algorithms on the other side. If only a point estimate (single number) is returned, this seems particularly dangerous.

This chapter continues the discussion of micromanagers and the automatic assessment of algorithms but pays attention to the intent of messages passed between them. I provide a brief introduction to some ideas from statistics that can help avoid misunderstandings.

7.1 Supervised Microprediction

I've suggested that in some mental models for micromanaging, discussed in chapter 5, one algorithm will pose another a question. What does that really mean? In English a reasonable prediction question might be

> When will the train arrive?

to which an answer might be "in about five minutes." An application might be written that parses and responds to vague questions such as this, but that application would probably find it convenient to call down to micromanagers who communicate in a more precise fashion about weather, related train questions, and so forth.

Let us say that a *microprediction task* contains a well-defined objective. It communicates both a question and a specification of how the answers to the repeated questions will be evaluated.

These tasks can be formulated in many ways, as also noted in chapter 5. However, there are some workhorse categories that are well understood, and they can be used to construct more elaborate patterns.

I will consider the task of hitting a target *truth*. The parent will challenge the child to provide a single number that is close to some future measurement. We know from chapter 2 that the use of the words *truth, measurement*, and *close* are quite broad.

We might call this a *supervised microprediction task* in keeping with the convention in machine learning—and I will content myself with that category. Although in passing, there is nothing to prevent repeated consensus games being established where the target involves the responses themselves. This is a common pattern in crowdsourcing labels for machine learning training data.

In contrast to the vague question about the train above, a well-formulated, supervised task might be the following:

> Provide me with an answer t, denominated in minutes, that will minimize, on average, the absolute value of the difference between your estimate t and the subsequently revealed truth τ that I will send to you later.

The command is a little unwieldy in English, but so are most precise things—just ask a lawyer. This phrasing of the *intent* to reward is described in a manner that allows the producer of microprediction (the responder to the question) to materially optimize their behavior in a repeated game.

We'll be assuming the responder will seek to minimize the average of their errors over multiple questions, although there is an important caveat....

7.2 Trust

Will the producer of prediction receive payment? It is simplest to assume that they know they will be rewarded as promised, which would allow us to proceed directly to the next section.

That's not going to be true in most cases in a microprediction web, but it likely doesn't matter. For instance, if the possibility of not being paid is unrelated to the game itself, and that cannot be influenced by the producer, then a score-minimizing strategy may yet coincide with a reward-maximizing one. The reward is merely discounted, but the game is otherwise the same.

Contracts are possible. The task above is written well enough to assist the writing of a contract and *could* be implemented as such—either by conventional means or as some variety of smart contract (as volumetrics permit). Some micromanagers could even play the role of escrow agents.

But in a rapidly repeating game, and in the presence of a microprediction web, we probably don't really need contracts of any kind. A producer of prediction who feels robbed of a promised reward can simply go elsewhere.

The famous prisoner's dilemma tournaments of Axelrod suggest that micromanagers who adopt relatively simple policies for cooperation might fare well, because it is easy for other micromanagers to understand their behavior.[1] (The prisoner's dilemma arises in our setting if a consumer decides whether to pay the promised microreward, whereas the producer decides whether to send an implicitly promised prediction. It's best all around if both act in good faith, but one can try to take advantage of the other.)

There is some dispute about whether Axelrod's findings are terribly general.[2] But they may be less relevant in a microprediction web in any case. A potential contributor has access to external decision-making power that algorithms in Axelrod's tournament did not have. It can request a prediction of whether or not some other player will cooperate. A micromanager can even request predictions of its future welfare in a game, as per chapter 8.

Trust swings both ways and applies at the outset of a relationship, not just in the steady state. A race-organizing micromanager might feel aggrieved if it incurs expense in the process of trying out another micromanager who purports to be able to perform a task (only to discover that the program fails to install). Every developer is intimately familiar with that pain.

Yet it isn't hard to conceive of a micromanager specializing in the prediction of reliability, or a reliability oracle that eventually ameliorates that annoyance.

The nature of the micromanager may dictate further considerations. For example, if a micromanager is a collider of some kind, in the broad category of exchange-inspired devices, then it is up to the active participants to exhibit trust, or not, as they choose.

So hereafter, I will assume that there is sufficient trust between the producers and consumers of microprediction to allow us to assume that one player's behavior mimics trust in an ex ante reward scheme established by the other.

This might even apply if supply is thin, as when few micromanagers turn up to a contest. In the limit of one producer, a useful bilateral

arrangement can evolve. Here we anticipate that the parent micromanager and child adapt to the other's behavior. The principal–agent problem
might inform our intuition.

We might suppose that principal (parent) and agent (child) make
epoch-based decisions. The agent needs to choose an effort, and the accuracy will respond. Meanwhile, the principal needs to decide how much to
reward the agent.

One is inclined to believe that in a hypercompetitive microeconomy,
the rewards paid by the principal to the agent would eventually settle
into a regular pattern deemed sensible to an outside observer.

That isn't always a given, though, as contract theory informs us (and
empirical labor pricing, arguably). There may be a race to the bottom, or
other pathologies.

However, formal versions of this problem suggest reasonable outcomes, and it can even be established that the principal's optimal policy
in some multiperiod games amounts to a consistent linear sharing of the
value unearthed by the agent.[3]

These considerations suggest we set the matter of trust and contracts
aside and focus on what else can go wrong.

7.3   Scoring

We hereafter restrict attention to a producer of prediction who, when
sending a single-number forecast, is trying to minimize or maximize a
score computed by the consumer of their predictions.

The theory of scoring rules provides us with a very good understanding
of the thorny issues that surround point estimate answers to prediction
problems. It provides ideas for crafting microprediction questions with
clearly interpretable answers. I use a physical system that I suspect will
be familiar to you to illustrate.

There is a radioactive mass in a laboratory. Every now and then, a
particle is emitted. We will observe these events and measure the time
between them. We assume a single emission will lead to the death of
a cat because this serves to make questions about events that transpire
morbidly exciting (and also more concise).

We choose to employ an oracle as our statistically minded lab partner.
Our objective is to understand the physical system before us. We suppose,
due to a deplorable absence of hardworking data scientists in the vicinity,
that the only way we can do this is to ask an oracle.

Ours isn't a speaking oracle, unfortunately, and it will only provide a repeated prediction of some quantity. You will only receive a number, and based on the oracle's responses, it is you that must draw conclusions about the system.

In this example, we play parent to the micromanager we are calling an oracle, and we might suppose for discussion that it is a race organizer of some kind. It wants to maximize its reward. It is probably well served by a clear task with clear interpretation, because it can then relay the exact same task to contestant micromanagers who will also maximize their rewards, as they undertake the real grunt work.

(In passing, we note that this isn't absolutely necessary, and a micro-manager might exist purely to translate potentially confusing tasks into less confusing ones. We'll see why it might find a lot of business in a moment.)

I will make one assumption, however, and that is that you know enough physics to call an exponential oracle (one that assumes numbers follow an exponential distribution), not any garden variety.

That domain knowledge aside, this example is chosen because of its philosophical simplicity. Because there is only one number that completely determines the physics, there should be no question as to whether we succeed or fail to "understand" the system. Pushing Schrödinger and quantum mechanics to one side, if we get that one number right, we have the right physical model. Get it wrong and we don't.

The single number is the hazard rate, representing the likelihood an emission event will occur at any moment. For simplicity, we will assume that the rate, as yet unknown to us, is unity. One emission per second.

There are many different ways to design a sequence of prediction tasks and corresponding revealed truths that might be fed to the oracle. A question is an incomplete task, as noted, but here are some anyway.

1. Seconds to live?
2. Probability of surviving for one second?
3. Survive next second?

To turn these into tasks, we should also tell the oracle how it will be scored. For example, question 1 could be accompanied by the following *scoring rule*:

$$score = (\overbrace{\tau}^{actual} - \overbrace{t}^{predicted})^4 \tag{7.1}$$

Table 7.1
Examples of oracle answers, some more easily interpretable than others.

Q#	Question	Rule	Oracle	Truth
1	Time until next	$(\tau - t)^4$	1.5961	1.0
1	Time until next	$(\tau - t)^2$	1.0	1.0
2	Prob. survive	Brier	0.6232	0.6232
2	Prob. survive	Modified	0.5450	0.6232
3	Do we survive?	Unweighted	1.0	?
3	Do we survive?	Weighted	0.0	?

It is not hard to see how the rewarded game will influence the oracle's answers. The oracle will accumulate evidence and initially give responses that are noisy, but after a large number of samples, these answers will start to converge on ... 1.5961.

Perhaps not the number you were expecting? This malfunction occurs because the oracle will worry about the long right tail of the exponential distribution and the possibility of being heavily penalized, so it returns a higher number to guard against this.

There isn't anything necessarily wrong with this arrangement, but we can agree that 1.5961 is a number requiring very careful interpretation given that the *intent* of the questioner might have been a more *direct* revelation of the actual physical mean time until emission, namely, 1.0. I think it is fair to say that if we were to uncritically accept this number as "the" hazard rate, then we will have failed in our mission.

If, on the other hand, we were to tell the oracle it will be judged based on the squared error rule

$$score = (\overbrace{\tau}^{actual} - \overbrace{t}^{predicted})^2 \qquad (7.2)$$

then, as indicated in table 7.1, an oracle will eventually provide an answer close to the true value of 1.0. Most people would prefer that lab partner.

Evidently, it is possible to set a "good" task or a potentially confusing one. In general, the burden lies with the user of the oracle or with any micromanager establishing a contest. After all, why would the score-minimizing answer just happen to coincide with some tacit assumption in the question?

Asking a different kind of question does not free us of our responsibilities to define the task carefully. In question 2, the oracle is asked for a probability p of an outcome rather than an example of an outcome.

One takes a hint from the success of the squared error rule in the previous example. If we encode $(0, 1)$ to be emission and $(1, 0)$ no emission, as well as encode a probabilistic prediction $(0.8, 0.2)$ the same way (this means 20 percent chance of emission), then we can think of both prediction and score as pairs of numbers and use the square error just as before—applied to a 2−vector this time.

For example, if an emission event does occur and the probability assigned was 20 percent, then the score would be

$$score = (\overbrace{0}^{actual} - \overbrace{0.8}^{predicted})^2 + (\overbrace{1}^{actual} - \overbrace{0.2}^{predicted})^2$$

which is named after Brier. Notice that this score would have been lower had the probability assigned been 20 percent or 0 percent. Alternatively, under the modified Brier score, invented for the purpose of making our point, the result would be

$$score = (\overbrace{0}^{actual} - \overbrace{0.8}^{predicted})^4 + (\overbrace{1}^{actual} - \overbrace{0.2}^{predicted})^4$$

As also shown in table 7.1, only the Brier score using the squared error encourages the oracle to reveal (in an obvious way) its true estimate for the probability.

Notice that in every other way, this example is set up to succeed. There is an explicit shared knowledge about the nature of the distribution. Yet confusion may still abound because of reward-seeking behavior.

7.4 Spring Theory

Scoring rules that solicit "honest" responses are termed *proper*.

Proper scoring rules are a well-established method for parameter optimization of models that describe some probability of an outcome. Given some historical data, we wiggle the parameters to try to minimize the score.

This approach is more general than likelihood estimation and less general than M-estimation, topics that will also interest some readers building devices to insert into the microprediction web.[4]

It might strike the reader as a suspicious coincidence that participants have no incentive to bias their answers up or down when squared error is used (but not for some other exponents, evidently). This can be checked using elementary calculus, but as an alternative, there is a physical explanation.

Imagine a universe in which some particles are connected to others by perfect invisible Hookean springs, which is to say that the force of attraction exerted by the spring is proportional to the length of the spring.

Force ∝ *Distance*

And consequently, potential energy in each spring is

Energy ∝ *Distance*^{2}

The Hookean universe shares with the gravitational one a useful notion of *center of mass* (and also a related concept from physics called *reduced mass*, while we are on the subject). But this is something of a coincidence, and it is only this fortuity that allows us perform force or energy calculations for a cloud of particles *as if* all the mass were at a single point. That point is the statistical mean.

We can now see why asking an oracle to return a point estimate to minimize a squared error will lead the oracle to answer with (its best estimate of) the mean and why sometimes it won't.

We won't know the full extent of the oracle's belief, which might be visualized as a fine mist of particles, but we do know that it is trying to minimize the potential energy stored between its answer and every particle in that mist, and we know in turn that this energy is equivalent to a trivial calculation

$$Energy \propto (answer - \overbrace{center\ of\ mass}^{mean})^2$$

with an obvious solution: return the mean as the answer.

Choose a random exponent other than 2 and the oracle will still minimize the score, but you won't be able to relate it to the mean so easily—the concept of center isn't useful in the same way. (You might get something else though. If energy is proportional to distance rather than distance squared, then the oracle can return the median, or something close to it.)

In the case of a Brier score applied to probabilities of outcomes, the visual is no different, except that the action occurs on the line from $(1, 0)$ to $(0, 1)$ in two dimensions. More generally, we can ask the oracle for probabilities to assign to n mutually exclusive events and expect an answer somewhere on the simplex.

7.5 Everything That's Proper

Squared error serves us, but it can't be the end of the story.

Suppose we define a score as follows, where again t is a prediction of cat death time and τ is the subsequently revealed ground truth.

$$score \propto \phi(t) - \phi(\tau) - \phi'(t)(\tau - t)$$

We first assume that ϕ' exists and also ϕ is convex. For example, if $\phi(x) = x^2$, then we notice

$$score \propto \phi(\tau) - \phi(t) - \phi'(t)(\tau - t)$$
$$= \tau^2 - t^2 - 2t(\tau - t)$$
$$= \tau^2 + t^2 - 2t\tau$$
$$= (\tau - t)^2$$

recovering squared error. But it turns out that any such scoring method is proper. This family was introduced in a landmark paper by Leonard Savage.[5]

Actually, his set of scoring rules is more general than I have described because ϕ need not be differentiable (if it is not, ϕ' need only be a so-called subgradient, which is to say that it is less than the slope no matter which way you head).

What is most notable, however, is that this family exhausts the possible proper scoring rules. There's still an infinite number, of course, since they are parameterized by choice of ϕ and ϕ'. Despite the variety, you won't recover a score of $(\tau - t)^4$ or $|\tau - t|^5$, just to make the connection to the previous section.

7.6   Helpfulness

When a micromanager solicits responses from other micromanagers in a repeated prediction game, there is another way to view the use of proper scoring rules that directly reflects on the usefulness of the predictions to the parent.

To illustrate, I shall relate proper scoring rules to market making, layering a bit of my personal interpretation on top of the insights provided by Ehm, Gneiting, Jordan, and Krüger.[6]

For consistency, I will maintain the notation t, τ for estimated and actual cat time of death, respectively. But some readers not in the habit of wagering on feline fatality might prefer to view τ and t as referencing the value of an asset.

Suppose that instead of my judging you based solely on some function of your estimate t and the actual time of death τ, I complicate matters by introducing some benchmark time of death θ that I devise.

I will take your estimate t and throw away most of the information. I only care whether you think my estimate θ is too high or too low. If $t > \theta$, you suggest the latter, and if you are right (i.e., if $\tau > \theta$), I will give you a score of zero. Conversely, you also get zero if $t < \theta$ and also $\tau < \theta$.

However, if you are wrong, then I will assume a score equal to $|\tau - \theta|$, which you will notice is the absolute error in *my* estimate, not yours. You can't control this quantity, only whether you incur this penalty or not. You must pick the right side of my guess θ to avoid it.

This situation is reminiscent of adverse selection in trading. Your estimate is interpreted by myself, playing the role of a trader, as a directional hint. If you are right, no harm is done. But if you are wrong, an adversary will pick me off and the financial penalty will be proportional to the discrepancy between θ (my price that I am willing to transact at) and τ (the fair value, somehow known perfectly by the adversary).

Your task, in this scenario, is to protect me. Somehow you need to get in front of this dangerously knowledgeable foe—perhaps by stalking the same WallStreetBets subreddit. You may be hard-pressed to get this right every time. If θ is "wild" (far from any reasonable guess of τ), it is easy to guess the direction. But when θ is close to the true value, it is more difficult. On the other hand, the penalty for being wrong is larger when the task is easier.

In passing, you might ask how it could possibly make sense to throw away most of the information in t when assessing its accuracy. (An information theorist passing by might find this almost as excruciating as Matthew McConaughey's efforts, in the movie *Interstellar*, to download black hole data using only Morse code.)

But let's not disregard this scoring technique offhand, because it is analogous to the operation of most markets—and they are generally regarded as good at aggregating information.

Moreover, as we take the next step to relate trading to statistical accuracy, I can reclaim the lost information by simultaneously assessing you using many different θs. I could assign a different weighting to each score, and generalizing this, I could even judge you based on an integral across different thresholds instead.

$$\mathrm{score}(\overbrace{t}^{guess}, \overbrace{\tau}^{truth}) = \int_{\theta=-\infty}^{\infty} |\theta - \tau| 1_{wrong}(t, \tau, \theta) dH(\theta)$$

where $1_{wrong}(t, \tau, \theta)$ is equal to 1 if you are "wrong" (i.e., θ lies between τ and t) and zero otherwise.

The surprising finding is that this construction is general. There isn't any proper scoring rule that can't be broken down into this integral of one-sided penalties. It is a stunning connection between statistical contests and trading.

Ah, but you say, we already had a characterization of proper scoring rules in the previous section. You are right, and we must make the connection. Fortunately, it is right there in front of us, and it can be established that $dH(\theta) = \phi'(\theta)d\theta$, where ϕ is the same function in Savage's representation of the proper scoring rule, so we are choosing any convex ϕ in both cases (and also ϕ' if ϕ is not differentiable).

To summarize, we view the elementary score

$$|\theta - \tau|1_{wrong}(t, \tau; \theta) = \begin{cases} |\theta - \tau| & \text{if } \min(t, \tau) \le \theta < \max(t, \tau), \\ 0 & \text{otherwise} \end{cases}$$

as a quantification of the helpfulness, revealed by truth τ of an price estimate t to a market maker with parameter θ. Then by integration in θ, we conclude that any proper scoring rule is a metric quantifying "mean helpfulness to different market makers."[7]

Keep that in mind if you decide to offer spread bets on when cats will die or trade just about anything on a repeated basis. Accuracy is directly related to the number of times you lose your shirt.

7.7 Summary

The old joke runs that if you ask a weatherman for the probability of rain and they say 40 percent, they can never be wrong. But we've seen what the real problem is: depending on incentives, you don't even know what probability the weatherman really believes in. Penalize error too severely and the answer you get will be biased upward on most days, even in Portland.

This chapter has suggested that if micromanagers communicate clearly to others how they will be judged, in keeping with what is generally regarded as best practice, they may receive more help than they otherwise would. A possible counter to this argument is that micromanagers using only a single scoring rule may eventually lose out to micromanagers capable of *also* inferring information from predictions whose statistical goal, if any, is unstated.[8]

That caveat aside, I've discussed proper scoring rules and their motivation, as it seems likely that a choice of scoring rule may frequently be included in the protocols that help algorithms find and assist each other.

I've emphasized the intuition behind squared error, although this is just one example, and a longer treatment would discuss efficiency and other critiques of the Brier score.[9] The logarithmic score is also popular.

Savage provided an elegant description of the family of all proper scoring rules. Ehm, Gneiting, Jordan, and Krüger describe a decomposition with several possible interpretations. I've chosen to view the elementary scoring rules in that study—averages of which comprise the full complement of proper scoring rules—as measures of how helpful a stream of predictions is to a dealer.

I hope that assures the reader not already familiar with scoring rules that micromanagers informed by theory can be as clear as humans—likely more so—when it comes to tasking reward-seeking algorithms with repeated prediction. They have a variety of very well-understood ways to establish scoring, interpret terse answers, and benefit from them as they go about producing their own value-added predictions.

8

Decisions

Is operational AI really synonymous with microprediction?

Having presented a vision for how microprediction might be collectively commoditized, I return to this assertion. My goal is only to introduce those not already familiar to *value functions* and *advantage functions* (the difference between two value functions). I discuss how oracles change the decision game by providing both.

Value functions are often the missing link between frequently repeated prediction and business applications. It's strange but true, however, that the PGA Tour, a golfing organization, has provided a more pedagogically useful incarnation of a value function than any of the world's well-funded AI companies.

So it is without apology that I provide a nonstandard introduction to oracle-based decision-making that is built in large part around that old game. I won't presume the reader is versed in optimal control or reinforcement learning because you can pick up the central ideas as we go. If you follow my mildly contrarian emphasis, you might come away with a better decision engine—one that is eventually hard to beat.

8.1 Conditional Prices

I begin with a trick every golf professional can try the next time they are in contention but faced with a 213-yard carry to an island green from a bunker. Pull a three-wood from your bag and make a practice swing. Have your caddy check your probability of winning according to Betfair, then put the club back, pull a wedge, and see how the market reacts. (Betfair is a U.K.-based betting exchange that operates a central limit order book. Market-implied probabilities of a player winning a tournament can readily be inferred in real time.)

In our examples, we'll be swapping out the betting market for a microprediction oracle, but that's a detail. What's more important is that Betfair pundits are being tricked into answering a *conditional* question—although this particular stunt might not work repeatedly. We'll come to view the probability of winning the tournament as an example of a *value function* and the change as indicative of an *advantage function*.

Perhaps you think I'm being cute, but actually, the only thing special about this club selection example is that a live market exists for golf outcomes, whereas competitive prediction does not exist for the vast majority of quantities of importance to industry (despite the fact that in many cases, the monetary significance of decisions is as high, if not much higher).

What a shame. I hope I've started to convince you that competitive live microprediction has the *potential* to drive diverse commercial activities— including many things not ordinarily associated with the term *prediction*, as we saw in chapter 2.

That's true, to briefly revisit the thesis, if competition can be achieved in a more streamlined fashion, as discussed in chapter 5, and if reuse of algorithms, automated navigation of algorithms to problems, and fragmentation of tasks into smaller ones can drive down the marginal cost of repeated predictions. Then, an equilibrium can arise where accurate prediction doesn't require the kind of money we see in financial exchanges, or golf ones for that matter.

When it comes to repeated decisions, we need competitive *conditional* prediction because optimal decision-making is a hard task. Certainly, it is as open-ended as any other prediction task and also requires a search in a near-infinite space of exogenous data.

This is illustrated by the fact that the humans who might influence prices on Betfair, in this example, assimilate information of various types, such as wind, previous shots by other players, history of responding to pressure, and so on. The micromanagers must do the same, on analogous problems in industry, but with the key advantage that in a near-frictionless supply chain, any given micromanager only needs to contribute part of the solution, as we discussed in chapter 5.

There are a few very special cases like chess where the system appears to be closed. Even there, exogenous data might matter, as I will suggest, in high-stakes situations.

8.2   Immediate Feedback

Let's try to hold ourselves to a new, high standard in the engineering of decision systems. Let's make it a constraint that whatever we build must constantly benchmark itself against the world, eventually drawing in all relevant data and models.

We could even label it "intelligence-free" application development. That isn't to suggest it won't be intelligent, merely that all intelligence will be sourced externally, from the prediction network. In building it, we don't have to be clever, merely modest enough to seek help from an oracle.

Decision-making is not only feasible in the presence of a microprediction web but, in some cases, very straightforward. For one can request conditional predictions such as "What will X be if I make choice C_1?" where X is some measure of our well-being. One is free to ask the oracle many such questions, within reason, for different choices $C_1, \ldots, C_n$ and choose the action resulting in the highest forecast of X.

As an example, this pattern is good enough to help you find a desirable seat on the train—even if this isn't directly instrumented. I'll suppose that in the morning, you stand on the platform wondering whether you are really in the best spot. Which car will be the most sparsely populated, you wonder, with both comfort and fear of COVID-19 in your thoughts?

As the application author, I can't ask a vague question to an oracle on your behalf. But I can send it a question like, "What is the probability that this phone will be horizontal when it next starts moving in excess of twenty miles per hour?" That's probably a good proxy for whether you have found a seat—unless you are given to sitting on the floor in the vestibule, or your legs are very long.

Perhaps we further assume that over many months, your phone betrays the geometry of the train platform (or other passengers' phones do, for they might be using the application too). One question could split into ten. One of those ten questions might be, "What is the probability that your phone will be horizontal when it next starts moving in excess of twenty miles per hour *assuming* you walk fifty feet down the platform right now?"

The action-conditional probabilities that are returned by the oracle can then influence your decision-making. The accuracy of these predictions will depend on how routinely you use this application and how often other people do. Most of the conditional outcomes cannot be assessed—only the one you choose. But over time, it is still conceivable that your chance of getting a seat will improve.

The use of conditional prediction can be a powerful tool if, as in this example, the result of our actions will quickly become apparent. For then the result, conveyed to the oracle, provides feedback for the algorithms and people behind it.

Suppose you commute by car instead and need to choose whether to take the upper or lower level of a congested bridge. To a first approximation, this is one decision only. You and your quantum twin will split apart and take different paths, only to recombine quite quickly right after the bridge exit. The loop is closed.

Similarly, if you have the discipline to enter a rating after the fact, an oracle could choose a wine for you or steer your Netflix binge watching. One can predict whether one style of interface will engage a potential customer more successfully than an alternative.

Perhaps an oracle can assign a probability of a bad reaction to a message sent via text to someone you wish to flirt with. And there are plenty of manufacturing or digital applications where an intervention is expected to have immediate effect.

Pandora runs a recommendation engine, but it is far from perfect. You could send your personal stream of thumbs up and thumbs down to an oracle to see if it can determine if there is room for improvement.

In that example and many like it, we are predisposed to assume large companies are the best placed to perform the microprediction tasks (labeled as recommendation, quite often). However, the time might come when the tables are turned and consumers keep their data locally.

Eventually, consumers might be *better* placed than companies because they can join their own personal information that those companies don't have (heart rates, time since use of the home coffee maker, ambient noise created by kids, and so forth). They won't miss out on the predictive power of collaborative filtering or other ways to benefit from others' preferences, because they will be able to participate in collective recommendation using techniques discussed in chapter 9.

8.3 Delayed Feedback

I won't comment further on the case where the result of an action brings immediate feedback. However, this chapter considers the difficulty that arises when the outcome is not obviously measurable, at least immediately, and when the result of that action is obscured by *many other subsequent actions* occurring prior to some final, unequivocal quantification of the outcome.

Consider the taxi driver who asks an oracle whether to turn left, continue straight, or turn right at an intersection while cruising for passengers. A conditional prediction question sent to an oracle might take the form, "How much money will I make today if I turn left?" *In theory*, the oracle can provide slightly different responses to each question.

In practice, we can expect this to be very flawed. By placing the quantified result far in the future, we have introduced so much noise into the outcome that the oracle may struggle to provide useful information. Algorithms may fail to differentiate themselves from lessor algorithms, and clearly, the judging will depend on thousands of other driving decisions, not to mention exogenous factors such as the afternoon's weather, which lie in the medium-term future.

This conflation of short- and medium-term effects might very well prevent an incremental, specialized contribution. For example, an algorithm that can process images of traffic and pedestrians, or is aware of some "fleeting knowledge" by other means, might helpfully steer a taxi driver toward a throng of exiting concertgoers.

But, if this same algorithm doesn't possess an excellent longitudinal model for the driver's typical day, or if it isn't hooked into special event broadcasts and doesn't know about a United Nations conference on the other side of town, its predictions might be well off. In the absence of a very clever micromanager, its contribution may never be recognized, rewarded, or encouraged.

With this in mind, an ad hoc shorter-term metric could be constructed instead. For example, we might judge the decision to turn left, turn right, or continue straight based on fares collected in the next two minutes. Unfortunately, this introduces censoring. The driver might pick up a passenger to take them to the airport, a ride taking more than twenty minutes to complete—and that won't register a reward tied to the action.

A larger problem is that even if obvious corrections are made—such as accounting for the fact that a passenger just opened the door—other subtler biases may persist. An oracle might instruct a driver to cruise in such a way as to pick up passengers going uptown rather than downtown because the probability of pickup is higher.

This strategy may prove myopic, however, if there are fewer return trips likely from uptown than from downtown. A more careful evaluation would consider the value of the car's position and how this influences the likelihood of future revenue.

8.4 Value Functions

Enter the concept of a value function. What we shall do is ask the oracle a question of the form, "What will V be if I make choice C_1?" where V represents a miraculous measure that transforms seemingly myopic optimization into percipient forward-looking strategy.

Fortunately, the V we want is entirely standard—at least in the abstract. It is the core concept underpinning techniques from dynamic programming, optimal control, and (sometimes) reinforcement learning. The phrase "value function" has been used since at least the time of Richard Bellman.

Bellman's principle of optimality explains the role of the value function and defines it. His principle expresses the notion that sometimes it is possible to put one foot after the other even when navigating mazes, playing poker, or optimizing a micromanager's behavior.

An optimal policy has the property that whatever the initial state and initial decision are, the remaining decisions must constitute an optimal policy with regard to the state resulting from the first decision.
—Bellman optimality principle

The key word is *state*. If we are able to express mathematically the relevant features of the world that impact our decision-making and call that state, then we can talk about a value function V defined on that state that is specific to our strategy and, conversely, must satisfy certain properties given that the strategy is best.

For example, the taxi driver might define state to be multidimensional and include numbers such as accumulated earnings minus fuel and running costs, location, time, and current passenger trip if any. The driver's value function can be defined as total cost-adjusted earnings for the day.

Given an accurate way to compute the expected value of this value function at any moment in time, optimizing a driver's behavior over the course of the day could be equivalent to optimizing a single decision: whether to turn left, continue straight, turn right at the next intersection.

The value function isn't given to us—it is more an aspiration toward internal consistency. It isn't always easy to formulate and refine the problem faced. The state and set of decisions will always be open to critique.

Perhaps the driver's set of actions might be broadened to include stopping for breaks or to conserve fuel and where to stop. Perhaps the driver's state might include many more items such as hunger, fatigue, bladder pressure, and, heaven forbid, injury.

Let's not make the perfect the enemy of the good. Sometimes ad hoc intermediate reward functions can get the job done. And the truth is that we spend all our days, and all our careers, solving optimal control problems without knowing it. So how hard can it be?

That's true of taxi drivers but also hospital administrators, teachers, bakers, and candlestick makers. It's definitely true of racing car drivers and athletes of all varieties, professional or amateur. Yet humans are pretty good at solving reasonably tough problems quite accurately.

You solve an optimal control problem when you ride a bike in a time trial. Does it make sense to up the wattage on the hills? Yes of course. You intuit one characteristic of the solution of Bellman's equation. You know to spend more energy where it hurts, pedal over the crest, and then take a breather on the way down. Humans intuit how to harvest nonlinearities.

Let's say that in this cycling example, the Bellman state contains four components. It is the distance traveled, lactic acid buildup, your glycogen reserves, and your velocity. The value function can take these four variables and report the expected finishing time.

In this cycling example, we try to get by with one space dimension and one velocity dimension, but if you are focused on a different aspect of the task, such as cycling down Alpe d'Huez without losing your life, then the state must be expanded (another spatial dimension at least—probably two). You might want to include tire wear and pressure as well.

Sir Lewis Hamilton, seven-time winner of the F1 World Driver's Championship, might be considered a value function genius—that is if we continue to pursue an approach to repeated decisions slanted slightly more toward control theory than reinforcement learning.

Let's consider for a split second, literally, Hamilton's decisions and their impact on the state of the car from one spot in position-velocity space to another. Bellman suggests that we don't need to wait for the end of the race to appreciate his talent.

Imagine that you are thrown into his hurtling car and allowed to drive it for one-twentieth of a second. Hopefully, that is a short enough time to avoid disaster, and we'll assume that at the end of that short period, Hamilton will be reinstated as controller of the car.

What will be the impact of your temporary usurpation on Hamilton's lap time? Suppose that at the moment when he relinquishes control, his expected time to complete the lap was thirteen seconds. If you are as good as he is, that time will drop by one-twentieth of a second during your stint—the same as the wall clock time elapsed. But in all likelihood, it will reduce by *less* than one-twentieth of a second.

Perhaps you failed to break quite as aggressively as he would have. Hamilton's virtual car, superimposed over ours, might appear to trail behind during that brief moment. However, position on the track isn't the only determinant of expected time to lap completion. That may be an increasing function of speed—and your distance gain will be more than lost when Hamilton is forced to break harder half a second later.

Racing cars suggest quite complex value functions, but in other contexts, the value function can be quite simple—at least to a first approximation. Most businesses wrestle with inventory—management. The state might simply be the inventory held, to first approximation.

The levers they use to control inventory include purchasing decisions and pricing of their finished goods. There is a cost to holding inventory—it might be a physical storage cost or a funding cost per unit time. There is also a risk that the price of the good you store will change value.

Adding to the nuance of inventory value functions, there is a more subtle benefit of holding inventory that works the other way. The more inventory you hold, the greater the value of the next trading opportunity. We shan't go into the weeds, but one can arrive at a "true" inventory cost that takes all of this into account in a sneaky, self-referential manner using Bellman's equation.

Perhaps the simplest value functions to talk about don't depend on inventory, however, but space. The NFL field of play comes close to providing a clean, single-variable state (how far down the field the team has progressed)—although down counts and yards-to-go enlarge the state.

I went looking for a more "pure" value function on the reader's account, and you may be surprised at what I've found.

8.5   The PGA Tour Value Function

The PGA Tour provides a value function for every golf course where professionals play. The construction of this wonderful collection of decision-guiding numbers begins when hardworking volunteers use position finders to record the final resting position of every golf ball hit by every player in every hole of every tournament.

Smoothing that data, the Shotlink folks estimate the average number of shots it takes a professional golfer to complete a hole from any position.[1] This procedure creates a function $S()$ defined everywhere on the golf course.

A couple of quick examples. It takes roughly 1.5 shots to finish the hole when a professional putts from eight feet away, so the 1.5 isobar might look very roughly like a circle with that radius around the hole. (Although as we know, greens are not flat, breaking putts are harder than straight ones, and uphill is preferred to downhill. You can imagine how the value function isobars might stretch and distort.[2])

Now let's walk back down the fairway. On average, it might take 3.2 shots to finish the hole when a professional plays from the left side of the fourteenth fairway, some 230 yards from the green—we shall imagine. Similarly, we might assign a value of 2.4 to the middle of a greenside bunker.

It is the Markovian nature of golf that allows us to use the golf course as the state. That's to say that the position of the ball captures *everything we need to know about what has occurred before.* That last errant shot is forgotten as the professional makes his recovery shot.[3]

The PGA needs an estimate of shots to finish the hole so that the granular performance assessment of every shot can be computed. This is merely a difference of those estimates, adjusted for the shot taken.

$$shot\ quality = S(before) - S(after) - 1$$

This measures the number of "shots gained," as the Tour refers to it, relative to the average player. For example, a player sinking an eight-foot put gains half a shot on the field as follows:

$$shot\ quality = \underbrace{1.5}_{S(before)} - \underbrace{0}_{S(after)} - 1 = 0.5$$

Conversely, missing an eight-foot putt will typically constitute a shot quality of -0.5, unless we miss so badly as to have another eight-foot putt coming back, in which case the shot quality is -1.

It's my understanding that at the prompting of Mark Broadie, professor at Columbia Business School, the PGA Tour introduced this approach in order to provide fans with meaningful statistics about player performance. This was much needed. Hitting bad approach shots that narrowly miss the green had been the best way to top the putting statistics.

I'd invite you to view the shot quality metric as an intermediate reward. A distinction can be made between the number of shots to finish the hole, which I've called S, and the accumulated shot quality.

Since the difference is deterministic for a fixed number of shots (the difference is the shot count), it doesn't matter which you optimize. So I'll be loose with that distinction and feel justified in labeling the PGA

Tour's approach a "value function" or certainly an "intermediate reward" technique.

I note also the tiny departure from Bellman's definition because the PGA Tour's estimated number of shots to finish the hole applies to the mythical average player—or a team formed by all Tour players, under a format where a player is selected randomly to take the next shot. But we'll return to that momentarily.

8.6   Three-Wood or Driver?

Setting player statistics aside, the real reason we need value functions is not to passively measure performance but to change the actions we take. I'd suggest that even the most astute golfers might benefit.

Phil Mickelson became the oldest winner of the PGA Championship in 2021. In theory, he should by now be the wisest golfer in the PGA—capable of nearly optimal course management. (Okay, not exactly his reputation.)

When Mickelson teed off on the final hole of the 2006 U.S. Open Championship needing only a par to win, things didn't go so well. Mickelson's errant drive set up a tragic chain of events ending in a double bogey that allowed Geoff Ogilvy to win. Mickelson's club selection on the tee would draw criticism subsequently—mostly from Mickelson himself. "I just can't believe that I did that. I am such an idiot. I can't believe I couldn't par the last hole. It really stings." *Sports Illustrated* covered the tragedy under the headline "The Crack-up."[4]

Poor Phil! But he makes for a good value function illustration. And we ask, in generality, do golfers choose their clubs correctly? (This decidedly First World problem might not be worth the reader's time, I reiterate, had the PGA Tour not invested more heavily in control theory pedagogical devices than all the world's machine learning research groups.)

So Phil can turn to the value function—the one defined for every spot in the rough or the fairway, every grain of bunker sand, and every playable or unplayable position a ball may come to rest—be it behind a tree or in the ball-washer. Phil could have used the hidden accounting measure for golf that provides the immediacy required to make decisions.

Every club and shot choice can be evaluated by imagining thousands of swings with that club and then averaging the value function at the final resting place of the ball. A few of those imagined shots are in the lake, but most are not. Nobody's suggesting that this mental integration is trivial.[5]

But at least we only have to simulate one shot. That key simplification is provided by the value function.

Indeed, if you want to understand the link between microprediction and business optimization, you need only imagine Phil looking through a range finder and seeing a course lit up with value function numbers—not yardages. It borders on a restatement of Bellman's optimality principle to say that the value function does the looking forward for Phil, so he doesn't have to.

It puts a new spin on the age-old golf adage: "one shot at a time."

8.7 A Bespoke Value Function

As far as convincing you of the power of oracles goes, we could potentially stop here. After all, you can ask the oracle to predict the Tour's value function after your shot, if you are the average Tour player.

But that would be only half the story, as we'll see. And it would considerably undersell the options at your disposal when the world fills with microprediction oracles. It would also leave you with the problem of constructing your own value functions. Unfortunately, the PGA Tour data scientists—as good as they no doubt are—are rather too busy to create a special one for whatever small business you happen to run.

So let's dig a little deeper, starting with the observation that at the end of the tournament, Phil also needs a tailored value function—just like you.

Indeed, I used a little sleight of hand in that last example because Phil Mickelson's end-game problem is not the mean shot quality maximization task for which the PGA's value function is designed. He needs to take into account his personal monetary and nonmonetary payoff of winning, and the end is too close to get away with a linearity assumption.

Phil's value function will be driven by his utility function, to rephrase, which is rather complex I am sure. In 2006, it related in some small way to the prize money from finishing first outright (par or better), entering a two-man playoff (bogey) or tie for second (double bogey), and so forth.

In the interest of a more precisely calculated last-hole strategy, what Phil needs to do is replace the PGA Tour's value function with a slightly different function W defined on a slightly different state space—one that includes both the number of shots taken as well as the position of the ball.

We might visualize Phil's augmented state space as a multideck golf course—a little like a multistory parking garage. Each floor is labeled with a number indicating the shots taken thus far—from zero to four. You can visualize Phil hitting from one floor to the floor directly above each time, advancing the ball down the course but also up a level.

What values should he see through his range finder? Reading Phil's reaction, I will assign a value of 1.0 to winning the tournament but negligible rewards for anything else. Then W stands for "win," and if so, that eight-foot putt on level 3 would be marked as 0.7 because the odds of making the par putt are roughly fifty-fifty (but he could also win in a playoff).

And so it goes. The same putt one floor up is marked 0.2 because we assume a 50 percent chance of Phil winning a three-way playoff. And to round it out, the same putt on floor 2 would be marked 0.995 because a professional needing a two putt to win a major will lag the putt, not try to make it. Even Phil.

Phil's work is cut out for him. He needs to work backward from those easily computed values and determine his value function on approach shots, and all the way back down the fairway. Oh yes, he better compute the value behind a tree too.

Only then, standing on the floor zero tee box, Phil can look at the values taken by W on the first floor of the golf course. He can consider the spray of his driver and three-wood, respectively. Or he can ask an oracle.

1. Dear oracle. What, on average, will my value function W be *after my shot* if I choose a three-wood?
2. Dear oracle. What, on average, will my value function W be after my shot if I choose a driver?

Phil has still done the work to estimate W, but at least he is spared the integration over all possible trajectories of driver and three-wood.

8.8 Oracle-Defined Value

Next, we're going to make Phil's life even easier.

What if Phil let the oracle *define* the value function? After all, W is a mean of a future quantity, so an oracle can tell Phil that. Let's denote by $\tilde{W}$ an oracle prediction of W at the end of the tournament.

Notice here that the only data input is how much Phil hates to lose. All that value function work done by him (analogous to the PGA Tour's work computing V) is now unnecessary.

In this thought experiment, we imagine algorithms behind the oracle using perturbations of the PGA's value function, ideally with access to the same data but taking the analysis further. They might also reach out to exogenous sources of data, meteorological or otherwise.

If we're fortunate, data going back fifteen years might still have relevance and tournament play could include 50,000 data points or so, with plenty of room for imaginative feature engineering. Phil asks:

1. What will $\tilde{W}$ be after my shot if I choose a three-wood?
2. What will $\tilde{W}$ be after my shot if I choose a driver?

If this is a general-purpose oracle, this takes on a semicircular appearance, along the lines of "What will you think W will be after my shot?" That isn't actually more circular than Bellman's principle of optimality, but there are some pitfalls we will come to.

For now, let's appreciate the elegance.

8.9 Advantage

That's a lot of golf talk, but I hope it's clear how the same logic applies to a program that steers a ship across an ocean. It likely comprises two separate components: a value function analogous to Phil's and some prediction machinery.

In this light, it is clear that the ship *might* get to port faster, or use less fuel, if predictions of its internal value function are performed by an oracle—one providing a portal to more powerful prediction models and data than exist in the in-house program.

The shipping company could use oracles to wholly or partially construct a value function, instead, and then again source predictions of the same.

Notice that the compound question ("What will you think $\tilde{W}$ will be after my shot if I choose three wood?") implies two types of question: an action-conditional estimate of a value function $\tilde{W}$ and also an unconditional estimate of W itself at a future time (which here will be used to judge the former).

These are tasks whose challenges are quite different. They ask for estimates placing emphasis at different points on the state space. Estimating the expected value of W calls on knowledge of Phil's short game ability. Whereas when it comes to the conditional estimation of $\tilde{W}$, the difference between Phil's first and second question suggests we focus attention on what might happen three hundred yards off the tee.

Actually, conditional and unconditional estimates are inherently different even if they apply at the same spot on the golf course. We cannot deny that these are mathematically related. Dropping tildes to unclutter:

$$\overset{\text{unconditional}}{\widetilde{W(\cdot)}} = \sum_{club \in bag} \overset{\text{choosing a club}}{\widetilde{P(club)}} \; \overset{\text{conditional}}{\widetilde{W(\cdot|club)}}$$

but the unconditional estimate $W(\cdot)$ of the value function when we stand on the tee requires us to estimate the probability $P(club)$ that Phil will choose a driver or a three-wood. The conditional value function $W(\cdot|club)$ does not require this estimate.

It seems eminently plausible that some people and algorithms will be better at estimating $W(\cdot|club)$ and others will be better at estimating $W(\cdot)$ and thus specialization is achieved. Naturally, there will also be specialization on the other side of the oracle, as already discussed in chapter 3. Weather, wind, and other factors can enter the supply chain.

To rephrase, all Phil really needs to know is the *advantage* of using the driver over three-wood, which is to say

$$\overset{\text{advantage}}{\widetilde{A(driver)}} = \tilde{W}(\cdot|driver) - \tilde{W}(\cdot|three\text{-}wood)$$

that we all suspect, with a little hindsight bias, might be a negative number for Phil's famous shot.

8.10 Specialization

I suggest to you that the construction of value and advantage functions is a specialized task.

This isn't a terribly outrageous claim to begin with and, turning to video games, I find researchers who agree with this position. Support for the idea that advantage function estimation is related but different from the value function estimation is found in an article by Ziyu Wang and others working at Google DeepMind.[6] (The citation engine Mendeley assigns over a hundred authors to this particular article so perhaps there is widespread support.)

Therein a reinforcement learning algorithm is trained to play the Atari racing car game Enduro. Two different but intertwined related neural networks are deployed. One network learns the value function for the game.

Another set of calculations branches off from the first and separately estimates the advantage.

The authors of this article then compute the value function and advantage function saliency for every pixel on the screen, which is a measure of how important each pixel is to the calculation and therefore indicative of where the computer is looking.

Rather strikingly, the Enduro value function looks far down the road (to see if the next bend is to the left or right, and so forth), whereas the advantage function takes a shorter view (avoiding hitting other cars).

The moral would seem to be: don't assume the value function and advantage function need to be sourced from the same calculation, the same algorithm author, or the same continent. They are different tasks, so in the microeconomy for microprediction of value functions, they will likely have interrelated but distinct supply chains.

8.11 ... and More Specialization

Now to baseball.

We have been leaving out an important question. Is what we have been doing the best way to ask an oracle for an advantage function? How is the oracle going to be able to discern good advantage function estimates from bad, given that only one outcome unfolds?

Consider the decision made by a baseball catcher when calling the next pitch. We let W denote the probability of the team winning the game. The impact of any play can be measured as the change in winning probability—the postplay value of W minus the preplay value of W.

We will suppose the pitching team has a lead in the game but the opposing team has occupied bases. The count is two balls and two strikes. The catcher must call one of ten plays to the pitcher. He seeks to maximize the expected impact of the play.

To be more precise, the oracle-as-catcher will determine W after the play by the usual means and use this to judge pitch-conditional predictions of W that are made before the play. So as with golf, the predictions sourced break down into two kinds.

1. Unconditional estimates of W
2. Conditional W estimates

We'll suppose that one rather clever micromanager has this all covered. It will receive both kinds of estimates from other algorithms. One approach it might try is adjusting the supplier's estimates for the second

Table 8.1
Baseball pitches and conditional value functions W. Also shown are pitch selection probabilities p and centered advantage functions A.

Action	W	p	A
Four-seam	0.91	0.1	0.0525
Two-seam	0.90	0.05	0.425
Cutter	0.90	0.20	0.425
Forkball	0.87	0.05	0.0125
Curveball	0.93	0.05	0.0725
Slider	0.85	0.1	−0.0075
Slurve	0.86	0.1	0.0025
Screwball	0.80	0.05	−0.0575
Changeup	0.78	0.15	−0.0775
Palmball	0.85	0.05	−0.0075
Circle	0.81	0.1	−0.0475

question up or down so that their weighted mean across all possible pitches equals the answer to the first question. They can then be judged against the postplay value of W.

Here the respondent's answers are arbitrary up to a constant, so they are really supplying advantage functions shown in table 8.1. We are throwing away information in their response—but it all depends on whether there's really information in the mean.

There is an analogy in the election polling. Suppose a pollster has a lowly reputation due to large error and bias. Suppose, however, that it is somehow good at picking up on changes in polling patterns near the very end of the election. Those pollsters might clue you to a possible late Trump surge, whereas others that are typically more accurate might not.[7]

Now that isn't the only way the oracle can evaluate advantage functions or exploit the differential ability of algorithms and people. One reasonable supposition is that with a careful design, we can hope to take advantage of different modeling strengths of different algorithms and different people, just as the AI Enduro driver benefits from a distinct value function and advantage function estimation.

Those choices may depend on the state. One observes that it is a different modeling activity to estimate game-winning probability W at the end of a play than at the end of an at bat. The same can be said of modeling winning probability at the end of an inning versus the end of a play.

Some fans will prefer to focus their modeling effort on longitudinal performance and will prefer to inject their intelligence at moments when

Table 8.2
Analogy to finance.

	Oracles	Finance
Underlying	Value	Stock
Derivative	Advantage	Option

there are no runners on base or even no outs. There is some state carried from one inning to the next due to the rotation of batters, how long a pitcher has been in, and so forth.

One could go on. Some state complexity also vanishes at the top of each inning versus the bottom, since the relative number of innings remaining for each team is the same. Further complexity arises if we change the horizon and look beyond the game—defining W to be the probability of winning the World Series.

The variation in modeling task suggests that oracles will have an advantage computing advantage functions, and therefore guiding decisions, as compared to approaches that don't tap the world's people, machines, and data.

8.12   Pitfalls

Is this too circular?

I remark on one potential flaw with the setups we have described thus far: instability arising from the subjective nature of the estimates of the value function. Our pattern has been to ask an oracle (and thereby many combinations of people and machines) for an action-conditional estimate of what will result from another call to the oracle to estimate the value function after the decision is made.

In doing so, we are asking people and machines to predict what other people and machines will predict. This is a commonplace idea and directly analogous to buying a call option on a company's stock (a wager that the price of the underlying stock will rise above a prespecified level). You could say the same thing about trading in and out of the market at high frequencies.

Adopting the financial terminology shown in table 8.2 suggests some relevant work. We might refer to the unconditional value function $W(\cdot)$ as the "underlying" and to the action-conditional prediction of the same as "derivative" microprediction. Thus, for example, we refer to the paired micropredictions suggested in section 8.9 as follows:

1. *Underlying:* Unconditional estimates of $W(\cdot)$
2. *Derivative:* Conditional $W(\cdot|a)$ estimates

The notation $W(\cdot|a)$ denotes the conditional value function estimate for an action a. It might, in the case of a discrete number of actions, be visualized as a vector of value functions.

The estimates of conditional value functions $W(\cdot|a)$ will still only be as good as the yardstick against which they are judged, namely, the next occurrence of an estimate of the unconditional value function $W(\cdot)$. At the risk of drowning out the immediate decision against future decisions, it sometimes makes sense to judge $W(\cdot|a)$ against a longer horizon that allows the game to play out.

8.13   Chess

For the remainder of this chapter, I consider this issue of circularity, switching games to keep it fresh. Chess is often cited as the quintessential example of complex decision-making requiring a mixture of tactical and strategic foresight, so it is perhaps a good test for whether layering oracle predictions is likely to succeed.

Due to the amazing energy put into chess-playing programs, the game is probably a good indicator of how much decision-making in other fields could be improved (assuming similar effort was put in or oracles arrive).

The chess progress comes with a ready-made yardstick: the Elo rating system. These ratings document an almost perfectly symmetrical reversal in fortunes between man and machine. Grandmasters had a 1 percent chance of losing to computers thirty years ago. Now, they have a 1 percent chance of winning.

Chess computers are now racing through the Elo 3000s, but one would be tempted to assign an Elo rating to business decision-making near the 1400 mark today—since that is the level of an average registered chess player. At least chess players know what game they are playing. Many traders, in comparison, haven't realized they are solving a value function problem.

The recent success of chess-playing program AlphaZero follows other high-profile success stories involving self-play value function estimation. Rightfully making its way onto the covers of popular magazines, an algorithm that learns the intricacies of chess in fewer than twenty lines of (core) code represents a new benchmark for elegance.

Indeed, we might measure the advances in chess-playing decision-making by the number of ad hoc topics in chess position evaluation, prior to their obsolescence at the hands of DeepMind creations—there are at least sixteen subjects wiped from that curriculum.[8,9]

So let's use chess to critique our pattern of oracle usage involving conditional estimates of value functions $V(|a)$ judged against the next unconditional oracle prediction $V()$, as we have laid out in section 8.9. At the same time, we might hope to discern some advantages of opening up the problem to the world and unleashing the oracle's data-finding capability, even though this seems like the one example where that would be least likely to help.

8.14   Which Value Function Can You Trust?

The diagram is taken from the "Match of the Century" played between the brilliant but unpredictable American Bobby Fischer and reigning world chess champion, Russian Boris Spassky, in Reykjavik in 1972. Because this battle was an allegory for the cold war itself and formed the premise for the musical *Chess*, you may be at least vaguely aware of it.

To evaluate the match's most famous move, you need to know that the story did not begin well for the American facing down the Russian world champion. Fischer all but gave away the first two games to go down $0-2$, a margin that today would leave any challenger with few hopes of fighting back. Needing to mix things up, Fischer played the Benoni defense in game 3 and sought an unbalanced position with the black pieces.

Commentators have pinpointed Fischer's eleventh move as the turning point of the match. But as you can see from figure 8.1, the position itself appears relatively quiescent. There are no obvious tactical complications, and no undefended pieces are attacked. Only three possible captures are available to white and three to black. In chess middlegame terms, the sea could not be much calmer.

Why the fuss then? Fischer had moved his black knight to square $h5$ on the edge of the board. This was a surprise to onlookers and his opponent in equal measure. It violated a maxim about knights on the edge of the board and, more importantly, invited Spassky to take the knight with his bishop ($e2$) and destroy black's pawn formation around his king.[10]

Would a computer, even a very good one, have advised Fischer to play Nh5!? The answer would seem to be "probably not," and the reason illustrates nuance in the use of oracles for decision-making.

Although few computers would have played Nh5!?, I'll suggest that some oracles would have done so (although not all). I submit evidence

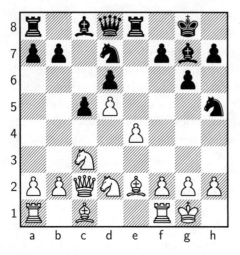

Figure 8.1
Spassky–Fischer World Chess Championship game 3, 1972. Position after Fischer's anti-positional move 11 ... Nh5!?

Table 8.3
Evaluation of the position after black's moves (positive scores suggest white is winning) in the infamous Fischer-Spassky game 3. Fischer's 11 ... Nh5!? might well have been the turning point of the match, but not according to a minimax evaluation.

Move	Value	Move	Value
12	+0.39	19	−0.24
13	+0.25	20	−0.16
14	+0.40	21	−0.39
15	−0.18	22	−0.41
16	−0.04	23	−0.33
17	−0.00	24	−0.61
18	−0.35	25	−0.66

in the form of position evaluations in table 8.3, as the subsequent moves were played.[11]

If we are sticking with our scheme from the previous section, only the first entry in this table is relevant. That shows a positional evaluation of +0.39. This means white is winning by almost half a pawn, Fischer's alleged brilliancy notwithstanding. The historical narrative is a fraud. Send back your Nh5!? swag.

However, an oracle *could* have been asked to predict the computer evaluation *five moves ahead*. Or, it could have been asked to predict what an oracle would predict five moves ahead, five moves ahead.

Either way, an oracle, or rather the algorithms, people, and data feeds behind it, could take into account the number of beads of sweat on Spassky's brow or the intensity of the television camera lights. Perhaps they might have arrived at what most chess historians regard as a situational brilliancy.

No doubt Fischer himself would have ascribed a lower value to Spassky's position. Not only could Fischer have taken into account deep positional insight, and a complex assessment of the likelihood of Spassky finding the precise sequence of moves to counteract Fischer's piece activity, but also some psychological impact of novelty that, as it turns out, probably did pack some punch in this high-pressure setting.

I suggest that an oracle using the simplest derivative pattern might not always be best and that, therefore, moving beyond chess, we should judge conditional estimates $V(state|action)$ against *future oracle answers*, not only the next value estimate $V(state)$, unless there is some strong reason to have great faith in $V(state)$.

That's not controversial, and in fact, I'm taking a leaf out of the temporal difference learning literature. Here is an example of a truth that might be generated ex post. We ask algorithms to aim at a target that is a weighted combination of future position evaluations:

$$target = (1 - \lambda) \sum_{k=1}^{\infty} \lambda^{k-1} V(k \text{ moves ahead}) \tag{8.1}$$

for some choice of λ between 0 and 1. For example, with $\lambda = \frac{1}{2}$ the forward target would read

$$target = \frac{1}{2} V(1 \text{ move ahead}) +$$

$$+ \frac{1}{4} V(2 \text{ moves ahead}) +$$

$$+ \frac{1}{8} V(3 \text{ moves ahead}) +$$

$$+ \frac{1}{16} V(4 \text{ moves ahead}) +$$

$$+ \cdots$$

whereas with $\lambda = 0.95$, we weight future move evaluations more heavily:

$$target = \frac{95}{1000} V(1 \; move \; ahead) +$$

$$+ \frac{90}{1000} V(2 \; moves \; ahead)$$

$$+ \cdots$$

$$+ \frac{60}{1000} V(10 \; moves \; ahead)$$

A micromanager might choose $\lambda = 0.25$ and another manager might choose $\lambda = 0.95$, say, with only the latter rewarding those who judged the game to be going in Fischer's favor immediately after $11 \ldots Nh5!?$.

I will not go deeper into the possible interplay between oracles and reinforcement learning—for I feel this is a greenfield and we will learn as we go. Nor does space permit a dive into the mathematics of real-time decision-making and techniques for looking further ahead, including Monte Carlo methods. Suffice to say that tricks from this literature could inform micromanager design.

For example, rewarding can demand some careful accounting. In equation 8.1, as written, the feedback to the oracle will be delayed ... in principle until the end of the game. Again the literature helps. This is not a new kind of problem, and the issue of delayed gratification is tackled in reinforcement learning in various ways, such as the use of eligibility traces. We're also helped by the statistical literature relating to recursive (online) calculations, as well as the financial literature that treats running expectations of future rewards and margins as discussed in chapter 5.

8.15 Summary

In this chapter, I've tried to describe in lay terms the key connection between repeated decisions and repeated prediction, moving beyond the obvious situations where the impact of a decision is quickly revealed.

When the value of position is computed for every blade of grass on a golf course (and it is), we convert a problem where the impact of an action is not obvious to one where it receives some intermediate assessment.

When oracles are abundant and powerful, they can also create the positional values. This leads to potentially labor-saving self-referential oracle patterns for decision-making that I feel are deserving of future study.

I have drawn analogy to derivative markets in finance, to help identify strengths and weaknesses of layered use of oracles. Patterns we find in reinforcement learning can also inspire the design of real-time decision-making applications, potentially addressing some drawbacks.

Repeated decisions are crucial to many operations and directly impact bottom lines. And as noted earlier, the provision of sufficiently cheap but effective decision-making can also create a virtuous cycle in a prediction web, since micromanagers themselves need to make all sorts of decisions for themselves.

If oracles become ubiquitous, control and reinforcement learning might be enhanced considerably. Current approaches are rarely engineered in such a way that they can be improved by anyone, anywhere, without their asking permission.

Current approaches can't expect to take advantage of all outside expertise and data, and they don't always allow the possibility of advantage function and value function estimation being performed by entirely different people or algorithms with different approaches and ideas.

Only a microprediction microeconomy can foster that level of specialization.

9

Privacy

Collective microprediction would seem to work best on open, public data. But can it work its way into private use, given the intellectual property and data privacy walls that separate us all?

In this chapter, I discuss how a combination of simple technique and privacy-preserving computation could see predictive capability pass between firms and individuals, even though in many cases, data will remain in place.

9.1 The Open-Ended Problem

I began this book asking you to assume that at some point in the future, the problem of repeated near-term prediction was definitively solved. I'm not sure if your most conditionally likely scenario has converged in any way toward my own, but to close the circle, I will start by presenting my own hypothetical that ties together ideas we have seen.

To emphasize the role of real and perceived risks, I will assume, this time, that you run a large global company with real-time operations assisted in some material way by predictive analytics. Quite possibly you have invested vast sums of money in combinations of people and machines that provide thousands, millions, or billions of short-term predictions.

The engines that drive your profit and loss might literally be engines. Or they might be intelligent applications advancing sales, trading, navigation, recruitment, or customer satisfaction. Inside these engines is a common ingredient: bespoke repeated prediction. Those predictions are created by data scientists you employ. They try to gather relevant models and data.

Because your bottom line is driven by an intelligent application of some flavor, and because that is in turn driven by repeated short-term

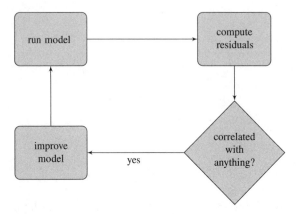

Figure 9.1
A highly stylized depiction of ongoing analytical model improvement.

prediction, a highly stylized depiction of your company's never-ending quest is presented in figure 9.1.

Of course, no prediction is perfect. The difference between your model predictions and the revealed truth is computed every time. By these means, you produce a flood of individual ex post model residuals. You search for data sources or new transformations of existing data that are correlated to these residuals.

If your employees find a new well-motivated statistical relationship, you might include the features in your model. The process repeats. The spend never ends. There may be no absolute or even relative notion of what you are getting for your money.

9.2   The Oracle Arrives

One day you are presented with something that seems like a free option. It is touted as a mysterious source of predictive power. It exists inside your company's firewall and can be used in a variety of simple ways.

This particular oracle operates in conversational style. You send it a question and it provides a prediction. You hope it will help you speed the cycle in figure 9.1. You could, it occurs to you, see if the oracle can predict your model residuals (which by definition you cannot).

What's not to love? Well, one concern is privacy. You are told that this oracle invites machines and people to predict your data. That is why it is so effective and constantly improving. The marginal cost for an algorithm to attack your data stream is close to zero, since it was designed to address several other problems as well. No human involvement is required.

As it happens, you do not consider your model residuals to be highly proprietary. Nobody is likely to reverse their meaning, and nobody has your model. You can send only a subset of residuals and, as a kicker, you are assured by experts in privacy-preserving machine learning that nobody will ever recover your residuals (even if they were to care about them, which is unlikely).

Indeed, nobody will learn *anything* about these numbers, even statistically speaking. And yet this oracle will allow you to benefit from both data and models in the outside world that you might not otherwise discover.

So you give it a spin. For a while, the oracle returns a sequence of zeros. You've told it that you are sending model residuals. It cannot determine with any confidence that zero is not its best estimate of your model residuals, so it merely returns zero. You shrug, but there is no harm done.

But then one day, the oracle starts returning small numbers. It does not do this for every prediction. Most are still zeros, but just a few are not. Over time, the numbers get slightly larger and the number of zeros fewer yet.

The oracle, whose construction you will learn about only later, is trying to identify the statistical bias in each and every prediction your model is making. The oracle does not predict the entirety of your errors—to do so would be to imply perfect prediction. However, by subtracting the numbers the oracle returns to you from your existing model predictions, you are able to create a new prediction that reduces the error.

Well, you say, isn't that something? But the world is full of spurious correlations.[1] For a while, you and your team are skeptical whether the oracle's performance will continue to be strong.

Sensibly, you limit the use to cases where thousands or tens of thousands of predictions are made daily, in order to reduce the likelihood that the oracle's apparent prescience is a ruse. You steer away from asking the oracle for long-term predictions of singular events, most commonly associated with the world "prediction."

You don't try to use the oracle to generate "alpha"—excess returns in the stock market. You focus on the bespoke predictions that help your business. The oracle continues to perform. Day after day. In fact, it gets even more accurate.

9.3 Tentative Steps

This is your first introduction to the prediction web, whether you realize it or not. Only later you will discover that the search performed by this oracle is not miraculous but merely basic economics and that you have tapped into a collective statistical construction that will one day power *all* AI applications—in one way or another. You are using it without taking on any real business risk.

But for now you are still skeptical. You are not prepared to throw out your model and rest entirely on the oracle for real-time business decisions without knowledge of its inner workings. You receive pushback from compliance, dampening your enthusiasm. Is it worth it?

Meanwhile, you're making yourself unpopular with some data scientists and some managers of data scientists. They mention privacy a lot, but what they are really thinking is, *oh Lord, this is a potential mark-to-market event for my skill set and my entire group*. You ask your quants to explain why their model residuals are proprietary—as compared with merely being closely guarded.

They go quiet but drag their feet. Sending your residuals out for inspection feels a bit too much like posting a stool sample to a cancer screening company. You know you should do it, but you are fearful of the results.

The oracle is unperturbed by the machinations of your company. It simply keeps doing its job. The length of the time series you have created keeps growing. The history is more informative. Unbeknownst to you, it is patiently discovering new sources of data, new transformations of that data, and new approaches to processing it, storing it, and, of course, applying advanced mathematical models to it.

Its tentacles—the graph of computation performed by disparate micromanagers behind the scenes—stretch outward from the other side of the oracle. They reach transport data, financial data, and the internet of things. They use data sources you will never know about or never need to.

You revisit your concerns. It occurs to you that because you have focused on streaming prediction problems, the risk is reduced substantially. Both the economic benefit and downside accumulate over thousands or millions of decisions, each one of manageable size.

So you create a hybrid. You enforce a rule stating that the prediction you use will always lie within a fixed distance from an approved in-house model. This amounts to bounding the residual thresholds. Since very few predictions trigger this rule, you retain 95 percent of the economic benefit, while ensuring that any increase in your economic risk is immaterial.

9.4 Infection

Slowly, the prediction web begins to worm its way into every aspect of your operations. You migrate some of the intelligence behind the oracle into your model. By using the oracle, you become aware of a source of data you never imagined would help you. After carefully incorporating the new source, the oracle's residual estimates go down.

This proves to be rather addictive, yet you hunger for a faster process, one freed of the limitations of your quantitative practices. Your engineers start to implement some hooks behind the oracle, adding new levels of functionality without jeopardizing your data privacy. You are now able to ask the oracle for predictions of data you supply it, going well beyond your starting pattern: the use of model residuals only.

You become more confident in the underlying technology and begin to ask the oracle to predict things for which you have no existing model. The instrumentation of your business comprises a collection of numbers intended to provide up to the minute information deemed critical. You realize that any such number, produced for your benefit at some cost already, can be enhanced with a forward-looking estimate of the very same number for almost no additional cost on the margin.

Still later, you examine the inner working of your decision-making algorithms powered by control theory and reinforcement learning methods. You identify various points in these calculations where a parameter is set using the minimization or maximization of some predictive criterion.

You start to incorporate oracles into darker places such as intermediate value function calculations used to navigate, set prices, and solve logistic problems on the fly. You start to outperform your competitors because the brain that powers your business is an analytical supply chain. Every step in the chain is constantly improving.

Whether you realize it fully or not, you are finally free of the most important limitation of your existing practices—the models were comprehensible to a single person and thereby constrained by human cognitive capability.

Your business is now powered by something far more potent—a global prediction web that sees more and more exogenous data every day and whose artificial fauna match every conceivable algorithm to the specific task you have at hand.

And it costs you next to nothing. Indeed, sometimes you get paid. It turns out that one sequence of true data points you need predicted is valuable to somebody else's prediction capability. Sometimes, the economic value of the data you inject into the grid exceeds the rapidly falling cost of bespoke prediction you have called upon the oracle to perform.

You are being rewarded in a small way for helping to solve the modern-day tragedy of the commons—the lack of an extant real-time feature space usable by anyone, including companies much smaller than your own.

Unbeknownst to you, independent cinemas, bakeries, nonprofits, and individuals are contributing tiny amounts of money, or eyeballs, to the same prediction web you use. Algorithms automatically resuse themselves. The power of data is automatically shared.

Next you contribute a model. Some nonproprietary feature generator that one of your data scientists had open sourced grows legs. It navigates across the prediction web, on its own, and finds a dozen places where it adds value.

In the process, other algorithms analyze it and assess its relative worth in different situations. The additional experience suggests improvements. You discover that when contributing to the open-source community, you get back more than you put in.

You and your company are now part of the prediction web in every sense. You are contributing to a collective solution to the *almost* intractable problem of search in the space of models and data, at least as it applies to optimization of real-time business processes. You will be entangled, now, and for as long as you operate. And so will everyone else in your industry, sooner or later.

9.5   What Will We Give Up?

So ends my speculation as to the manner in which collective prediction latches hold of your business.

And I ask, what really stands between us and free artificial intelligence, given the topics we have visited thus far? The customary answer is privacy. Most readers may anticipate that the use of a tremendously powerful prediction utility is just another privacy trade-off—although I hope the just-so story hints at why this isn't the case.

It's true that in this day and age, we surrender a lot of our privacy in the name of convenience. We do this because other companies have scale and the ability to use that data, and analytics, more effectively that we do.

But I'm not going to make the argument that a common utility of immense power justifies a similar bargain. I'm sure there can be an element of that, but it mostly undersells the potential. In this last chapter, I have invited you to come at things from a different direction and ask if anything, really, needs to be given up.

In fact, there are a slew of techniques that you can use to avoid betraying commercial intent, surrendering data, or otherwise making a Faustian bargain. Some are very simple—so simple I won't discuss.

But not everything is obvious. Mathematics has a lot to contribute to this conversation. We are on the cusp of a new age of privacy-preserving federated computation. Nobody doubts that. It is a reality.

And all of the techniques that work in macroscopic ways (as with privacy-preserving consortia for medical records, to pick one) will also work in the tiny belly of the micromanager. They are just algorithms, after all.

The use of mathematics to protect privacy while preserving predictive power is not intuitive. It will take a while before the world (accustomed to identifying data with the predictive power of data and to viewing private firms as separated by information barriers) unscrews its head and screws it on again backward.

So I'd say you have a good chance to get out in front.

9.6   A Trade Secret

We'll get to what mathematics has to say momentarily, but first let's dive into an example where it might not be required.

I'll pretend that you have a trade secret. Your trade secret is knowledge of a relationship between particulate matter in New York City (X) and same-day equity returns (Y). You believe X has a causal effect on Y, and you would like to leverage this knowledge without compromising your amazing discovery. (Drat ... the impact of air pollution on stock prices has been studied in Levy and Yagil (2011) and Wu et al. (2018), among others.)

It's reasonable to ask whether use of a microprediction oracle that shoots your data into the public domain (there are safer kinds) can actually be useful to you. Will you not be giving away your interest in X, your interest in Y, or knowledge of their relationship? For now, let's suppose we are brave souls performing naked public prediction.

It isn't by any means a foregone conclusion that we'll mess up. I would say that it is a matter of technique. Rather than directly asking the oracle for predictions of recorded air pollution, X, you might instead ask an oracle to predict one or more quantities *caused* by X—such as hospital admissions, recorded crime levels, the grammatical complexity in speech, performance on standardized tests, light sensor readings, temperature, solar electricity generation, or even bike-share trip durations.

You might be pleasantly surprised when the chain of micromanagers this gives rise to grows more complex over time and when, eventually, particulate matter readings show up in the feature space.

At this point, elsewhere in the web, predictions of particulate matter emerge—because as with our mosquito example from chapter 5, its always better to have forward-looking predictions of regressors if you can find them (and, as a consequence, almost everything in the web will be predicted).

And so, in this manner, you have brought about the prediction of a quantity you care about but with considerably reduced risk of anyone sniffing around your theory—since the prediction of particulate matter was initiated by someone else.

Now maybe you get braver, flushed with success. And perhaps you try to be a little sneakier, too, and create a micromanager where the compensation scheme is based not only on the accuracy of predicting hospital admissions but on the predictive value of submitted data as it relates directly to stock returns—or something else you keep private.

In doing so, you make an entirely different discovery—one you never anticipated. You realize that in part, the relationship between X and Y can be partially explained away by a third variable Z, which appears to cause both. The realization has come to you with relatively little risk, and without the prediction web, you might never have arrived at this insight at all.

9.7   Structure-Preserving Obfuscation

Despite these possibilities, naked crowdsourcing isn't for everyone. I'm going to consider far more defensive attitudes.

One possibility is the use of transformations that disguise your data but preserve enough structure that outside algorithms can continue to help you.

If the intent is mostly to source model insight, not data, and the machines on the other side of the oracle aren't going to try to interpret the data (merely predict it), there is little to be lost by transforming the data in a way that makes it unrecognizable but, at the same time, almost preserves addition and multiplication.

Because multiplication and addition are almost preserved, so are most things, hopefully, including linear algebra and machine learning techniques built upon that base.

Going beyond obfuscation, strong encryption that preserves addition and multiplication is emerging from the labs at long last. It has been a journey since the surprising study by Gentry in 2009 established the possibility.[2]

A structure-preserving transformation is called a homomorphism, so the techniques are referred to as homomorphic encryption. Who can say how powerful they will be a few years hence? I had no trouble locating 131 studies on the subject published in the past three months (Q1 2021) alone.[3]

This approach comes with the drawback that others might not be able to help you with exogenous data search—although you could arrange for that separately. This kind of two-pronged approach is favored by hedge fund Numerai, for example, who separately crowdsources signals and algorithms.

I suggest that in the context of using oracles, *almost* homomorphic obfuscation will often be more than sufficient. It is not necessary to preserve all structure *precisely* when the objective is statistical prediction. Nor is it necessary to *completely* encrypt all data if the original reason for its protection falls short of the most sensitive categories. (Almost encrypted market data is not market data anymore, to pick one example.)

An example of a homomorphic transform is multiplication by your grandmother's age. Perhaps we throw in a rotation, or some portion of a neural network that has been trained to learn the identity mapping. The practical matter is that your "data," which might actually be model residuals, is often less than a military secret.

It is entirely possible that you are accidentally already performing a structure-almost-preserving pretty-good-obfuscation as part of your existing pipeline.

9.8 Algorithm-Preserving Noise

Adding noise in clever ways can help too, provided it does not defeat the purpose. It is becoming commonplace to see differential privacy employed when data is passed from one party to another.

The idea is that an information budget is tracked, allowing a differential privacy layer to determine if individual record-level information has been leaked over the course of numerous interrogations of the data.

Unfortunately, what sometimes happens in practice is that the information budget is reset and new data introduced. This can defeat the ambition of keeping data private for a long period of time.

However, in the fast-flowing domain we care about, it is often the case that the commercial value of live data and its sensitivity degrades extremely quickly over time. So methods that work only for a limited time can be rather useful.

And the research never stops. For every possible complaint we might raise about a given privacy-preserving technique, there are no doubt several groups working to ameliorate it. For example, the use of local differential privacy may help with data sets that grow.[4] Differential privacy can be applied to algorithm results, not the data itself.[5]

9.9   Those Precious Residuals

I don't take privacy lightly, but I do expect it to fade in the minds of many as an obstacle to collective prediction. The key question might be whether everyone decides to send their model residuals to the micromanagers or not.

For as you will discern from the plausibility story that began this chapter, I predict that model residuals will be an important driver of prediction web adoption.

There are some situations where residuals could betray intent, portfolio holdings, or something else—usually with simple workarounds. But for every one of these potential blunders, there are a hundred situations where protection of model errors is precious, self-serving, and disingenuous (if you really want to know how I feel about it)—aimed only at an attempt to prevent others from establishing the limitations of one's own modeling attempts.

Despite these comments, I will proceed as if the differences between your in-house model predictions and revealed ground truths are, in fact, the crown jewels. This helps us assess an ultra-defensive stance.

Let's embed model residuals into a high-dimensional space. The lagged values of any univariate time series can be considered a vector, as shown in figure 9.2, where each coordinate is the value taken at a different time. The figure represents only three dimensions, of course.

The time series of your model residuals is the ϵ vector shown. The exogenous data can be represented on the same plot as well, and it is *likely* to be useful if it points in the same general direction as your data. I say that without too much loss of generality. Also, I am assuming that all your data is regularly sampled at the same times as your model residuals.

Putting these caveats aside, we have a "Geometric Hypothesis of the Oracle Skeptic"—one who declares that it is not possible to use micro-prediction oracles to improve your modeling due to privacy concerns.

Specifically, the skeptic will argue (I suppose) that an oracle cannot predict your residuals *unless* the actual residuals themselves are sent through that portal—and that would be such a terrible thing, right?

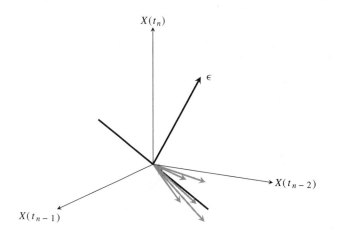

Figure 9.2
Model residual time series ϵ represented as a point in Euclidean space. Also shown is a gray vector that is very nearly orthogonal to the residuals and thus not terribly useful.

Let us look to the outside world and ask if there is public data that can help us. Each of those time series can also be represented by a point in space, but where are they?

By definition of model residual, we have at our disposal only vectors that are mostly useless. An example is the gray vector in figure 9.2. It is close to the hyperplane perpendicular to your data. For otherwise you would have included this data in your model, the hyperplane would move, and we'd be back to the start of the argument.

The skeptic finds it plausible that all the data is perpendicular. Let's set that aside and give them a pass, because the next question is tougher. Is it plausible that all the data that one might use to *predict all data in that plane* will *also* be perpendicular? What if we keep repeating?

By starting with time series that were rejected predictors of ϵ (rejected at some level of significance, say) and then sourcing new data that predict *them*, and then new sources of data that predict those, and so on, we are going to have a tough time staying in the space orthogonal to ϵ. A possible progression is shown in figure 9.3.

Now we should be careful about making arguments in high-dimensional spaces as our intuition is usually poor. It is also true that if $X \perp \epsilon$, then a predictor of X is a lot less likely to be a good predictor of ϵ than a randomly chosen vector X'.

Nonetheless, I think the prediction web and the relevance of its data to your predictions will sneak up on you. It's just a matter of time.

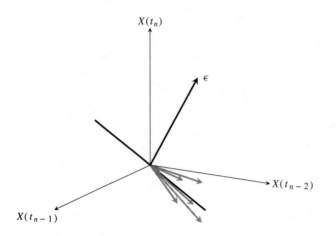

Figure 9.3
A collection of public data and regressors for the same. Will it stay in the hyperplane perpendicular to the model residuals ϵ?

As an aside, this geometry helps us visualize the role of *weak universal data feeds* as noted in section 2.4, and I would argue that the skeptic might require quite elaborate contortions to cling to their position.

That's because one data feed can be used to create many *approximate* truths, including whether it is raining, windy, or congested. By seeding other predictions, you encourage an eventual filling in of the space, as I noted in chapter 2.

9.10 The Data Lives of Others

I'm not sure if the preceding discussion will convince every hardened skeptic. After all, maybe your model residuals (or something causally related to them) are correlated with some other source of data—but that data is owned and kept private by someone else.

You don't realize that. They don't realize that. The end?

There are other versions of the same romantic tragedy. A vendor thinks they have data that is valuable to you. You suspect it is. But you cannot make a determination of this, and then effect a trade, without taking possession of the data.

There are some traditional approaches to this last quandary, naturally, such as trial subscriptions, but they are far from perfect. The inability to know the predictive value of data is the old lemons problem. The value of the data might lie in part in its historical record, so sometimes that can't be given up in advance of a trade.

Other times, the vendor can try to demonstrate value before the sale. But this too is problematic. The firm that might benefit from a new data source may be reluctant to reveal the intended use and certainly not the model in which the data is used, as we have discussed.

The inability to know the predictive value of others' data to you is one of the largest trade frictions. But there is another friction of trade that may be even more significant—although less apparent.

I'd suggest that the real (perceived) "problem" with the trade of data is the fact that the seller of data thinks they need to provide the buyer with the data *after the sale*. If that sounds like a problem that cannot be solved, read on.

I won't try to estimate the size of this problem, but of course, we know that in recent times, sizable investments have been made by buy-side firms in predictive technology and data. There are more than one thousand companies that collect and sell alternative data to hedge funds, for example, over and above the existing enterprise data industry.[6]

What if there was a way to discover a potentially mutually benefi-cial arrangement without the risk of revelation of commercially sensitive intent or commercially valuable data?

9.11   Secret Sharing

We can couch this in a more general setting. Party A, party B, and party C each possess data a, b, and c that they have no intention of divulging to anyone. However, all parties have an interest in learning the result of a calculation $f(a, b, c)$ that requires knowledge of all three data sets.

A collection of devious methods for effecting this begins with party A performing a random masking of data a and a splitting of it into, say, three intertwined secrets a_1, a_2, and a_3. For example, if we suppose for simplicity that a is an integer modulo $p = 7$, then party A can use a random-number generator to produce a_1, a_2, and a_3, satisfying

$$a_1 + a_2 + a_3 = a \bmod p$$

In a similar fashion, parties B and C can also split their data into related secrets:

$$b_1 + b_2 + b_3 = b \bmod p$$
$$c_1 + c_2 + c_3 = c \bmod p$$

Party A now sends a_3 to party C and sends a_2 to party B, retaining a_1. Likewise, party B sends b_1 and b_3 to party A and party C, respectively, and finally party C sends c_1 and c_2 to party A and party B, respectively.

This communication is yet to compromise the private number a held by party A, or likewise b or c held by parties B and C, respectively. Yet collectively, the information needed to reconstruct a, b, and c exists in distributed form.

In principle, depending on what the function $f(a, b, c)$ comprises, it *might* be possible to arrange for rounds of communication, and more secret passing such as this, that eventually arrives at the computation of $f(a, b, c)$.

To prove this can sometimes be done, consider addition. More precisely, f is the sum of the numbers $f(a, b, c) = a + b + c$ modulo p. Since this sum is also equal to the sum of all the distributed secrets by construction, it will be immediately revealed if all players add up the secrets currently in their possession and announce the answer to the other two parties!

The question needs to be asked at this juncture: has anything been revealed that should not have been? The answer is no, although it requires careful checking. (For example, party A is in possession of b_1 and c_1, and retained a_1, so it will announce $a_1 + b_1 + c_1$. But party B can't do much with the number $a_1 + b_1 + c_1$.)

There are also some weaknesses with the protocol. It requires all parties to honestly report, for example, and collusion among any two players is all it takes to leak information.

Still, this simple example should immediately alter our mind-set. Clearly, data is not the same as the use of data. There is immense potential of this rapidly moving field, known as secure multiparty computation.

The reader might like to ponder how multiplication might be achieved. A clue is provide by the expansion

$$(b_1 + b_2 + b_3)(c_1 + c_2 + c_3) = b_1 c_1 + b_1 c_2 + \cdots b_3 c_3$$

where it is observed that all terms require knowledge of two secrets only.[7] Of course, if we can achieve addition and multiplication, then many things follow—even gradient descent.

Returning to our discussion of discovering the value of someone else's data, it is now clear that the computation of inner products in a secure manner can sniff out causal relationships or at least suggest them. Here f can be Granger causality, for instance.

Furthermore, if *f* is a machine learning model, then the use of an exogenous regressor in a prediction is not predicated on ownership of that data. Nor is it predicated on *revelation* of that data. The predictive power of data is completely divorced from the knowledge of the data itself.

To me, the use of entangled secrets is reminiscent of quantum effects near the event horizon of a black hole. One photon from a pair passes through the horizon while the other escapes. In this prediction web analogy, even the most secretive of firms will, I predict, not be completely black. They will emit a kind of Hawking radiation.

9.12   Luring Adaptive Algorithms

Perhaps in the future, as algorithms get smarter, firms will establish the AI equivalent of human resources departments. Therein, people and algorithms will be charged with attracting high-quality adaptive algorithms to work on private data (inside their "event horizons").

As with the human equivalent, the artificial resources department will assist the algorithms with this transition—making them comfortable and productive (as well as assuring them they are now part of the world's most exciting, open, and ethically superior company in the whole of Northern California).

But their real role is recruiting. And that boils down to a privacy-hampered version of the race manager. A relatively easy problem, arguably, is the modification of that algorithm to work on internal systems, if we could somehow know in advance that it will work well.

This is no different, in principle, to the problem of knowing whether a human candidate will perform well on a future task, given that it might not be appropriate to put them at the helm of a nuclear submarine immediately. Interview questions or other screening activities play the role of synthetic data—used to assess algorithms before they can see the real stuff.

Synthetic data generation is problematic, admittedly, and a field unto itself. But even imperfect synthetic data can be a sufficient lure, one hopes, for adaptive algorithms capable of transferring *some* knowledge to unseen private data. In machine learning, the study of meta-learning, multitask algorithms, and few-shot and transfer learning is proceeding at a breakneck pace.

In the limit, as this generalized analytic ability improves, there will be no privacy issue at all. Data sensitivity issues only arise due to externalization of learning—for instance in a loop involving a human making occasional program updates. But if the algorithms are clean slates or do all the learning themselves, this isn't an issue.

A possible interim solution involves a pair of race organizers. One of these micromanagers sits inside your firewall and has access to private data. The other sits outside and does not. They run very similar contests.

We presume that from time to time, a small fraction of contestants in the external contest can be cloned and transported inside the firewall where—unbeknownst to their authors—they will operate on private data *in addition to* the synthetic data used by the external micromanager.

Then, an iterative process can begin where ongoing refinements are made to the synthetic data used by the external micromanager. That process can be informed by the relative performance of algorithms on the external versus internal data sets. Modifications to the synthetic data bring into closer alignment the ranking of algorithms in the external versus the internal leaderboards.

I present this merely as an example of the kind of thing a human resources department for algorithms might do. Another idea is the design of testing sets that are calculated to fool algorithms that don't adapt— these test examples might be more extreme than the real-world data and cover more regimes.

These tests can act like centrifuges, hopefully, separating out the algorithms that don't really have any special adaptive intelligence. Those that remain are more likely to assist in tasks their authors are yet to see.

9.13 Keeping It Simple

I close by tabulating some approaches to privacy preservation that are mostly self-explanatory. It would be foolhardy to suggest there is one best way to address risk, regulatory or other concerns. For one thing, there isn't one concern. Are you concerned about theft? What about piracy?

Contamination of the data with a small number of erroneous data points (ignored by scoring rules) may deter unpaid commercial usage. Steganography can be used to make statistically insignificant yet traceable changes to the data, enabling a subsequent investigation to identify the precise participant who was the source of the stolen goods.

There are too many approaches to give names to, at least standard ones, but table 9.1 enumerates some issues and countermeasures. Some we have discussed. Others are self-evident. And some, like the use of contracts, are too obvious to even include in the table.

Table 9.1
Defenses against misuse of data supplied to participants (or not supplied as the case may be).

Concern	Example	Techniques
Intent	Sensitive targets	Weak truths Residuals (and many below)
Theft	Subscription data	Subsampling Contamination Dilution Blacklisting (and all below)
Piracy	Reselling	Steganography Bootstrapping Transformation (and all below)
Privacy	Proprietary data	Allowed list Private contests Obfuscation Differential privacy (and all below)
Secrecy	Classified data	Chumming Multiparty computation Structure-preserving encryption Centrifuge

It's worth noting that many of the concerns regarding microprediction also apply to alternative data, and that hasn't stopped that area from exploding in recent years.

9.14 Summary

Privacy and intellectual property are important. However, they do not preclude the growth of a microprediction web within and between private firms. Many sensible steps can be taken to avoid leaking commercial intent or intellectual property.

To grow, a microprediction web needs only to add value by leveraging the *predictive power of data*, which may be possessed and guarded closely by separate parties. But fortunately, this does not require those parties to reveal their data to each other.

Skepticism of collective prediction is understandable, but *predictive ability* will flow freely between firms much more effectively than it has in the past—even if private raw data stays where it should. Indeed, a network of micromanagers is precisely what we need to infect the world with privacy-preserving mathematics.

So, I close by suggesting that an effective way to visualize the potential for a microprediction network is to imagine that boundaries between firms do not exist at all.

Afterword

It is hard, you will agree, for any considering human to avoid forming a mental picture of the way that quantitative techniques will influence commerce, and society, going forward. Let's face it, *all future visions* of *just about anything* place mathematically driven automation in a central role. Even the fictional President Josiah Bartlett, of *The West Wing*, told us that the twenty-first century would be the century of statistics.

Evidently, my own vision includes a new type of utility. The task of catalyzing a prediction web is better addressed by code, not prose, (I really must get back to that) but I hope these pages have offered you an opportunity to consider the potential for competitive prediction in the "small."

As with computing prophesies of yesteryear that only saw enterprise use, I suspect we are mostly blind to what the equivalent of an in-house data science team will eventually be used for, once shrunk down to the size of a thimble. I'm sure I'll look back on these pages in a few years and kick myself for missing something obvious.

I'm reminded too of how difficult it is to overcome our mental inertia, especially on the matters of cost—the central obsession of this book. Many years ago, my undergraduate professor, filling out a form to acquire me a university computer account, listed "email" as the only justification. I was shocked at the time as computers were expensive. It seemed unlikely that an administrator would allocate precious computation and bandwidth to someone whose only stated use was so frivolous.

Needless to say, I got that computer account, and how quaint that guilt seems now. In the same way, I think we will use a network of micro-predicting algorithms and data in ways that initially seem fatuous. Later, the exact same uses will be considered essential. The idea of not being able to map the near future, of everything large and small, will seem as antiquated as a car that cannot see the road ahead.

Admittedly, we won't all use microprediction at the lowest level of implementation detail, but that's okay. We aren't all experts in the TCP/IP internet protocols, either. Whatever your preferred level of abstraction is, I hope you are interested in helping to create an incredibly inexpensive alternative to the "data science project." A universal source of intelligence, despite the limitations I've stated, could be the next great utility.

To emphasize one last time, I have concerned myself with the microprediction domain only, for reasons that I hope are now clear. It is not *the* future of AI. It is not *the* future of statistics. It is not the future of general artificial intelligence—merely half the things branded AI. As I write these words, the world is experiencing a dreadful pandemic. It needs thoughtful inferential statistics to interpret a dire situation, make medium-term forecasts, and approve vaccines.

This kind of statistics will never be replaced by a microprediction network, but a substrate where algorithms travel can help in surprising ways—as with the sourcing of surrogate models for disease spread, or crowd sourced approximations for long-running molecular simulations.

And *in addition* to medium-term prediction, or the things we usually associate with the word *prediction*, the world also needs inexpensive, accessible, but accurate microprediction to drive operational efficiency in every industry. This is well within our collective ability. The prediction web is ambitious in some ways but rather mundane in others. It almost feels like busywork.

Recently, I came across a paper whose subtitle summed up the ambition nicely:

All models are wrong, but some are somewhere useful. (Yao et al. 2021)

Perhaps you have such a model but aren't quite sure of all the places it might add value.

I've suggested that given the right infrastructure, algorithms that manage algorithms can collectively solve this problem for you—and that they will be empowered by all the results from game theory, contest theory, auction theory, sequential experimental design, and anything else that assists. They don't need humans.

Or perhaps you are one of many who drive the data science contest participation rates well beyond the Nash equilibrium. I can offer you a challenge much closer to real-world work.

For those of you who picked this book up hoping for some new algorithmic breakthrough, I'm sorry I've disappointed. But we can do a lot with what we have. Algorithms merely need access to problems. They need businesses to hold their hands up and say "*Sure, I'll give this explicit microprediction thing a shot.*" Maybe you can do that.

Like models, all visions of the future are wrong, but maybe some are (somewhere) useful. I hope that's true of mine. My main goal has been to provoke you into contemplation of the fundamental contradiction at the heart of machine learning—or at least its artisan production. The efficacy of data-hungry methods counters the very notion that humans should be hand-managing them.

I thank you for your suspension of disbelief and hope to interact with you, or your autonomous brain-children, at a future date.

Acknowledgments

This book owes its existence to Adrian Banner and the larger Intech Investments family, who granted me the opportunity to advance the vision in a combination of prose and code while juggling other responsibilities. Christine Ardito, Jaime Cangiano, and Andre Prawoto helped present and socialize the idea.

I thank Michael Zierler of RedOx Editing for helping move the book to its present shape, Christine E. Marra for managing the editorial production, and Noah Springer of the MIT Press for advancing it to publication. I'm grateful for specific suggestions from Vaikkunth Mugunthan, Ganesh Mani, Dan Caroll, Ian Klasky, and my wife, Anne, who has constantly reminded me of the agony suffered by all authors (I doubt I would have pushed through without her encouragement). Several anonymous reviewers also helped immeasurably by providing detailed feedback and suggestions on the text.

As the late comedian Clive James reminds us, timing is everything. That is also an excellent excuse for poor prophesy and we'll see how the singular, long-term prediction on these pages fares. Regardless, I'll be grateful to early contributors in the microprediction community including, in addition to some mentioned above, Eric Lou, Rusty Conover, Fred Viole, Bob Smith, Aaron Soellinger, and Graham Giller.

If 2022 isn't the right time for a prediction network, 2013 probably wasn't either. But it was nice to be invited to Oxford by Forbes Elworthy to discuss "nano-markets," as I termed them at the time, over an extended period—bending the ears of numerous kind people including Michael Stein, Charles Elworthy, and Stephen Maddle. David Ferrarin, Steven Callander, and Gareth Moody heard little else from me around the same time.

The necessity of earning a living notwithstanding, I've failed since that time to free myself of the possibilities for collective data science. For this disease I should probably thank Anthony Goldbloom, who opened my eyes to a new demographic in 2012 when I ran a Kaggle contest (or really, Dan Glaser did on my behalf).

Since then I've been energized by conversations on related topics; and by people who have initiated projects inspired by some part of the thesis; by technologists who have worked late nights and hobbled through the snow on crutches; by those who have helped socialize the goals; and by a thousand people too numerous to mention who have participated in real-time contests, or supported microprediction in its infancy, or drip-fed me unsolicited encouragement on social platforms.

I single out Stephen Luterman and Jim Driscoll in particular, for their ability to instantly grok the microprediction web, and for the intellectual support they have provided me. But I've benefited from discussions and interactions of different kinds with many people including Antoine Toussaint, Charles Reyl, Jonathan Larkin, Daniel Szeredi, Dimitar Jetchev, Joseph Langsam, Qi Wei, Thomas Malone, Kathleen Kennedy, Robert Lauchbacher, Gianni Giacomelli, Bengt Holmstrom, Antigoni Polychroniadou, Richard Smith, Gene Fernandez, Daniel Szeredi, Ilya Uts, Markus Lampinen, Newcomb Cole, Tim Paine, Jose Marques, Deepankar Sharma and Iheshan Faasee.

Also Derrick Johnson, Myron Scholes, Jordan Brandt, Alexander Petric Cissp, Charles Williamson, Gael Reinaudi, Tad Nygren, Don Hausch, Liliya Simkahyeva, Christopher Carroll, John A. Cardinali, Derreck Johnson, Andrew Calderwood, Tim Berners-Lee, Patrick Quade, Ed Bishop, Ken Baron, David Edelman, Robbie Waterhouse, Kevin Armstrong, Virginia Edelstein, Darko Matovski, Karen Qin, Maksim Sipos, Adam Craig, Lidia Mangu, Ben Sylvester, Timur Sahin, Justin Wright, Kenneth Ng, David Schofield, Len Laufer, Vassilios Papathanakos, Ashwin Alankar, John Brown, Ilya Minevitch, Lance Campbell, Jian Tang, Afsheen Afshar, Roberto Spadim, Richard Yasenchak, Peter Memon, Kevin Armstrong, Tian Gan, Valerie Azuelos, Dustin Cone, Manuela Veloso, Sean Arendell, Michael Salita, Alex Castro, Neville Kadwa, and many others whose egregious omission will be rectified on the web site.

Notes

Chapter 1

1. Silver et al. (2021).
2. Cotton (2021c).
3. Domingos (2015).
4. Coase (1937).
5. The insult is from Captain Redbeard, of *Blackadder*.
6. HOV are high-occupancy lanes, elsewhere called transit lanes and carpool lanes.
7. Conover (2021).
8. Cotton (2020b).
9. See Cotton (2020d) for a description of the badminton example.

Chapter 2

1. DTCC (2019). At the time of writing, the left-hand panel of the SDR real-time dashboard contained "slice" files that, when unzipped, are comma-separated files containing one trade per row. The comments in the text refer to the prices listed in these files.
2. For an example of how microstructure complicates econometric estimation, see Hansen and Lunde (2006) and O'Hara (2015).
3. "Nibblefish" was once a candidate name for the prediction web project, with rather mixed focus group results. I urge the reader to consult the Scottish Health Protection agency report on risks associated with *Garra rufa* fish pedicures before engaging in that activity. (Health Protection Agency n.d.).
4. Definition of redlining is from Wikipedia.
5. Mendez et al. (2011).
6. Credit redlining is discussed in Cohen-Cole (2011). Groceries in Eisenhauer (2001). See Lang and Nakamura (1993) for further discussion.

7. The New York City Council passed legislation on December 11, 2017, according to an article published by the UCLA (Richardson 2017).

8. Peck et al. (2013).

9. Adler et al. (2017).

10. Turek (2017). Also emphasized is the enabling of human users to understand, appropriately trust, and effectively manage the emerging generation of artificially intelligent partners.

11. Kastellec (2010).

12. See Forrester and Keane (2009) for a survey of surrogate methods for optimization, although plenty has occurred since.

13. Crites and Barto (1998).

14. In the taxonomy, I'm drawing upon numerous sources, including some mentioned in chapter 6. Kaggle provides more data than most (Kaggle Inc. 2014).

15. McKinsey & Company (2011).

16. McKinsey & Company (2011).

17. Cotton (2019b).

Chapter 3

1. Yuling Yao et al. (May 2021).

2. Cotton (2021d).

3. Malone (2018).

Chapter 4

1. Wikipedia was also directly inspired by Hayek's essay. Tucker (2017).

2. The mentioned course is offered by Stanford University and Coursera.

3. See Freider et al. (n.d.) for an example of a pipeline tool.

Chapter 5

1. Fuller (1987).

2. Goetschalckx et al. (2008).

3. Janisch et al. (2020).

4. Cotton (2021b).

5. Cotton (2021d).

6. Examples of model search frameworks include Auto-Sklearn (Feurer et al. 2015), H20 AutoML (Candel et al. 2015), autoxgboost (Thomas et al. 2018), FLAML (Liu and Wang 2021), oboe (Yang et al. 2019), LightAutoML (Vakhrushev et al. 2021), GAMA (Gijsbers and Vanschoren 2019), TPOT (Olson et al. 2016), MLJAR, Hyperopt-Sklearn (Komer et al. 2014), AutoKeras (Jin et al. 2019), AutoGluon (Erickson et al. 2020), and PyCaret (Ali and Baum 2020).

7. Cotton (2020b).

8. Cotton (2020b).

9. Abramowicz (2007).

10. Baron and Lange (2007).

11. Moffitt and Ziemba (2018).

12. Cotton (2020a).

13. Wang et al. (2019b).

14. Zhenlin Yang and Min Xie. Process monitoring of exponentially distributed characteristics through an optimal normalizing transform. *Journal of Applied Statistics*, 27 (8), 2000. ISSN 0266–4763.

15. Box and Cox (1964).

16. For instance, Sakia (1992) and, more recently, Hossain (2011).

17. Proietti and Lütkepohl (2013).

18. Cotton (2019a).

19. Kaplan and Rich (2017).

20. VanderWeele (2017).

21. Miller (2012).

22. Cotton (2021b).

23. Cotton (2020c).

24. Strongly performing Python-ready optimizers include Nevergrad (Bennet et al. 2021), DLIB King (2009), PySOT (Wang et al. 2019a), BayesOpt (Martinez-Cantin 2015), Scikit-Optimize (Timgates42 2020), UltraOpt (Tang 2021), and Py-Bobyqa (Cartis et al. 2019). However, the reader is referred to live ratings (Cotton 2021a) for many more possibilities, and the likely staleness of this advice merely highlights the need for more micromanagers.

25. Examples of meta-data tooling include the DataHub and Amundsen packages.

26. Duan et al. (2020).

27. Conlon (1997).

28. See Byrne (2018) or Holowaychuk (2017) for discussion of why lambda memory is useful in other contexts.

29. Cotton (2021e)

Chapter 6

1. McKinsey & Company (2011).

2. Hurtgen, et al., (2020).

3. Forrester Research (2016).

4. Other competitive sites more focused on evaluation of participants (rather than solving industry problems) include Hackerearth, Interviewbit, Hackerrank, Code-Ground, Codeforces, Sphere Online Judge, UVA online judge, and Code Chef.

These collectively add another million or so users. Numbers have increased substantially since compilation or the date of sources used. I was not able to find estimates for some notables such as WorldQuant, Numerai, or Quantiacs and apologize for any omissions.

5. The description of the Common Task Framework echoes Donoho (2015).

6. Stolfo (1999) and Bennett and Lanning (2007).

7. Kaggle reported a 340 percent accuracy improvement, which sounds good, even if I can't help you parse that number.

8. GE Flight Quest (2013).

9. Cotton (2019a).

10. The TopCoder case study seems no longer to be available. Here is an extract originally taken from the TopCoder website.

> Harvard Medical School enlisted TopCoder to help find a faster, more accurate solution for a tool that calculates the edit distance between a query DNA string and the original DNA string. This is critical for making high-precision, high-throughput readouts of the immune system. Prior to the TopCoder contest, the best known solution, MegaBLAST, processed 100,000 sequences to a high degree of accuracy, yet required 2, 000 seconds to execute. A full-time, Harvard resource that spent a year on this unique problem was able to produce an improved outcome, reducing the computational time to 400 seconds.
>
> With $6,000 in total prize money, 733 registrants and 122 members submitting working algorithms, TopCoder provided HMS with a winning solution that performed hundreds of times faster and at a higher degree of accuracy, reducing the time to execution to just over 16 seconds.

11. Makridakis et al. (n.d.).

12. A longer response to the future of forecasting paper can be found in Cotton (n.d.).

13. Donoho (2015).

14. See Breiman (2001) for extended discussion. I have used Donoho's "prediction culture" terminology as I find it more suggestive of the connection to microprediction. Breiman referred to this side of statistics as "algorithmic modeling culture" and to inferential statistics as "data modeling culture."

15. Introne et al. (2011).

16. von Neumann and Morgenstern (2007).

17. The theoretical contest results in this chapter are from Vojnovic (2016), where the reader can find generalizations with arguably more realistic Nash equilibria.

18. As a technicality, and very much beside the point, this reduction to two players assumes that when we rank players by their desire (i.e., subjective prize value $v_1 \geq v_2 \geq \ldots$), there is no tie for second place. For example, if all players value the prize the same (or in the equivalence game have equal ability to translate work into output), then everybody plays.

Chapter 7

1. Axelrod (1980).

2. Rapoport et al. (2015).

3. Holmstrom and Milgrom (1987).

4. A review of extremum estimation is provided in MIT Open Courseware (2008).

5. Savage (1971).

6. Ehm et al. (2016).

7. These comments apply to scoring rules used to elicit estimates of the mean. See Ehm et al. (2016) for generalizations to quantiles and expectiles.

8. An example of judging predictions that are made in the absence of some pre-specified scoring rule is the use of Murphy diagrams. The idea is that predictors are scored across a number of different scoring rules (such as the basis suggested by Ehm et al. [2016] used in the decomposition of scoring rules).

9. Assel et al. (2017).

Chapter 8

1. The recommended technique starts by creating an estimate on grid points using exponentially smoothed averages. Next, splines are fit to isobars to eliminate rough edges (Stöckl and Lames 2011).

2. For a longer discussion of putting value functions, see Yousefi and Swartz (2013).

3. The Markov assumption for golf doesn't hold perfectly if the course is the state. For example, professionals are more likely to sink a ten-foot putt for par than a ten-foot putt for birdie (Pope and Schweitzer 2011).

4. Shipnuck and Reilly (2006).

5. A Monte Carlo model for golf shots is considered in Broadie and Ko (2009).

6. Wang et al. (2015).

7. Cotton (2020e).

8. Traditional chess programs included custom logic such as negamax search, analysis functions, iterative deepening, alpha-beta pruning, principal variation search, aspiration windows, transposition tables, killer moves, history heuristic, quiescence search, quiescence width extension, internal iterative deepening, null move heuristics, futility pruning, razoring, and search extensions.

9. Frayn (n.d.).

10. Knights on the edge of the board have few options to move compared to those in the center, thus giving rise to the saying *a knight on the rim is dim*. The German version is no kinder. *Ein Springer am Rand bringt Kummer und Schand* (sorrow and shame).

11. The position evaluations in this example use a twenty ply search—ten moves taken by both players—using the Stockfish chess engine.

Chapter 9

1. Vigen (2015).
2. Gentry (2009).
3. For a recent survey of homomorphic encryption, see Alharbi et al. (2020).
4. Joseph et al. (2020).
5. For a survey, see Zhu et al. (2020).
6. For a listing of alternative data vendors, see YipitData (n.d.).
7. This introductory example of secret sharing, and the solution, is taken from Cramer et al. (2015), where the reader may find a discussion of attacks, generalizations, and applications.

Bibliography

Abramowicz, Michael. 2007. "The Hidden Beauty of the Quadratic Market Scoring Rule: a Uniform Liquidity Market Maker, with Variations." *The Journal of Prediction Markets* 1(2): 111–125 http://www.ingenta connect.com/content/ubpl/jpm/2007/00000001/00000002/art00002.

Adler, Philip, Casey Falk, Sorelle A. Friedler, Tionney Nix, Gabriel Rybeck, Carlos Scheidegger, Brandon Smith, and Suresh Venkatasubramanian. 2017. "Auditing Black Box Models for Indirect Influence." *Knowl Inf Syst* 54, 95–122 (2018). https://doi.org/10.1007/s10115-017-1116-3

Alharbi, Ayman, Haneen Zamzami, and Eman Samkri. 2020. "Survey on Homomorphic Encryption and Address of New Trend." *International Journal of Advanced Computer Science and Applications* 11(7) https://doi.org/10.14569/IJACSA.2020.0110774.

Ali, Moez, and Antoni Baum. 2020. "PyCaret Python Package." https://github.com/pycaret/pycaret.

Assel, Melissa, Daniel D. Sjoberg, and Andrew J. Vickers. 2017. "The Brier Score Does Not Evaluate the Clinical Utility of Diagnostic Tests or Prediction Models." *Diagnostic and Prognostic Research*. https://doi.org/10.1186/s41512-017-0020-3.

Axelrod, Robert. 1980. "Effective Choice in the Prisoner's Dilemma." *Journal of Conflict Resolution* 24(1); 3–25. https://doi.org/10.1177/002200278002400101.

Baron, Ken, and Jeffrey Lange. 2007. *Parimutuel Applications in Finance*. Palgrave Macmillan, New York. https://doi.org/10.1057/97802 30627505.

Barto, Andrew G. and Robert H. Gates. 1996. "Improving Elevator Performance Using Reinforcement Learning." *Advances in Neural Information Processing Systems*.

Bennet, Pauline, Carola Doerr, Antoine Moreau, Jeremy Rapin, Fabien Teytaud, and Olivier Teytaud. 2021. "Nevergrad." *ACM SIGEVOlution* 14(1). https://doi.org/10.1145/3460310.3460312.

Bennett, James, and Stan Lanning. 2007. "The Netflix Prize." *KDD Cup and Workshop* 9(2): pp. 3–6. https://doi.org/10.1145/1562764.1562769.

Box, G. E. P., and D. R. Cox. 1964. "An Analysis of Transformations." *Journal of the Royal Statistical Society: Series B (Methodological)* 26(2). pp. 211–52, https://doi.org/10.1111/j.2517-6161.1964.tb00553.x.

Breiman, L. 2001. "Statistical Modeling: The Two Cultures." *Statistical Science*. Institute of Mathematical Statistics, 2001, 16(3) pp. 199–215, https://doi.org/10.2307/2676681.

Broadie, Mark, and Soonmin Ko. 2009. "A Simulation Model to Analyze the Impact of Distance and Direction on Golf Scores." In *Proceedings— Winter Simulation Conference*. https://doi.org/10.1109/WSC.2009 .5429280.

Broman, Karl. 2013. "Data Science Is Statistics." https://kbroman.word press.com/2013/04/05/data-science-is-statistics/.

Byrne, Jason. 2018. "Persistent Data in Lambda. It Works!" https:// engineering.flosports.tv/persistent-data-in-lambda-it-works-ca0c1b25 879e.

Cartis, Coralia, Jan Fiala, Benjamin Marteau, and Lindon Roberts. 2019. "Improving the Flexibility and Robustness of Model-Based Derivative- Free Optimization Solvers." *ACM Transactions on Mathematical Soft- ware* 45(3). https://doi.org/10.1145/3338517.

Coase, R. 1937. "Nature of the Firm." *Economica*, 4: 386–305, https:// doi.org/10.1111/j.1468-0335.1937.tb00002.x

Cohen-Cole, Ethan. 2011. "Credit Card Redlining." *The Review of Economics and Statistics* 93(2): 700–713 http://dx.doi.org/10.1162 /REST_a_00052%5Cnhttp://www.mitpressjournals.org/doi/abs/10.1162 /REST_a_00052.

Conlon, Brian. 1997. "Totalizator History." http://members.ozemail.com .au/~bconlon.

Conover, Rusty. 2021. "Predicting New York State's Electricity." https:// rusty.today/posts/predicting-ny-electricity-with-julia-and-tensorflowjs.

Cotton, Peter. (n.d.). "The Future of Forecasting, According to the Experts." https://www.microprediction.com/blog/future.

Cotton, Peter. 2019a. "Self Organizing Supply Chains for Micro-Prediction: Present and Future Uses of the ROAR Protocol." Thirty-first Conference on Neural Information Processing Systems, Long Beach.

Cotton, Peter. 2019b. "How to Respond to an RFQ." https://github.com/microprediction/winning/blob/main/docs/How_to_respond_to_an_RFQ.pdf.

Cotton, Peter. 2020e. "Why Liberals Should Be Terrified Right Now—How a Trump Surge Can Sneak Past the Election Models." https://www.microprediction.com/blog/election.

Cotton, Peter. 2021b. "Inferring Relative Ability from Winning Probability in Multientrant Contests." *SIAM Journal on Financial Mathematics* 12. pp. 295–317, https://doi.org/10.1137/19M1276261.

Cotton, Peter. 2021a. "HumpDay Optimization Package." https://github.com/microprediction/humpday.

Cotton, Peter. 2021d. "The Only Prediction Function You'll Ever Need?" https://www.microprediction.com/blog/forever.

Cotton, Peter. 2020a. "The Lottery Paradox." https://www.micropredic tion.com/blog/lottery.

Cotton, Peter. 2020c. "Popular Python Time-Series Packages." https://www.microprediction.com/blog/popular-timeseries-packages.

Cotton, Peter. 2021e. "Time Machines Python Package." https://github.com/microprediction/timemachines.

Cotton, Peter. 2021c. "Is Facebook's Prophet the Time-Series Messiah, or Just a Very Naughty Boy?" https://www.microprediction.com/blog/prophet.

Cotton, Peter. 2020d. "Where Will a Badminton Player Move to Next, and How Should We Adjudicate Predictions of the Same?" https://www.microprediction.com/blog/badminton.

Cotton, Peter. 2020b. "Microprediction.org." https://www.micropredi ction.org.

Cramer, Ronald, Ivan Bjerre Damgård, and Jesper Buus Nielsen. 2015. *Secure Multiparty Computation and Secret Sharing.* Cambridge University Press, August 2015. https://doi.org/10.1017/CBO9781107337756.

Crites, Robert H., and Andrew G. Barto. 1998. "Elevator Group Control Using Multiple Reinforcement Learning Agents." *Machine Learning* 33, 235–262, https://doi.org/10.1023/a:1007518724497.

Domingos, Pedro. 2015. *The Master Algorithm. How the Quest for the Ultimate Learning Machine Will Remake Our World*. New York: Basic Books.

Donoho, David. 2017. "50 Years of Data Science." *Journal of Computational and Graphical Statistics*. 26. 745–766.

DTCC. 2019. "DTCC Swap Data Repository Realtime Dashboard." https://rtdata.dtcc.com/gtr/.

Duan, Jiexin, Xingye Qiao, and Guang Cheng. 2020. "Statistical Guarantees of Distributed Nearest Neighbor Classification." *Advances in Neural Information Processing Systems* 33, pages: 229–240. https://proceedings.neurips.cc/paper/2020/file/022e0ee5162c13d9a7bb3bd00fb032ce-Paper.pdf.

Ehm, Werner, Tilmann Gneiting, Alexander Jordan, and Fabian Krüger. 2016. "Of Quantiles and Expectiles: Consistent Scoring Functions, Choquet Representations and Forecast Rankings." *Journal of the Royal Statistical Society. Series B: Statistical Methodology*. 78(30): 505–62, https://doi.org/10.1111/rssb.12154.

Eisenhauer, Elizabeth. 2001. "In Poor Health: Supermarket Redlining and Urban Nutrition." *GeoJournal* 53(2):125–133. https://doi.org/10.1023/A:1015772503007.

Erickson, Nick, Jonas Mueller, Alexander Shirkov, Hang Zhang, Pedro Larroy, Mu Li, and Alexander Smola. 2020. "Autogluon-Tabular: Robust and Accurate AutoMl for Structured Data." *arXiv preprint arXiv:2003.06505*.

Candel, Arno, et al. 2015. *H20 AutoMl* https://github.com/h2oai.

Feurer, Matthias, Aaron Klein, Katharina Eggensperger, Jost Springenberg, Manuel Blum, and Frank Hutter. 2015. "Efficient and Robust Automated Machine Learning." *Advances in Neural Information Processing Systems* 28: 2944–2952 http://papers.nips.cc/paper/5872-efficient-and-robust-automated-machine-learning.pdf.

Forrester, Alexander I. J., and Andy J. Keane. 2009. "Recent Advances in Surrogate-Based Optimization." *Progress in Aerospace Sciences*, 45, (1–3) 2009, pp. 50–79, https://doi.org/10.1016/j.paerosci.2008.11.001. (https://www.sciencedirect.com/science/article/pii/S0376042108000766).

Frayn, Colin. n.d. "The Chess Brain Project." http://chessbrain.net/.

Freider, Elias, Erick Bernhardsson, Arash Rouhani, and Dave Buchfuhrer. n.d. "Luigi Package." https://luigi.readthedocs.io/en/stable/.

Fuller, Wayne A. 1987. *Measurement Error Models*. New York: Wiley.

GE Flight Quest. 2013. http://www.gequest.com/c/flight/details/winners.

Gentry, Craig. 2009. *A Fully Homomorphic Encryption Scheme*. PhD thesis, Stanford University Department of Computer Science.

Gijsbers, Peter, and Joaquin Vanschoren. 2019. "GAMA: Genetic Automated Machine Learning Assistant." *Journal of Open Source Software* 4(33). 1132, https://doi.org/10.21105/joss.01132.

Goetschalckx, Robby, Kurt Driessens, and Scott Sanner. 2008. "Cost-Sensitive Parsimonious Linear Regression." In *Proceedings—IEEE International Conference on Data Mining*, ICDM. 809–814. https://doi.org/10.1109/ICDM.2008.76.

Hansen, Peter R., and Asger Lunde. 2006. "Realized Variance and Market Microstructure Noise." *Journal of Business and Economic Statistics* 24(2). pp. 127–61, https://doi.org/10.1198/073500106000000071.

Hayek, F. 1945. "The Use of Knowledge in Society." *American Economic Review*. Vol XXXV, pp. 519–30, https://doi.org/10.1257/aer.98.5.i.

Health Protection Agency. (n.d.). "Guidance on the Management of the Public Health Risks from Fish Pedicures." https://assets.publishing.service.gov.uk/government/uploads/system/uploads/attachment_data/file/322420/Fish_Spa_guidance.pdf.

Holmstrom, Bengt, and Paul Milgrom. 1987. "Aggregation and Linearity in the Provision of Intertemporal Incentives." *Econometrica*. no. 2, pp. 303–28. https://doi.org/10.2307/1913238.

Holowaychuk, T. J. 2017. "AWS Lambda Lifecycle and In-memory Caching." https://medium.com/@tjholowaychuk/aws-lambda-lifecycle-and-in-memory-caching-c9cd0844e072.

Hossain, Mohammad Zakir. 2011. "The Use of Box-Cox Transformation Technique in Economic and Statistical Analyses." *Journal of Emerging Trends in Economics and Management Sciences* 2(1) pp. 32–29.

Hurtgen, Holder, Sebastian Kerkhoff, Jan Lubatschowski, and Manuel Möller. 2020. "Rethinking AI Talent Strategy as Automated Machine Learning Comes of Age." *McKinsey*, August 14th, 2020. https://www.mckinsey.com/business-functions/mckinsey-analytics/our-insights/rethinking-ai-talent-strategy-as-automated-machine-learning-comes-of-age/egy-as-automated-machine-learning-comes-of-age/

Introne, Joshua, Robert Laubacher, Gary Olson, and Thomas Malone. 2011. "The Climate CoLab: Large Scale Model-Based Collaborative Planning." In *Proceedings of the 2011 International Conference on*

Collaboration Technologies and Systems, CTS 2011, pp. 40–47, https://doi.org/10.1109/CTS.2011.5928663.

Janisch, Jaromír, Tomáš Pevný, and Viliam Lisý. 2020. "Classification with Costly Features Using Deep Reinforcement Learning." *Machine Learning*. 109. doi: 10.1007/s10994-020-05874-8.

Jin, Haifeng, Qingquan Song, and Xia Hu. 2019. "Auto-keras: An Efficient Neural Architecture Search System." In *Proceedings of the ACM SIGKDD International Conference on Knowledge Discovery and Data Mining*. https://doi.org/10.1145/3292500.3330648.

Joseph, Matthew, Aaron Roth, Jonathan Ullman, and Bo Waggoner. 2020. "Local Differential Privacy for Evolving Data." *Journal of Privacy and Confidentiality* 10(1). https://doi.org/10.29012/jpc.718.

Kaggle Inc. 2014. "The Home of Data Science." http://www.kaggle.com.

Kaplan, Edward H., and Candler Rich. 2017. "Decomposing Pythagoras." *Journal of Quantitative Analysis in Sports*. no. 4, pp. 141–149, https://doi.org/10.1515/jqas-2017-0055.

Kao, S. C. and Ho, C. 2007. "Monitoring a Process of Exponentially Distributed Characteristics through Minimizing the Sum of the Squared Differences." *Qual Quant* 41, pp. 137–149, https://doi.org/10.1007/s11135-005-6214-8

Kastellec, Jonathan P. 2010. "The Statistical Analysis of Judicial Decisions and Legal Rules with Classification Trees." *Journal of Empirical Legal Studies* 7(2):202–230. https://doi.org/10.1111/j.1740-1461.2010.01176.x.

King, Davis E. 2009. "Dlib-ml: A Machine Learning Toolkit." *Journal of Machine Learning Research* 10, pp. 1755–58.

Komer, Brent, James Bergstra, and Chris Eliasmith. 2014. Hyperopt-Sklearn: Automatic Hyperparameter Configuration for Scikit-Learn. In *Proceedings of the 13th Python in Science Conference*. 32–37, https://doi.org/10.25080/majora-14bd3278-006.

Lang, William W., and Leonard I. Nakamura. 1993. A Model of Redlining. *Journal of Urban Economics* 33(2): 223–234 https://doi.org/10.1006/juec.1993.1014. URL http://linkinghub.elsevier.com/retrieve/pii/S0094119083710144.

Levy, Tamir, and Joseph Yagil. 2011. "Air Pollution and Stock Returns in the US." *Journal of Economic Psychology* 32(3) pp. 374–383, https://doi.org/10.1016/j.joep.2011.01.004.

Liu, Xueqing, and Chi Wang. 2021. "An Empirical Study on Hyperparameter Optimization for Fine-Tuning Pre-trained Language Models." (pre-publication) https://doi.org/10.18653/v1/2021.acl-long.178.

Makridakis, Spyros, Chris Fry, Fotios Petropoulos, and Evangelos Spiliotis. n.d. "The Future of Forecasting Competitions: Design Attributes and Principles." *INFORMS Journal on Data Science.* https://arxiv.org/abs/2102.04879.

Makridakis, Spyros, Michele Hibon, and Claus Moser. 1979. "Accuracy of Forecasting: An Empirical Investigation." *Journal of the Royal Statistical Society. Series A (General)* 142(2) pp. 97–145, https://doi.org/10.2307/2345077.

Malone, Thomas W. 2018. "How Human-Computer 'Superminds' Are Redefining the Future of Work." *MIT Sloan Management Review*, July 1, 2018.

Manyika, James, et al. 2011. "Big Data: The Next Frontier for Innovation, Competition and Productivity." https://www.mckinsey.com/business-functions/mckinsey-digital/our-insights/big-data-the-next-frontier-for-innovation.

Martinez-Cantin, Ruben. 2015. "BayesOpt: A Bayesian Optimization Library for Nonlinear Optimization, Experimental Design and Bandits." *Journal of Machine Learning Research* 15 pp. 3735–3739.

McKinsey & Company. 2011. "Big Data: The Next Frontier for Innovation, Competition, and Productivity." *McKinsey Global Institute*, June, 156. https://doi.org/10.1080/01443610903114527.

Mendez, Dara D., Vijaya K. Hogan, and Jennifer Culhane. 2011. "Institutional Racism and Pregnancy Health: Using Home Mortgage Disclosure Act Data to Develop an Index for Mortgage Discrimination at the Community Level." *Public Health Reports* 126(suppl. 3). pp. 102–14, https://doi.org/10.1177/00333549111260s315.

Miller, Steven J. 2012. "The Pythagorean Won-Loss Formula and Hockey: A Statistical Justification for Using the Classic Baseball Formula as an Evaluative Tool in Hockey." *arXiv preprint arXiv:1208.1725.*

Moffitt, Steven D., and William T. Ziemba. 2018. "A Method for Winning at Lotteries." Papers 1801.02958, (prepublication)arXiv.org.

O'Hara, Maureen. 2015. "High Frequency Market Microstructure." *Journal of Financial Economics* 116(2):257–270. https://doi.org/10.1016/j.jfineco.2015.01.003.

Olson, Randal S., Nathan Bartley, Ryan J. Urbanowicz, and Jason H. Moore. 2016. "Evaluation of a Tree-Based Pipeline Optimization Tool for Automating Data Science." In *GECCO 2016—Proceedings of the 2016 Genetic and Evolutionary Computation Conference*, New York: Association for Computing Machinery, pp. 485–492, https://doi.org/10.1145 /2908812.2908918.

MIT Opencourseware. 2013. "Review of the Asymptotics of Extremum Estimators." *Time*, Series Analysis, https://ocw.mit.edu/courses/econo mics/14-384-time-series-analysis-fall-2013

Peck, Tabitha C., Sofia Seinfeld, Salvatore M. Aglioti, and Mel Slater. 2013. "Putting Yourself in the Skin of a Black Avatar Reduces Implicit Racial Bias." *Consciousness and Cognition* 22(3):779–787. https://doi .org/10.1016/j.concog.2013.04.016.

Pope, Devin G., and Maurice E. Schweitzer. 2011. "Is Tiger Woods Loss Averse? Persistent Bias in the Face of Experience, Competition, and High Stakes." *American Economic Review* 101(1) pp. 129-57, https://doi.org /10.1257/aer.101.1.129.

Proietti, Tommaso, and Helmut Lütkepohl. 2013. "Does the Box-Cox Transformation Help in Forecasting Macroeconomic Time Series?" *International Journal of Forecasting* 29(1) https://doi.org/10.1016/j.ijforecast. 2012.06.001.

Rapoport, Amnon, Darryl A. Seale, and Andrew M. Colman. 2015. "Is Tit-for-Tat the Answer? On the Conclusions Drawn from Axelrod's Tournaments." *PLoS ONE* 10(7) https://doi.org/10.1371/journal.pone .0134128.

Forrester Research. 2016. "Data Science Marketplaces Unlock Advanced Analytics for the Masses." https://www.forrester.com/report/Brief-Data -Science-Marketplaces-Unlock-Advanced-Analytics-For-The-Masses/ RES127081.

Richardson, Rashida. 2017. "New York City Takes on Algorithmic Discrimination." https://www.aclu.org/blog/privacy-technology/surveillance -technologies/new-york-city-takes-algorithmic-discrimination.

Sakia, R. M. 1992. "The Box-Cox Transformation Technique: A Review." *The Statistician* 41(2). pp. 169–178, https://doi.org/10.2307/23 48250.

Savage, Leonard J. 1971. "Elicitation of Personal Probabilities and Expectations." *Journal of the American Statistical Association* 66(336), pp. 783–801, https://doi.org/10.1080/01621459.1971.10482346.

Shipnuck, Alan, and Rick Reilly. 2006. "The Crack-up." *Sports Illustrated*, June 26.

Silver, David, Satinder Singh, Doina Precup, and Richard S. Sutton. 2021. "Reward Is Enough." *Artificial Intelligence*, vol. 299, https://doi.org/10.1016/j.artint.2021.103535.

Stöckl, Michael, and Martin Lames. 2011. "Modeling Constraints in Putting : The ISOPAR Method." *International Journal of Computer Science in Sport* 10(1992).

Stolfo, S. J. 1999. "KDD Cup 1999 Dataset." UCI KDD repository. http://kdd.ics.uci.edu.

Tang, Qichun. 2021. "Ultraopt: Distributed Asynchronous Hyperparameter Optimization Better Than Hyperopt." https://doi.org/10.5281/zenodo.4430148.

They Might Be Giants. "Ana Ng," *Lincoln*. 1988.

Thomas, Janek, Stefan Coors, and Bernd Bischl. 2018. "Automatic Gradient Boosting." In *International Workshop on Automatic Machine Learning at ICML*.

Timgates42 Tim Head, Holgar Nahrstaedt, and Manoj Kumar, 2020. "scikit-optimize." Scikit-Optimize Python Package github.com/scikit-optimize.

Tucker, Jeffrey A. 2017. "Wikipedia Is the Wonder of the World That Wasn't Supposed to Work." https://fee.org/articles/wikipedia-is-the-wonder-of-the-world-that-wasn-t-supposed-to-work/.

Turek, Matt. 2017. "Explainable Artificial Intelligence." https://www.darpa.mil/program/explainable-artificial-intelligence.

Vakhrushev, Anton, Alexander Ryzhkov, Maxim Savchenko, Dmitry Simakov, Richin Damdinov, and Alexander Tuzhilin. 2021. "LightAutoML: AutoML Solution for a Large Financial Services Ecosystem."

VanderWeele, Tyler J. 2017. "On a Square-Root Transformation of the Odds Ratio for a Common Outcome." *Epidemiology*. 28 (1).

Vigen, Tyler. 2015. "Spurious Correlations: Correlation Does Not Imply Causation." https://www.tylervigen.com/spurious-correlations.

Vojnovic, M. 2016. "Contest Theory: Incentive Mechanisms and Ranking Methods." Cambridge: Cambridge University Press. https://doi.org/10.1017/CBO9781139519366

von Neumann, John, and Oskar Morgenstern. 2007. *Theory of Games and Economic Behavior*. Princeton: NJ. Princeton University Press, https://doi.org/10.2307/3610940.

Wang, Qiang, Li Zhang, Luca Bertinetto, Weiming Hu, and Philip H.S. Torr. 2019a. "Fast Online Object Tracking and Segmentation: A Unifying Approach." In *Proceedings of the IEEE Computer Society Conference on Computer Vision and Pattern Recognition* 2019, pp. 1328–1338, https://doi.org/10.1109/CVPR.2019.00142.

Wang, Yi, Ning Zhang, Yushi Tan, Tao Hong, Daniel S. Kirschen, and Chongqing Kang. 2019b. "Combining Probabilistic Load Forecasts." *IEEE Transactions on Smart Grid* 10(4) https://doi.org/10.1109/TSG.2018.2833869.

Wang, Ziyu, Tom Schaul, and Matteo Hessel. 2016. "Dueling Network Architectures for Deep Reinforcement Learning." *Advances in Neural Information Processing Systems* 2017-Decem(2016).

Wu, Qinqin, Ying Hao, and Jing Lu. 2018. "Air Pollution, Stock Returns, and Trading Activities in China." *Pacific Basin Finance Journal* 51, https://doi.org/10.1016/j.pacfin.2018.08.018.

Yang, Chengrun, Yuji Akimoto, Dae Won Kim, and Madeleine Udell. 2019. "OBoe: Collaborative Filtering for AutoMl Model Selection." In *Proceedings of the ACM SIGKDD International Conference on Knowledge Discovery and Data Mining*, pp. 1173–1183. https://doi.org/10.1145/3292500.3330909.

Yao, Yuling, Gregor Pirs, Aki Vehtari, and Andrew Gelman. 2021. "Bayesian Hierarchical Stacking: Some Models Are (Somewhere) Useful." https://arxiv.org/abs/2101.08954.

YipitData. n.d. "Alternative Data Catalog." AlternativeData.org.

Yousefi, Kasra, and Tim B. Swartz. 2013. "Advanced Putting Metrics in Golf." *Journal of Quantitative Analysis in Sports* 9(3):239–248. https://arxiv.org/10.1515/jqas-2013-0010.

Vehtari, Aki, Andrew Gelman Yuling Yao, and Gregor Pirs. 2020. "Bayesian Hierarchical Stackign: Some Models Are (Somewhere) Useful." https://arxiv.org/abs/2101.08954.

Zhu, Tianqing, Dayong Ye, Wei Wang, Wanlei Zhou, and Philip Yu. 2020. "More Than Privacy: Applying Differential Privacy in Key Areas of Artificial Intelligence." *IEEE Transactions on Knowledge and Data Engineering*, p. 1, https://doi.org/10.1109/TKDE.2020.3014246.

Index

Page numbers followed by f and t indicate figures and tables, respectively.